FAIRYTALES
AND
STREET FIGHTS

How To Give Your Inner Warrior Wings

RAMONA BAXTER

FAIRYTALES AND STREET FIGHTS
How To Give Your Inner Warrior Wings

Copyright © 2024 by Ramona Baxter

Inspired Legacy Publishing is a division of (DBA) Inspired Legacy, LLC
PO Box 900816
Sandy UT 84090-0816.

ISBN 979-8-9904095-0-7 (paperback)
ISBN 979-8-9904095-1-4 (hardcover)

Printed in the United States of America.

What People Are Saying

"What truly sets this memoir apart is its authenticity. The author doesn't sugarcoat her experiences or present herself as flawless. Instead, she embraces her imperfections, using them as stepping stones toward growth and self-discovery. In doing so, she not only empowers herself but also empowers readers to embrace their own humanity."
  –Ramona DeHoyos Stark

"Ramona's vulnerability and honesty throughout her book are what make it so powerful. She bares her soul, sharing both her triumphs, as well as her darkest moments. It takes immense courage to reveal oneself in such a raw and authentic way, and she has done so with grace."
  –Dennis A. Conforto, Podcast Host & Producer of Just Saying The Obvious

"I would encourage anyone to read this book about life's ups and downs, building resilience of the human spirit, and empowerment through self-love and kindness."
  –Janet Schmidt, International Best Selling Author of *Journey to Self-Awareness and Hope*

"Ramona has recreated her world from a very early age and shared it with all of us like a beautiful secret. Her words and her story are so powerful that I can't count the times I laughed and cried during this amazing journey."
  –Misti Mazurik, Director of Operations, RHG Media Productions

"I found this book to be well written, describing how a person can make their dreams come true with focused determination. It is an honest account of a life being lived and finding peace with it, especially with the ones she loves."

–Steve Zeiger, International Best Selling Author to My Lights

Today is a day for gratitude. This book is dedicated to all the incredible people who have graced the various chapters of my life. I want each of you to understand just how profoundly significant you are to me and the immense gratitude I hold for the roles you've played. I have lived such an amazing life, and it's been amazing because all of you were in it. Thank you from the bottom of my heart for being part of my world and this crazy experience we call "life."

CONTENTS

NOTE TO MY READER

As you can tell by the title, this is not your run-of-the-mill light reading. This is meant to be an engaging, transformational, self-help memoir that rawly expresses the crazy machinations of a closet addict and the astonishing miracle that freed her. Through self-deprecating humor, it teaches the value and power that can be gained from our darkest moments.

For me, life often resembled a street fight after I shattered the bulletproof bubble of my upbringing. Clueless and unyielding, it was a battle for survival. Life, akin to a street fight, demands confidence beyond measure. We all wear our bravest faces, navigating through new challenges with bluffs. Ultimately, victory belongs to those who refuse to surrender. It's not always about intelligence or wisdom in the beginning, but about the unwavering grit to endure and find solutions amidst the struggle. A big part of that is ultimately embracing humility and absorbing the profound lessons that life eagerly offers based on our actions. You might think "embracing humility" is contradictory to "unwavering grit." It's been my experience that *both* were crucial in my life.

I'm writing to a reader who is no stranger to intense emotional pain but is primed for deep personal growth. I shine a light on my most shameful experiences in order to proclaim that while our pain can be crippling at times, that pain in retrospect can provide inspiration and solutions. I want my readers to find and live their most spectacular version of life.

I call the badass in me a "Winged Warrior" because she's a *Superhero*. And right now, that's exactly how I feel . . . like a *Superhero*! When you're on the playground—and about to get your ass kicked—wouldn't you want a badass on your side? In my sadness, I found strength. In my pain, I found power.

That being said, I owe my readers a little warning. Although my life has unfolded just as intended and in Divine Order, it hasn't exactly been G-rated. I never realized I had grown up in such a sheltered bubble–until it burst.

To the fearless radicals who will stick in there with me . . . I salute you. Welcome to my wolf pack! To all the beautiful souls I might offend with the language in this book, say a prayer for me, dear readers–and keep on reading. You'll be praying for me often. Cursing is just a drop in the bucket when sharing the story of "me." I welcome you just the same! It took me a long time to decide if I'd keep the f-bombs in this book, and it came down to recognizing that any-one who can resonate with what I have faced will understand and embrace each word. It's not my intention to offend–only to be completely authentic.

While I'm at it, here's a little spoiler alert: some of you might become uncomfortable when I mention religion. It's played an enormous role in my life. Rest assured, you have nothing to fear. I'm not a hater. Everyone has their own personal journey regarding religion, and what a journey mine has been! I have the utmost respect for any peaceful religion that we as human beings choose to make a part of our life experience. Spirituality and religion are a part of my life to this day.

Because of my respect for all peaceful religions, I'm not going to use the actual name of the religion I grew up in, nor the exact region in which I grew up. As you will see, my vernacular is one of a small-town girl. And let's just call my faith "The X-Factor." Identifying any particular religion has no merit in my story. I've come to believe in a solid truth; we all get to choose, and we all get to be right in choosing our personal beliefs. I'm not being patronizing; I mean that literally. Hallelujah, God bless America, amen, and hurrah!

Each person has a unique narrative that has led them to where they stand today. My story is no exception. However, I see my life through a different lens now, a beautifully clear and powerful lens. Having reached this juncture– with a new badass mentality and miracles in my wings, I find myself excited to share my perfectly imperfect story with you.

CHAPTER 1

Wamona and Gowiath

I stepped off the front porch, ready to do battle. My light brown, pixie-cut hair rustled in the hot breeze coming up the street–as if it were high noon in our western town. The grit stung my light blue eyes, but I was still determined. Even though I didn't have a single weapon in my arsenal, I strode out onto the grass–barefoot and brazen.

Today, I would face him again, with all the dramatics a four-year-old could possibly muster, and somehow, I would win. Too little to understand the definition of insanity, I "girded up my loins," ready to return to the trenches of combat.

Glancing behind me at the small, A-framed brick house tucked away in a cul-de-sac in an older part of town, I ensured my two older siblings were nowhere in sight. Rita was the oldest, five years older than me; next, Kyle was just three years my senior. My baby brother wasn't on my radar yet, since I was only worried about losing face to siblings higher in the ranks. *Good.* I was glad there would be no witnesses to the slaughter.

The phrase, "I'm going to tell my daddy on you," didn't apply to my world. My dad was big and strong, a person I admired from a distance, but he rarely spoke to me. In fact, my only real memory of him at that age was watching him shave every morning. He whistled the song *Raindrops Keep Falling on My Head* as he skillfully moved the razor across his square jaw . . . his big, broad shoulders taking up the entire bathroom. The smell of *Old Spice* cologne would linger long after he was gone.

So alone, I balled my fists and stepped onto the driveway. My enemy was already there, grinning at me with his yellowed teeth and smelling of motor grease from working in his garage. This was a true David and Goliath battle; Goliath went by the name of Mr. Hampton, and he lived next door.

Mr. Hampton was old, but he had the gruffness of a drill sergeant. He wore thick, black-rimmed glasses that did little to conceal his bushy, gray eyebrows underneath. I knew what was coming. Glaring at him defiantly, my arms folded across my tiny chest, I stood my ground–daring him to make a move.

"Ramona," he stated venomously, peering down at me through those thick glasses, squinting as he prepared for the assault, "Say, 'The rickety rabbit ran across the rocky road!'"

BOOM!

Without even thinking, I blustered back like clockwork, "The wickety wabbit wan acwoss the wocky woad!"

Mr. Hampton began to laugh, a loud, thundering sound that tore through my soul. He knew I had a speech impediment and went straight for the jugular as any worthy opponent would. I couldn't even say my own name–I was "Wamona," and while that made everyone laugh, I hated it when *he* laughed most of all.

Right on cue, I turned and fled, once again crushed and crying out to my mother. To make matters worse, Mr. Hampton stood outside–right under my window, and howled like a bloodhound, mocking me as he matched my wailing.

You would think this scenario could only occur one time. Perhaps my mother would step in and save me . . . nope, that wasn't happening. She was a very passive woman. Facing Goliath was my job, and mine alone.

It stands to reason that my four-year-old self would have eventually taken action, grabbing my stones and whirling them in my slingshot, shouting a preschool version of "Why don't you just shove it, Mr. Hampton?" But alas, no. That definition of insanity, doing the same things repeatedly and expecting a different outcome? Well, that started early with me.

Goliath and I were at the war front every day, ready to assume our positions and play out our melodramatic scripts. We played out the scenario like it was the first time our little confrontation had ever occurred. The drama alone kept it interesting.

The problem was my oh-so-dramatic personality. I forever just wanted to be seen–not stuck in the middle somewhere, invisible. Goliath was my nemesis; as long as I was back inside our chaotic house by the time it got dark, that was a win for my mother's passive parenting.

One day, my mother told me about a visitor I would have. His name was Glen. He was a college student who was going to help me say my Rs. At first, I didn't like the thought of talking to a stranger. I was already fighting to keep my head above water in the neverending conflict with my shrewd opponent, Mr. Hampton.

The first time Glen came to our house, he had a big bag of M&M's in his hand. The sight of those delicious morsels changed everything. My new best friend and I sat on the back porch, and he gave me a white styrofoam cup. All I had to do was repeat the words he would say. Every time I at least tried to say the word, Glen would drop an M&M into my cup. No laughing, no teasing. Glen talked to me and only me. He became my knight in shining armor.

Before I knew it, I could say my name. "Ramona," not "Wamona." I could finally say, "The rickety rabbit ran across the rocky road!" claiming victory and ruining Mr. Hampton's fun. As triumphant as this was for both me and my valiant teacher, Glen, when that battle finally dissipated, I had to seek out new ways to put myself smack dab in the middle of situations designed to produce the maximum amount of drama possible. Attention was a scarce commodity; one that demanded considerable effort on my part to obtain.

The first day of school marked a true rite of passage. My mother, being a skilled seamstress, had sewn me a red, knee-length dress with yellow rickrack adorning the gathered waist. I stood there grinning from ear to ear as Mom took my picture. Our neighbors, the Martins, who lived opposite Mr.

Hampton, took me to school with their daughter Chelsie, who was the same age as me.

Chelsie was physically handicapped, and I hadn't spent much time with her prior to our first school day. Until that point, my preference had been to roam around the neighborhood like a stray puppy. But from that day forward, Chelsie and I became the best of friends. Chelsie's arms and hands were misshapen, extending only about six inches from her shoulders. She also had difficulty walking, so Chelsie's parents often carried her; I envied the special attention my tiny comrade received.

But I also loved to dote on my adored friend; carrying her books or helping her hang up her coat made me feel important. Protecting her from any injustice in the world became my new, self-appointed task. Telling a kid at school to "shut up!" (followed by a menacing glare that no child dared to challenge) if they were saying unkind things to my beloved friend was a piece of cake compared to my days of battle with Mr. Hampton. The kids in our class didn't scare me–not one little bit.

Chelsie once spent two weeks in the hospital having surgery to help straighten her spine. I was so happy to finally see her when she came home! My sweet friend showed me a craft book she had made during her hospital stay. The cover was a picture of Chelsie, with yellow yarn for her hair, braided into two long pigtails with pink bows attached to each braid. It was the coolest book I had ever seen!

Lying in bed that night, I fantasized about being in a hospital with some horrific ailment . . . and having a book like Chelsie's.

When Chelsie could walk again, she had new shoes; they laced up all the way to her ankle. Without thinking anything, I told her, "Those look like baby shoes." I don't remember trying to be hurtful, but my mom spoke with Mrs. Martin on the phone that evening. When she hung up, Mom took me into her room. I knew it must be serious; my mother talking directly to me only happened once every blue moon.

My mother was a large woman. She always wore a house dress with an apron tied not at her waist but right under her bust line. Tonight, as the sun slipped behind the horizon, she sat in her big rocking chair and began to nurse my baby brother as she talked. "Ramona," Mom said in a stern voice, "today when you were playing at Chelsie's house, you called her shoes 'baby shoes.'"

I looked at my mother with wide eyes.

"Would you like it if someone said *you* had baby shoes?" she asked, looking at me pointedly.

I shook my head in shame, realizing that I'd made a big mistake. I felt terrible. This was my beloved friend whom I loved! How could I have done such a thing? I blinked as tears streamed down my cheeks.

"You need to go and apologize to Chelsie," Mom finished.

Huh? My eyes grew wider as real fear took over, and the heaviness of my actions began to settle in. This was the kind of attention I did not want! *How did I get myself into such a mess?*

By now, it was after dark, and usually, that would have been scary for me. However, as I reached the end of our driveway, my fear lifted, and bravery took over. My only thoughts were seeing my friend and making things better again. As I stood at the entry of Chelsie's house, I mustered every ounce of courage I had.

In a shaky voice, I squeaked, "I'm sorry I said your shoes looked like baby shoes," as new tears streamed down my red cheeks. Chelsie came over and hugged me. Her arms barely reached my back as her little cupped hands patted my shoulders to console me. She told me it was okay, and I hugged her tight as a wave of relief came over my body. Grateful to have the love and forgiveness of my sweet friend . . . everything in the world was right again.

After our long hug, Chelsie took me into her room and let me have a closer look at her new shoes. I noticed the sole of the right shoe was about four times thicker than the sole of the left shoe. "This helps me walk better," Chelsie explained.

At that moment, I understood how cool Chelsie's new shoes actually were. I felt so much love and compassion for my sweet friend who took the time to teach me about her unique needs, and the shoes made just for her. Our bond became more vital than ever. I felt like the luckiest girl in the world to have such a wonderful friend.

Warrior Wisdom:

Having the opportunity to do battle with Mr. Hampton was priceless. The things it taught me! I overcame being bullied by a scary old man. In doing so, I was brave enough to protect my most beloved friend, Chelsie, from the bullies at school.

At the tender age of five, I learned how words can hurt someone and felt the grace of forgiveness when Chelsie forgave me. I experienced the joy of redemption and gratitude for my most special friend, who helped me to understand why she was different. Creating a sacred trust between us as little girls and a friendship forged in fire.

CHAPTER 2

Drama, Drama, Drama!

E very child deserves a hero, and I had a great one. Her name was Grandma.

During the summers, my mother took me and my siblings to Canada to visit the dairy farm and home where she grew up. We stayed for six glorious weeks full of adventure. I couldn't wait to get there–and never wanted to go home.

The year I turned seven, as our station wagon turned onto my grandparents' road, the butterflies in my stomach whirred faster and faster as we drove along the tall poplar trees that protected my grandfather's wheat crops. Piling out of the car and inhaling the smell of the dairy, I rushed into my grandmother's arms. I felt her strong arms wrap tightly around me . . . and I was home. It was the happiest time of my life. To me, the smell of the dairy farm was one of the best smells on the planet (manure and all).

From that moment on, I became my grandmother's shadow; relishing the age of seven and feeling immensely cherished as I had her all to myself, without the need to share her with my other siblings who were either too young or off enjoying farm life with other activities.

We had been at the farm for over a week. I woke up early one morning like every other day, but today felt different. Suddenly and strangely, my older sister Rita was standing there; she wanted to play with me. Nothing miraculous had happened in the previous days to warrant her newfound interest in me. *Rita is paying attention to me!* I thought my little heart would burst.

Rita and I walked out to the calf barn, me skipping, to see the new baby calves. Once inside, I cautiously moved behind her, feeling grateful there was a gate between us–they were every bit as big as I was.

"Watch this, Ramona," Rita grinned knowingly. She held out her hand to one of the calves, and I watched in horror as it started sucking on her fingers. Rita, knowing very well that I was a drama queen, giggled as my jaw dropped in utter disgust and nausea. But the horror show had only begun; my sister then took her hand out of the calf's mouth, her fingers full of thick saliva, and dripped it right in front of my face. I immediately began to dry heave as Rita burst out laughing.

Mission accomplished: Rita 1, Ramona 0.

Just like my years of playing a role in commencing battle with Mr. Hampton, I never disappointed my audience. Any button they pushed, was exactly what I gave them. I ran back to the house with Rita's laughter echoing after me. Completely traumatized from the shocking scene that triggered my gag reflex right down to the tips of my toes, I couldn't wait to report the latest infraction against my fragile feelings.

Thankfully, Grandma was there to quickly validate my horror and get my mind on something fun again. Life was so much nicer with Grandma in my corner. She kept me close and quickly defused the drama that inevitably broke out between me and my sister.

My grandparents' modest farmhouse felt so wonderful. Although, the home without the people in it could have been viewed as something ordinary, rather than extraordinary. The basement had cement walls where I could smell and feel the natural, cold moisture in the air. But the whole place felt magical to me. My bed had layers of my grandmother's hand-sewn quilts to keep me warm. I shimmied under the heavy quilts every night, inhaling the intoxicating fresh smell of the line-dried linens. Exhausted and happy, I fell asleep in that most perfect place.

Although I had unconditional love from both my mother and my grandmother, they were quite opposite in personality, drive, energy, and affection. Even as a little girl, I marveled at the difference between them. My mother seemed to always be nursing babies; life *just happened* around her. Despite being seven years old, I curiously observed how she reacted to situations instead of controlling her surroundings.

Grandma, on the other hand, was very put together. She always wore a floral dress, and a clean white apron with delicate flowers embroidered on the corners. She had gumboots for collecting the morning milk and eggs from the barn, and sensible slip-on shoes for the house. She was a true master of her life and skilled in everything she did.

Compared to the chaos of my mother's house, the routine of farm life was terrific. Friday meant wash day. Today Grandma looked at me with her sparkling eyes and declared, "Okay, my little partner, let's get moving!" as she made a running gesture with her fists.

"O-kay!" I shouted excitedly, and she laughed at my enthusiasm. We both radiated happiness as I followed her into the laundry room . . . where an old-fashioned washing machine awaited. Gazing at it with wide eyes, it seemed like a contraption from the pages of a Dr. Seuss book!

I peered over the giant open vat of hot water as the laundry jerked back and forth. Elaborate visions of myself as Dr. Ramona, famous scientist, filled my mind as Grandma handed me detergent to pour into the batch of laundry. *This is serious business!* Next came liquid that smelled like flowers to pour in during the rinse cycle.

As we pulled the soaking wet items out of the open washer and fed them into the ringer, Grandma began to sing, "Watch your fingers in the house and your toes in the yard; how ya gonna count if ya lose one?" She chuckled delightedly as she watched me bounce along to her little song.

The icing on the cake was the smell of the lilac bushes in the backyard as Grandma and I hung the laundry on the line to dry. This simple life was my paradise.

As our visit drew to a close, I grew more somber. The last week at my grandparents' farm was always the hardest. I knew my time was coming to an end. I couldn't bear the thought of going an entire year before I saw Grandma again! She was my protector. When we were down to our last evening, inevitably, Rita and I got into a horrible fight.

As the sun glistened across the lake, edging towards the horizon, Grandma had entrusted me with the task of taking the clothes off the line while she delivered dinner to my great-grandparents' house, located just around the lake on their farm. I cherished the role of being my grandmother's helper; by example, she had taught me exactly what to do and how to do it.

As Grandma pulled away in her car, I happily went into the laundry room to grab the basket. But the basket wasn't there.

This isn't right. We had a system; the basket was always put away in the same spot. I decided to check outside by the clothesline. As I stepped out onto the porch, I saw Rita taking the clothes off the line instead of me!

What is she doing? This is my job!

"Stop!" I shouted. "Grandma told *me* to do that!"

"You're not old enough. I'm doing it," Rita announced coldly.

"Me and Grandma do this job! This is our job!" I cried.

Rita pushed me back and snapped, "Get out of here. I'm doing this for Grandma."

Grandma will think I didn't want to do my job . . . No! I can't let this happen! I plowed into Rita with all my might to push her away from the line.

Now Rita was angry. She shoved me again–this time much harder. As I fell to the ground, she began to take the laundry off the line as fast as she could.

I was blind with fury. *How dare you come in and try to do my job?* I leaped up and pulled at her shirt, ripping the seam. This made Rita just as furious as I was. She dropped the clothes and engaged in a battle of hitting and shrieking. After several high-pitched battle cries, Mom finally surfaced and broke us up.

Fresh tears welled in my eyes as my chest heaved up and down. Everything was ruined. There were clean clothes strewn all over the lawn. *How will I explain this to Grandma?* I cried to my mother, "This is *my* job!" But she didn't want to hear it.

"Go in the house, Ramona! Rita, you get these clothes picked up!" my mother yelled. I cried even louder. This was the most unjust predicament I had ever encountered!

When Grandma returned to the house, I was still sobbing. I skipped dinner that night. When she came to check on me, I immediately started to cry again. *Why did Rita have to come in and ruin everything?* Even as a little girl, I knew the bond my grandmother and I had was special.

Grandma stayed up with me for most of the night. Rocking me back and forth in her arms, she told me stories about my mother's childhood and what life was like back then. I sat and listened in amazement as Grandma described their house. It was the same house we were in, but it had started out with just a single kitchen and bedroom. And no running water!

My mother, being the oldest, was given the job of collecting water from the lake and bringing it up to the house on a little cart when she was just five years old.

My grandmother's life back then sounded so enchanting, like a story from *Little House on the Prairie*. They were a loving family, working hard and protecting each other to survive in the wilderness. My seven-year-old mind thought, *How I would have loved that!*

As my grandmother spoke about times long past, I clung to her. It felt so good to be held. I didn't want her to ever let me go. Her life had been magical, and she lovingly enveloped me into her world. I cherished her stories and attention above anything else. After that summer, my relationship with my grandmother became an unbreakable root, a fierce and protective bond.

We drove home, and that fall, I found myself embroiled in a cosmic game of "musical chairs." During the midst of first grade, my family relocated to a new home fifteen miles away. Transitioning to a new school, and making new friends, became my new reality. However, there was a silver lining; this home was at least four times larger than our previous one, and had just been built. It truly felt like rags to riches.

As I stood in my new room, looking at my closet, which was bigger than my parents' in our old house, I felt like I was in a dream. But it was one I didn't quite understand. My dad had bought new furniture for every bedroom. Mine was white with a gold trim. The four-poster canopy bed had a light purple satin comforter with a matching sheer canopy top.

As magical as it all felt, the sting of being away from my best friend Chelsie was heart-wrenching. While my mother took me to Chelsie's house for sleepovers on Friday night a few times, it was never the same again. The easy factor had disappeared from the equation, and closeness was impossible. That was only the beginning.

With our move came the shock of the news that my father was leaving. He had started a new business that took him from being fairly nondescript to disappearing completely from our lives. My siblings and I cried, standing next to Dad's car as we hugged him and said good-bye.

Mom tried to comfort us, saying he would be back. But from that day forward, my father never lived at home again. He came home for Christmas and would show up in between jobs for a few days. And over time, my mother managed to have two more babies. To my mother's credit, she never said a negative word about my father's absence. That made it easier to adapt to our new normal.

But *my* new normal had become a war zone. Mr. Hampton was a cake walk compared to what I was now facing. I had to go about my way every day on high alert, keeping a low profile the second I came out of my room. Rita had begun to resent my entire existence. We had always fought with sibling rivalry, but this was new. Now she acted as if she truly despised me. It was a hatred I didn't understand.

The truth was, my overwhelmed mother had piled the responsibilities she once carried directly onto Rita, who was just eleven, the moment my father quit living at home. While Mom nurtured and cared for the babies, Rita single-handedly cooked for everyone. Feeding a family of six was no small task. Why my mother chose to not give any responsibilities to Kyle or me is a mystery. Under my grandmother's wings, I had learned to do the laundry and garden; and I loved every minute of it.

But that was our reality; Rita cooked, no one cleaned–ever. Our house was in a constant state of chaos.

We only did one thing on a regular basis–Sunday dinner after church. Beyond church and our weekly meal together, nothing was ever asked or expected of me. I'd always been a free spirit, but now–I became this completely carefree, skinny little shit with absolutely no responsibilities.

Unfortunately, my cavalier attitude made me a prime target for Rita's frustration within our dysfunctional household. Rita was overweight as a child, and when we moved, making new friends had not been easy. She was angry at life and *oh-so miserable*. There was nothing fair or balanced about our situation, and my sister began to take out her rage of being so unhappy on *me*.

Here's some irony for you: My dear mother was president of the "Mother's Aid Association" within the congregation of our faith. This organization taught the principles of being faithful women, wives, and mothers within the church. Each time my mother left for a meeting, I got my ass kicked.

Rita had long fingernails that were natural and sharp. She grabbed my arm and dug her nails in until long after they drew blood. Once in her clutches, I could do nothing to escape it, and nothing my mother ever said prevented it from happening the next time she was out of the house.

This was my reality; Mom couldn't save me, and Rita wouldn't stop.

A few months later, however, the stars aligned and something miraculous happened. A family with a girl my age moved into our neighborhood just two blocks away. And it wasn't long before we became inseparable.

Her name was Sheila, and her household was as Beaver Cleaver as you could get. As quick as you could say, "Whew!," this became my sanctuary. Tagging along with Sheila to 4-H club and dance class became easy. It was a no-brainer; I spent every waking moment I possibly could at her *safe house*. And Rita was left to tolerate the enormity of dysfunction within our home all by herself.

That was my life in a nutshell through the elementary grades. At school, I was like an excited dog at the park who couldn't wait to get off its leash. I could have been the poster child for ADHD if it had been recognized back then. When the bell rang to go home, it didn't matter what the teacher had given us to do for homework; assignments never crossed my mind once I left the school. Why should they? I was never asked about school or homework once I got home. My mother never even asked to see a report card!

Sheila and I remained best friends; companionship was key to my survival. So when my comrade moved away to another state the summer after our fifth-grade year, my sense of security left with her–and my sanctuary along with her family. I had never felt so lonely, lost, and afraid.

As I walked into the colossal middle school fortress designed exclusively for the sixth and seventh graders, I was confronted with the harsh reality that I was friendless and utterly alone. Sheila and I had kept to ourselves in grade school. We had each other, and that was all we needed. Although I was mischievous, I was also painfully shy. I didn't have the slightest clue how to strike up a conversation with other girls or become friends.

I soon realized I was *not* one of the popular girls . . . not even close. Having a July birthday made me the youngest in my class–and by far the latest bloomer. I'm sure it was a no-brainer for my mother to start me in school so early, when the alternative was listening to Mr. Hampton howl outside my bedroom window as I pitched my daily fit after retreating from our battlegrounds.

Middle school was a completely different animal. People swore and sometimes fought–unleashing their inner sailors. The popular ones held hands in the hall because they were "going out," and everyone knew what social class they carried within the hierarchy. No one cared if I had kicked ass the year before in dodgeball at recess. I missed hitting any type of "class" whatsoever.

This was due to the status I established in my dreaded sixth-period gym class.

No, it wasn't because I wore a training bra and had absolutely no boobs (although that didn't help). *My* mother had decided I could "just wear Rita's old gym suit." It's hard to decide what to list first when explaining *why* my mother's decision was so-very-wrong.

Rita had been in middle school five years before me. Since that time, the gym suits had changed styles not once, but *twice*! I didn't get to wear the new, cute yellow short shorts with purple piping around the legs and a yellow V-neck top like most of the class wore. In fact, I didn't even get to wear the previous year's suit like a few of the less fortunate girls wore. A one-piece, light purple, jersey knit jumpsuit with a white ribbed jersey knit waistband. *Dare to dream!* Oh no, I was in a class of my own.

I got to wear the dark, eggplant purple, double polyester, one-piece jumpsuit with an extra-large white zipper that went from the belly button to the neck. And I can't forget the pointed collar that covered half my chest.

Because of me, the less fortunate girls who missed out on getting the latest gym design had a free pass to not be mocked. I took in all the shame for being the number one winner of the "least fortunate." The relief they must have felt! But wait . . . it doesn't end there. There was a bonus, if you will, an added layer of humiliation. Because Rita had been overweight then, the crotch of this fashionable gym suit went clear to my knees! From the first day of gym, I became the mascot of misfortune!

The whole situation was so ironic. Rita was thin now–and happy! Over the last two years, she had taken her weight issue head on and won, using nothing but sheer willpower.

Fortunately for me, in her empowered state, the drama between us had dissipated entirely. That was a huge bonus at home, but there I was where reputation and clothing mattered like life's breath . . . wearing this ridiculous suit of shame. As if my social awkwardness wasn't enough! My stomach churned over and above my regular state of stress every day as sixth-period gym class approached.

I should have just spilled the beans to my mom, but nooo, I decided to embark on a grand social experiment instead. Picture this: me, the star of a year-long reality show titled "Misfit Madness." There I was, braving the treacherous hallways as an outcast. There were no friendly faces at lunchtime, only judgmental gazes staring at me like I was a rare species whose unpopularity was contagious if they got too close. If only there had been a trophy for enduring the most bullshit!

The safety and love of my grandmother's home felt a million miles away.

Warrior Wisdom:

The time and attention my grandmother gave me by simply allowing me into her daily life had an impact that would stay with me forever. I was so desperate to be seen, heard, and loved. Grandma provided all of that for me effortlessly; under her care, I had no need for dramatic roleplay.

Recognizing the silver lining in my mother's parenting skills has been crucial in choosing power over victimhood. When my father left, I could have learned to be resentful and spiteful, growing up with feelings of being abandoned. Instead, I learned to make decisions without questioning myself, with the strength of knowing that I didn't need a man's permission to do anything.

I never knew how my mom truly felt about my father leaving home. For all I know, she could have secretly been doing a little jig when he left, or she could have felt completely abandoned and heartbroken. Nevertheless, I will always love her for not pushing that drama onto me as a little girl.

A parent can often overlook sibling rivalry because both participants are their children. As parents, every single action we take to protect or ignore our children makes a lasting impact on their self-worth.

When I think about my dear and oh-so-dysfunctional family, I wish I could return to that time. I would tell Rita how much I love her. I would tell her what a great cook she was and say "thank you" every night as we ate the food she prepared. I would tell her she didn't ever have to be alone–she would always have me as a friend. I would also wash the freaking dishes!

But I can't go back. Our life stories are what they are. My mother's actions spared me by never being vocal regarding how she felt about my father leaving home. However, my mother's choice to give her responsibilities to my sister Rita and no one else directly impacted me.

I understand my mother was doing the best she could. Reflecting on those times, I see them through a compassionate and understanding lens. God bless you, Rita! I know those years were hard for you. Understanding this brought up such a fierce, protective love for you, my dear sister . . . something that ultimately saved me . . . but we'll get to that later.

Having no friends in the sixth grade isn't a sad story. On the contrary, the experience of wearing that ridiculous gym suit gave me empathy and aware-ness as an adult. The connection I feel toward people in need is a constant drive in my life. The joy I feel when I can help another person is incredible.

Do I act when I encounter a situation that I deem unacceptable? You bet your ass I do! Without this core drive to choose action over indifference, I would be a mere shell of the person I am today. As I reflect on my past, it's been such a joy to recognize and understand the gifts I've been given through my experiences. The life gift from the hideous gym suit experience has been one of my greatest blessings!

CHAPTER 3

Mean Girls

I looked in my mirror for the final inspection of the insecure girl staring back at me. I would soon be in the presence of . . . my "friends." Their unpredictable nature was as unsettling as your typical serial killer. I had met Hannibal–I mean Hannah–a month before school started. Hannah was very petite, and her mother was even tinier than she was. Their household was small, with just two girls, and the polar opposite from my home, with five siblings. Needless to say, we always hung out at her house.

There was a downside to our friendship–Hannah had a best friend of her own, so I became the third wheel. Her name was Stephanie. Stephanie was also very tiny; she had a stunningly beautiful mother who did hair, so Stephanie's hair always looked perfect.

Hannah and I got along great when it was just the two of us, but when Stephanie was there, I was only tolerated at best. When school started again, I was so happy and relieved to *finally* have friends. Just having someone to eat lunch with was a huge improvement–no more stares from other kids as they walked by, so I took whatever my new friends dished out.

The three of us got along great for a while, and then one or both would decide to bully me. Stephaine was always the instigator. She loved to make snide little comments about my hair or clothes. I became ultra-sensitive with my actions, walking on eggshells around them to prevent an upset. I wanted to protect my "having friends" status at any cost.

I had enrolled in a private dance class that year. My mother drove me thirty minutes to and from every week. I loved to dance, and the local teacher in our small town taught mainly grade school ages. I was so excited the day Hannah and Stephanie came with me to my class; we had planned on going to the mall afterward. *They'll finally see me dance . . . I'll have their respect after today.*

To my disappointment, Hannah and Stephanie made a point to "not" watch me. They talked and snickered through the entire lesson. They had already decided where I stood within our group—and nothing I could do would ever change that.

One day at school, as I walked towards Hannah and Stephanie to meet them for lunch, they started running in the other direction. *What's happening? Are they running from me?* I ran towards them until I heard Stephanie let out a high-pitched shriek as she yelled, "Run!" to Hannah.

That stopped me dead in my tracks. Everyone was staring at me—I was so humiliated! I self-consciously tried to smooth out my bangs, suddenly becoming ultra-aware of everything I was wearing. *I hate these corduroy pants . . . they make me look fat! Why did I wear these socks? They don't even match my outfit!*

Walking down the school hall, away from the humiliation in the lunchroom—I was shaking. My already fragile self-esteem was shattered. As I opened my locker, a note fell at my feet. I opened it . . . my heart sinking as I read the words:

WE ARE BREAKING UP WITH YOU! STAY AWAY FROM US!
Stephanie & Hannah

I walked home that afternoon completely devastated, replaying the embarrassing scene in the lunchroom over and over in my head. My only value was being liked and accepted by those around me. Hannah and Stephanie held the keys to my survival within a society of peers who observed whether I was acceptable or not. I felt sick to my stomach.

Lying in my bed that night, I cried and cried. *What am I going to do now?* The next day at school was gut-wrenching. *I hate my life! I'm going to hide in the bathroom at lunch.* But to my surprise, my "friends" decided to throw me a crumb in the third period and spoke to me again. I was so incredibly grateful to be back in their presence.

I felt relieved knowing I wouldn't have to feel like such a freak by hiding in the bathroom when lunch time rolled around. It was only slightly comforting; however, I knew it would happen again. It always did. This behavior had become a pattern that occurred every couple of months.

Then, one afternoon, it happened again. It was the worst and *last* time their nasty bullying would demean and humiliate me. We were all sitting in Mr. Hunter's English class when I passed a note to Stephanie for both her and Hannah to read. They sat next to each other, precisely one row behind me.

My note said:

Hey, do you guys want to come to my house after school? My mom can give us a ride home.

Stephanie started writing a reply . . . and just kept writing. Finally, she passed the note back to me with a little *smirk*. I opened the message and began to read her hateful words that criticized everything from my hair to my clothes. My heart started to pound as my familiar nightmare unfolded.

Then I came to the sentence that broke me:

We can't get a ride to your house from your mom anyway. She's so fat she takes up the whole car.

I had experienced hurt feelings before, but that gutted me. It was beyond mean. As a wave of shame overcame me, I felt like my heart had just been ripped out of my chest. I had never experienced such crushing pain.

To my horror, I began to sob during Mr. Hunter's lesson. Desperately trying to hold back my tears, I finally left the class and hid in the girl's restroom. Even in the privacy of the bathroom stall, I couldn't stop crying.

Tyra, a girl from the class, came in to see if I was okay. All I could say to her was, "I'm trying to stop . . . I just can't stop crying." I covered my mouth to get control. I wept until I was exhausted.

An hour passed. Finally, I left the restroom a half hour into the next period. I was numb and past the point of giving a shit. When I opened my locker, another note fell out at my feet. It read:

WE'RE SO SORRY! IT WAS JUST A JOKE!

My heart was being squeezed again. I felt nauseous. I didn't speak to either of my so-called friends as we all sat in the lunchroom together. Hannah and Stephanie acted nervous. The possibility of getting into trouble for what our entire English class had witnessed was probably weighing heavy on their minds.

That hateful comment about my mother lit a fire inside me that day. Saying mean things to me was one thing—but being so cruel towards my mother had crossed a line. I felt a new power growing . . . something I'd never experienced before. My energy did a complete one-hundred-and-eighty-degree turn—it was palpable.

I was painfully aware that my mother was different from the other moms. They had pointed their fingers and made fun of the very thing I was most insecure about. I no longer wanted to hang out with these two little bitches at any cost.

The two "friends" I once clung to for meaning and approval in our middle school world had been exposed. Now, I just saw them as a couple little punks. Their masks were off. I realized I was tougher than both Hannah and Stephanie put together! I quit tip-toeing around them; I stopped apologizing for everything I did.

The fear of having no friends if I didn't submit to their bullying was gone. I found a peaceful confidence in my willingness to walk away from my so-called friends who had been so cruel. Things were different after that day–and I would be forever changed.

Once I started junior high, I noticed my new, empowered attitude was beginning to carry some weight among our society of shallow-minded, young sheep. The kids no longer looked to the reformed bullies in my tribe (Hannah and Stephanie) to determine whether I was, or wasn't, in fact, a leper that week. I held my own at school–I was tougher now . . . I had a callousness that hadn't been there the year before.

Just as I got my balance on the scales, my born-again besties took a giant leap and acquired jobs at the local Dairy Queen. This was the perfect opportunity for girls our age to socialize and meet boys. To my delight, Hannah spoke with the owner, and they also had a space for me. I was ecstatic!

I gave my mother a long speech about wanting to be responsible and earn my own money. "They'll even let me choose my own shifts, so I won't ever have to work on Sundays," I told her, confident that I had covered all my bases. *I wonder if she's buying this? I wonder if they'll really let us choose our own shifts? This is going to be such a great way to meet boys!*

My mother saw right through my pathetic attempt with the whole responsible/keeping the Sabbath Day holy speech. There was no way she was going to let me get a job at that establishment. As incredibly passive as she was, she felt the people who visited the Dairy Queen could be a bad influence on me, and she made that fact very clear.

Argh! I'm trying to fit in! Why don't I just start wearing a burka! I balled my hands into fists as Mom denied my request, consumed by my constant frustration. My mother had no idea how hard it was to maintain a position of having my peers deem me acceptable. Working at the Dairy Queen would have carried a lot of clout.

How am I ever going to get a boyfriend? Truthfully, I had carried a massive crush on one boy. It all began in the sixth grade. His name was Ryan

Richards, and he was beautiful . . . so much that I joined the school band just to be closer to him. Ryan played the tuba, so I decided to play the clarinet.

The sheer joy of staring at Ryan's beautiful face–with his muscular arms and perfect hair every day in the fifth period made band my favorite class. I had been in the school band for three years and still couldn't read music. Let's just say Ryan took up one hundred percent of my attention.

In the ninth grade, to my delight, Ryan had cast his eyes in my direction. We had been flirting back and forth the entire year. By flirting, I mean I would punch him in the shoulder when I passed him–and he would fake being hurt. I still had my braces on at that point, so I was really reaching. That spring, our school band went on the yearly field trip to an amusement park; and the two of us happened to accidentally-on-purpose get on a ride together. The day had finally come!

Ryan and I sat together in a two-seat cart. As it moved along the track, we went through a dark, scary part of the ride. Suddenly, I could feel Ryan's breath on my cheek. Terror instantly took over my body. *Wait! I'm not ready to kiss a boy!* I stared straight ahead like a stone . . . like my life depended on it–I didn't move a muscle.

News flash! Ramona is too chicken to kiss a boy . . . she's the biggest nerd, dork-snork on the planet! That amusement park ride was the beginning, middle, and end of my love relationship with Ryan. *C'est la vie.*

One afternoon, I had just nailed the technical tap dance I had been working on for months with my teacher. At that moment, I had an idea; I could teach dance lessons in the basement of our house! We had a billiard room with a parquet wood floor, and there was even an outdoor entrance. It was perfect! All I had to do was move the billiard table into the back corner while I did my lessons–felt legs on the table made it easy to slide around.

My mother was very supportive of this new idea, especially compared to my first plan of working at the DQ with my friends. In fact, she purchased a record player and all the dance records I wanted. Vinyl wasn't vintage back in those days, so I acquired a big collection easily.

I made flyers to hand out door-to-door throughout the neighborhood. I offered beginning, intermediate, and advanced classes for tap, ballet, and jazz–ages five through ten. I charged the same monthly price the local teacher charged (minus three dollars).

I ended up with twenty-six students. Growing up in a ninety-five percent X-Factor community (aka my religion), our church members believed whole-heartedly in procreation. We probably had more children per capita than any-where else in the United States. No kidding! So, I definitely had the numbers in my favor regarding kids who wanted dance lessons.

I taught dance after school on Tuesday, Wednesday, and Thursday every week. And I did it fearlessly. I did this through my sophomore year, making three times what Stephanie and Hannah made at the Dairy Queen. And I was good at it!

My sophomore year brought forth a new world for me that took my bud-ding confidence up another notch. I had finally grown into my teeth! I got my braces off . . . and what once had been an array of crooked teeth that looked way too big to fit in my mouth were now perfectly straight and beautiful. My awkward stage was over!

I had big, beautiful (not boobs) blue eyes, a massive smile, and now per-fect teeth. Life was looking up! And even though I had the tiniest boobs in the school, I had long legs and a great ass–thanks to all the years of ballet.

I was also very thin. I had assessed my lot in life, and my fear of falling into a realm that was anywhere near my mother was always on my mind. I loved my mother dearly–but I would never be like her. The summer before I started high school, I had come down with a bug that made it impossible to keep anything down for a few days. I couldn't believe how fast I became really thin!

This was my answer to ease my fears, and this is when bulimia first came into my life. My weight was one thing I actually had control over. It felt good to be thin. It felt even better to be in control. There was no way I was giving that up.

Despite the new and improved version of myself, when the first home football game rolled around that fall, that oh-so-familiar feeling of not fitting in reared its ugly head again. Hannah and Stephanie were both dating seniors–a fringe benefit from working at the Dairy Queen. Waiting on hot boys with big trucks was something my dance business would never provide.

Hannah and Stephanie sat at the big game with their boyfriends, cuddled close in the crisp air on the hard bleachers. Painfully aware of my fifth-wheel status, I sat at the end next to Hannah. It reminded me of a teenager who's embarrassed to be seen with their mother. *Shit! I'm the mother!*

One week later, by the grace of all that is holy, I was spared my gloomy, single status. I met a beautiful boy–even more beautiful than Ryan! His name was Byron Thomas. Byron was a senior; he drove a cool car, he was kind, had good values, and hung out with a bunch of other good kids. My mother adored him.

He would come over to my house and paint with my mother while I taught dancing; they were both artists and truly enjoyed each other's company. Byron called me his little "Romer."

Oh my heart!

Our relationship became my world–it was all I ever thought about. His love filled me up so much that I was in a constant state of euphoria, blissfully floating day after day. My mother would have to constantly repeat herself to get me to *tune-in* to what she was saying.

"Ramona . . .? Ramona! Did you hear one word I just said?"

"What? Huh?" I would answer after I drifted back to earth, my mind fixated on how wonderful it felt to be in Byron's big, strong arms.

Within my tiny tribe, I was definitely the oddball out. Hannah and Stephanie were two of the twenty-five people in our town who were not raised with a strong, religious overtone in their homes. I, however, was raised very strictly within the faith. My mother was a modest freak! I will never forget the incident of what came to be known as "The Slap."

It was a sound that would echo through the ages. An event that had occurred during the summer between my eighth and ninth grade year was still being talked about two years later!

I was lying out at the local pool (working on my tan) in one of Hannah's bikinis. A neighborhood friend of my mother's drove by the pool and saw my "practically naked body" (as my mother had put it). Horrified, the neighbor rushed home and called my mother to report the appalling scene she had just witnessed within the righteous bubble we lived in.

Upon receiving the shocking phone call, my mother jumped in her big red van and sped down to the city pool. The clock was ticking. She had to get to the crime scene before anyone else in town had a chance to see my scandalous behavior. What were the ladies in church going to say? She had just given her lesson on parenting teenagers in church last month. It was titled "Modesty = Chastity." This scandal would be gossiped about for weeks!

Lying on my beach towel, slathered from top to bottom in Hawaiian Tropic tanning oil, I blissfully inhaled the smell of coconut while basking in the hot sun. I fantasized about what it would be like to actually have boobs.

Suddenly, the sun's heat was gone . . . it got eerie and quiet. I opened my eyes . . . and there was my mother–standing over me. To say my mother was livid is a gross understatement. Furious? Crazed maybe . . . there was no way this situation would end well. My mind began to race, contemplating exactly how bad it was going to get.

In front of my friends, my mother hollered, "Young lady, you get in the van this instant!" The jaws of every teenager within earshot all dropped in unison. I was horrified! I quickly grabbed my beach towel and hopped up. Not because I was afraid of my mother, I knew the sooner I fled this unthinkable situation, the sooner *she* would be gone as well.

I would never live this down among the unpredictable tribe of sun worshipers–all staring at my mother in shock and disbelief. There was no coming back from an event like this. Little did I know, it was about to get a thousand times worse!

To add another layer of humiliation (one wouldn't think that was even possible), my mother slapped me on the butt as I passed her! The already opened mouths of every well-tanned witness to this horrific scene let out an audible gasp. Yup, my mom said that . . . she did that.

I thought her showing up and yelling at me in front of my friends was the worst thing that could happen. Boy, was I wrong! It felt like I was in the Twilight Zone as we drove home. Something this asinine just didn't happen to a girl my age. That was the first time I remember thinking, *You're a real fruitcake!* about my mother.

Warrior Wisdom:

Hannah and Stephanie–those little punks. Our joy and peace come from how we choose to interpret life. I invite anyone who was ever bullied growing up to find something you can take from that incredibly painful experience. What makes us different because of that experience?

Painful experience = new gift. Cha-ching! Empowerment–welcome to my life! The pain was so deep with the letter about my mother, I was presented with an opportunity to break through my belief system and see the situation for what it was. The only thing that changed was my belief about myself. I now emitted an energy that said, "I dare you! I dare you to ever mess with me again!"

Did I realize what was happening at the time? Unfortunately, no. Sometimes it's hard to see the significance of events as they unfold. Today, I can share with you that (in my own life) every experience I've gone through has had a purpose–without exception. Seek out the gifts you can find daily, especially those that show up as a result of a painful or challenging experience. When you notice these gifts, talk about them with your children–and what brought them about.

The earlier we learn to do this, the sooner we can become victorious in life–rather than a victim of it.

Growing up, I didn't always understand why my mother did what she did. Not allowing me to work at the Dairy Queen changed my life; it presented an opportunity for me to create something better. Although my mother was very passive, she never once criticized me or told me I needed to do anything "better." So, when it came to doing something bold, I was fearless.

God bless my mother! She supported me wholeheartedly with my little business. This was my first entrepreneurial venture that gave me a little tiny taste of being a leader and an economic badass.

The slap . . . what can I say? Sometimes things that were such a colossal embarrassment give us nowhere to go, but they sculpt us. Of course, I have forgiven my mother for that ridiculous incident. Right or wrong, my mother did her very best with what she knew—every single day. I appreciate the belly laugh it gives me whenever I think about it.

Is it okay to publicly shame your child? Never, never-ever. I don't care what they've done. Two wrongs do not make a right. To think you're teaching your child a lesson by humiliating them is ignorant and cruel. That being said, I don't think my mother set out to humiliate me that day–she was humiliated herself. And in the moment, she cared more about how it made "her" look within our righteous community than thinking about the impact it would have on me.

Boyfriends . . . Byron's love gave me a sense of self-worth I had never experienced before. A sense of self-worth I would wish for any teenager to have all on their own. With a first love, I think the feelings I had were typical. Byron was a kind, good young man. I was very lucky.

CHAPTER 4

Oh Yes . . . No! Yes! Wait, No!

S ex and guilt. Two things that shouldn't go together in a healthy love life. Yet as teens raised so strictly within the X-Factor faith, the dynamics of our religion brought about a very creative approach when it came to being in love. Byron was also raised in this faith, and it wasn't too long before we started having great X-Factor sex. This kind of sex is everything imaginable except penetration. If one had "that" kind of sex, they would surely need to go in and meet with their pastor/bishop/ rabbi/priest (take your pick) and confess.

Let me clarify; of course, our religion taught that "even light petting is forbidden." But in our teenage minds, my hunky boyfriend and I could handle the ever-so-slight guilt, come Sunday, of doing "everything but" without feeling the need to involve a third party. There was nothing we couldn't justify–love conquered all. Nothing was too brazen or outlandish, because *we* were going to be together forever.

Needless to say, the "heathen" girls like Hannah and Stephanie went right past the X-Factor sex. And without a hint of guilt or shame, moved right on to regular sex. Both Hannah and Stephanie became pregnant during our sophomore year. Within our small town bubble, most parents had indoctrinated one belief system–abstinence, which they passed on to their children from the time they could understand what they were saying.

Because Hannah and Stephanie's parents opted out of talking to their daughters about birth control (even though they weren't religious), the only other advice they received came from the school system within our righteous bubble. In lieu of sex education, we were taught in ninth-grade gym class,

"Just don't have sex." Within this particular belief system, the prevailing belief was this: to teach a teenager about birth control would be condoning it. End of story.

The racing hormones and finding a first love were never considered part of the equation by my community's church. Our faith taught that we would have great rewards in the next life if we followed church standards. That was it. There was no backup plan. Yes, we were taught about repentance and forgiveness, just nothing to do with how to prevent becoming pregnant other than abstinence.

I thought about the teachers in our congregation; I would have given anything to know how many of these adults had great X-Factor sex when *they* were teenagers; they probably could have written a book of their own! The disadvantage Hannah and Stephanie had—besides having no sex education like the rest of us, was the lack of religion classes to give them a guilty conscience.

Life had become very real for the girls in my tribe. Just like that, their lives were forever changed. I felt sorry for both of them. *My life is just getting started.* Our worlds had catapulted into different spectrums. And once again, I was in a school without a pack.

Thankfully, this time, making new friends was a bit easier. In my fifth-period dance class, the most beautiful girl in the school (and pretty much the entire U.S.) had been transferred in mid-term. Her name was Linda Hathaway. Linda looked like a runway model with long legs, a thin body, and long, chestnut hair. She looked like she could have been Cindy Crawford's prettier younger sister—except Linda had piercing light green eyes instead of brown.

Because I was a dancer, it was one of the few opportunities I had that allowed me to shine. Consequently, I got along well with all the girls in the class. Our fifth-period dance class had been together for over half the year. Within our class was a girl with an outspoken, alpha personality. Her name was Finley.

When Finley heard through the grapevine that Linda would be joining our class, she told everyone how stuck-up Linda was and how much she hated her. Then she announced we were all going to call Linda "fuck-face" behind her back. Finley's words settled heavily in my gut. *Why would I want to be so mean to someone I don't even know? How bad can she be?*

I stayed quiet, with no plans of including myself in Finley's little pact. When the incredibly beautiful Linda joined our class, no one spoke to her. The next day, I decided that was going to change, no matter what Finley had said. I offered a smile to Linda, and we started talking.

"You're a really good dancer!" Linda said. I just looked at her with wide eyes. That was literally the first compliment of my life! And it felt amazing! "Thank you," I replied sheepishly.

Becoming friends with Linda was a no-brainer. I broke the "secret pact" and became best friends with the most beautiful girl I had ever seen. In doing so, I became an arch-enemy of Finley's. Disobeying the rule she had imposed was the ultimate betrayal; she now hated *me* more than she hated Linda. I never told Linda why. She just knew we didn't get along.

Linda was a senior, and being more beautiful than any fashion model at the time, my popularity status catapulted overnight. I taught Linda how to tap dance, and we did a sexy tap dance (wearing tight blue jean overalls) with the two most popular girls in my grade for the dance recital. It was awesome!

That sophomore year was epic! I felt invincible. So, when my junior year rolled around, it was painfully void of everything that had made high school great for me so far. All the senior boys had graduated, this included Byron. And my best friend Linda had also graduated, so I was back to square one in the friend department at school. Again!

As fate would have it, one of the girls who had done the sexy tap dance with me and Linda just happened to be in my religion class at school. Her name was Brinley Bayles–and we were soul sisters from the start!

Meanwhile (just like all the other eighteen-year-old boys in our small town), Byron decided to do what was expected of him and went on an X-Factor pilgrimage for two years. He came clean with the authoritative figures in our religion regarding our creative sex. And before I knew it, he was considered worthy and ready to go. He gave me a promise ring before he left. I demonstrated all the dramatics for a teen romance–and then some! One would have thought Byron was going off to war. I was promised to a boy who would be gone for two years, the equivalent of twenty years for a teenager.

Because this was the norm in our small town, I simply slipped into our community's preoccupied way of life. I stayed home on the weekends to ensure I got my long, weekly letter written to Byron. I tried making him a tape once . . . but when I listened to it, it sounded like I was a prisoner of war–living in the most deplorable conditions. *Oh my hell! I sound so pathetic! This makes me want to hurl! Snap out of it, Ramona!*

My mother couldn't have been more pleased. Byron was an exceptional young man–any parent would have been proud to have him date their daughter. Having Byron choose to do a pilgrimage ensured that I was also falling in line with the belief system she had taught me. My mother loved me and truly believed the X-Factor way of life was the one and only way to happiness.

This situation brought about an awareness I had never noticed before. I noticed it because it *didn't resonate with me at the time*. In my heart, I was beginning to think this didn't have to be *my* norm. I was different from my mother. Nevertheless, not being the same as my mother brought about a feeling of being wrong. I was raised to be one way, worship one way, and live one way.

I associated our faith with how my mother saw the world; she had a temperate personality, never showing excitement or enthusiasm toward anything or anyone. And after two short months of Byron being away, I really didn't want to be doing any of that.

Becoming friends with Brinley was every bit as exciting as becoming friends with Linda had been. Brinley had been the most popular girl in our class since the sixth grade–she didn't even know I existed back then. And now we were BFFs. Life was starting to get really fun again! Brinley was not only very beautiful with her perfect chestnut hair, great body, and big smile, she was also incredibly kind. Her fun, optimistic personality was contagious.

Every Thursday night, Brinley and I used her fake ID to buy a six-pack of beer and a box of powdered donuts–the phony ID was just for the beer; you can actually purchase powdered donuts in my town if you're a minor. We drove to the local disco tech and pulled into the parking lot. As soon as all the beer and doughnuts were consumed, we stumbled in for "Country Night."

When Brinley and I got together, we were out of control. We had no fear, and our inhibitions became nonexistent after a few beers. Just like with birth control, the parents in our town never educated their children on the dangers of being drunk in a dance club or driving drunk–because their children weren't supposed to be drinking in the first place! It was simply forbidden. And, because most kids never dared drink openly inside the bubble, that was good enough for parents to say: "It doesn't happen."

Once I crossed the line of deciding I was going to drink, it put a very evident (but invisible) wall between me and my mother. We both played the role of denial very well. My mother never said one word to me about coming home drunk if she suspected it. And I still treated my mother with respect. I'm sure it was comforting for her to see that I wasn't biting the heads off chickens or some shit.

Warrior Wisdom:

When a community believes their way is the only way, it keeps the world small and the bubble strong. Premarital sex was considered a sin in my hometown. The real sin was failing to educate teenagers about birth control. Five girls had to drop out of school in my sophomore year because they became pregnant.

Parents and teachers who don't want to have an uncomfortable conversation with their teenagers because of a religious commandment are subjecting them to a possible life-altering outcome. Teaching our children about the amazing way our bodies are designed to work and that feelings of sexual excitement are natural is one of the most important lessons we can share. Birth control is essential to this lesson—whether we are teaching our children abstinence or not.

That being said, for me, male attention was like a drug. Unfortunately, I missed out on the experience of having a father who cherished and adored me. Fathers have the ability to make their daughters feel protected, valued, smart, loved, and cherished.

A teenage girl might not feel so desperate to go shopping for something she already has at home. I'm not saying that having an attentive father will safeguard all potential teenage craziness, but it certainly isn't going to hurt.

The ability to be completely open with our children is a gift, one we either did or did not acquire based on how we were raised. I had to break through my "wired-in," uncomfortable feelings to break the cycle and create an open space for talking to my children about anything and everything.

Linda Hathaway . . . if I had given in to a bully by following along with Finley, I would have missed the opportunity for a beautiful friendship. Because of my earlier life experiences, through the pain, I was armed with the gift of empowerment, *and through my loneliness, I received the gift of* empathy *for others. Having these gifts, I was able to create my own path (not the path of a bully) and expand my life experience by becoming friends with Linda.*

Religion . . . it's both noble and natural to teach a belief system we deem worthy to our children. As parents, we want the very best for our children. But when do beliefs turn into brainwashing? How many generations does it take to lose one's freedom of choice within a religious community?

If a teenager is never taught they were put on this earth to have their own life experience (not the experience their parents think they should have) and the diversity of choice, how can they know what truly resonates with them?

Ruling a household like a communist country is fear-based. Parents who do this also rob their teenagers of the opportunity to discover for themselves. The teenager may match their parents' beliefs, but end up much stronger because they got to choose.

What if we could allow our teenagers complete freedom to choose how they feel? I grew up with this area being entirely void because the choice was always made for me; it was never something I had the opportunity to seek out.

What if we could have acceptance for every peaceful way of life? How great would it be for our children to know they have our unconditional love and the freedom to choose a life that resonates with them—even if it's different from our own?

When parents can lead through example and unconditional love, no matter what path their child chooses as they mature—temporary or permanent, they can be assured that everything is in Divine Order and feel peace and comfort knowing they have done right by their children.

Whatever my children choose is right . . . because they choose it. *I respect their path and honor their journey. I have shared my life lessons in hopes of giving them insight. But I understand the value of allowing my children to create their own experiences, and they have my unconditional love.*

Even though the way of life in our small town did not resonate with who I was at the time, it was still all I knew. Not having an example to follow or guidance for anything that expanded outside my tiny bubble created a feeling of recklessness. It felt reckless because I was going into uncharted territory.

Everything I should have been educated about regarding alcohol was kept from me because of an ongoing, generational belief system. To stay ignorant about something kept the bubble strong. Our parents expected us to grow up with the same beliefs as them, keeping all education regarding things outside the bubble away from us. This wasn't hard to do in a town that was mainly X-Factor.

CHAPTER 5

Shenanigans

Before Facebook existed, teenagers would climb into their cars and *cruise*. Brinley and I, (with our friend Jody) went out one evening to do just that. Our perfectly feathered hair had enough hairspray to defy gravity, we wore size zero Lee jeans–so tight we had to do the zipper up with a pair of pliers, knit shirts that fit like a glove, denim jackets for that extra cool factor, and cowboy boots with a three-inch heel completed our sexy, small-town look. Every third time we approached the end of the drag, we pulled into the gas station and went inside the convenience store–long enough to give boys a chance to pull in and talk to us.

Halfway into the evening, I was coming out of the store; it was our third stop-and-chat for the night. As I walked towards our car, I stopped and stared. The most beautiful cowboy I had ever seen stood next to our car–a dark-haired version of Robert Redford with his thick mustache and cowboy hat. He was so good-looking it took my breath away! As I approached him, he looked at me with a smile; his ice-blue eyes were hypnotizing.

"Hi there," he said, tipping his hat. I thought, *Hold it together, Ramona!* Even as I got lightheaded. *Don't you dare be a dork!* Brinley and Jody were still in the convenience store, so I had this beautiful man all to myself for a few minutes. His name was Cory Curtis. He was confident (how could he not be?) and so charming! Cory and I made small talk for a few minutes, my heart pounding wildly until my sidekicks came out.

"Well, my friends are coming," I said.

"Okay, I'll let you get back to your friends. Can I get your number?" Cory asked.

Hell yes! I'll have your babies!

"Sure," I said instead, trying to keep my cool. I gave Cory my number and said good-bye. I was starstruck!

I had a complete nerd attack as the three of us drove away. "Oh my hell! What a beautiful man! He asked for my number! Holy shit!" I squealed. Brinley and Jody observed my scene with raised eyebrows and emotionless faces.

"Just breathe, Romer," Brinley said . . . as she and Jody looked at each other with a knowing, sympathetic look for tolerating and loving their extremely nerdy friend.

Cory called me the following weekend, and I melted at the sound of his voice. He took me to a party where I was introduced to all his friends. Unfortunately, it wasn't a fun evening for me. Cory's friends were all five years older than me–just like he was. I was just a seventeen-year-old hick from the sticks.

This group was an entirely different class of people. It wasn't right or wrong. That's just the way it was. They grew up in a city fourteen times the size of my small hometown and were more sophisticated than me in every possible way. Not one of them wanted to welcome me into their circle. The fact that I was completely intimidated by everyone at the party–not saying a single word the entire night, probably didn't make the best impression. I got home that night and let out a big, frustrated grunt as I threw myself on my bed. *Why do I have to be the poster child for nerds?*

I went out with Cory again the following weekend; we grabbed some beer and drove up the canyon to make out. That was the last time he ever called me. The real sting came a week later when I learned he had asked out Brinley. Brinley sheepishly told me she knew I liked Cory and didn't want to hurt my feelings or our friendship.

Suck it up, I said to myself. Then I told Brinley our friendship was far more important to me than any boy. *No matter how beautiful.* Brinley immediately agreed with me wholeheartedly; however, that didn't stop her from going out with Cory. Nevertheless, Cory liked Brinley, not me. I wasn't going to lose my best friend over it. Brinley brought so much more to the table through her kindness and friendship. It was something I cherished above anything else.

A couple months after Brinley started dating Cory, we got ourselves into the biggest predicament we had ever faced. Brinley convinced Cory to let her drive his beautiful, red Ford pick-up truck for the weekend. He was going out of town with his friends.

"Okay, Skinny-dip," Cory cooed, kissing the top of her head. "But be careful! It's only got liability insurance."

"I will," Brinley vowed.

Keeping her promise in mind, Brinley and I only drank a six-pack each before we decided to take Cory's truck up on the mountain to go 4-wheeling. Dressed in our cut-off shorts and cowboy boots, the evening lengthened, and the sky became black. As the stars came out, we were having so much fun . . . thinking we were *the shit!* Until we became slightly stuck, that is.

Brinley and I looked at each other. "I've got this, Romer," she insisted as she put the truck in reverse and floored it.

The wheels on Cory's truck started spinning, and then we were moving again.

"See, darlin'?" Brinley grinned, her white teeth flashing in the dark of the cab.

Suddenly, the truck slid sideways and down as we both screamed . . . then the truck abruptly stopped.

"Get out! Get out! Get out!" I cried in utter panic.

Brinley and I quickly scrambled out the door on the driver's side. It was after dark, so we couldn't see much at first. When our eyes adjusted, however, we both gasped . . . horrified, we noticed that we had been driving on a trail with a fifty-foot cliff on the passenger side. And then we saw what had just kept Cory's truck from sliding off the cliff: it was a teenie-tiny, baby tree.

The only thing holding Cory's beautiful red truck in place was a four-foot sapling! "Oh shit!" we both cried. Utterly panicked, Brinley and I started running down the mountain.

"I'm so dead!" Brinley kept repeating–reminding us that Cory's truck only had liability insurance.

Thoroughly thrashed and out of breath, Brinley and I burst into a convenience store at the mountain's base forty-five minutes later. We ran up to some cowboys in the store buying beer and blurted out, "You've got to help us!" Gasping for breath, it took us a minute to spit it all out. They looked at us like we were obviously exaggerating.

Needless to say, they still jumped at the chance to rescue two small-town hotties who were obviously in distress. Hero mode took over, and we were off. Brinley and I piled in their truck. We stopped at a house, and two cowboys got in their trucks to follow us.

The small caravan made its way up the mountain. The moment we got to Cory's truck, the cowboy in our vehicle shook his head; he turned and stared at us like, *What the hell were you thinking?*

"Oh, shit!" We heard from the cowboys around us, almost in unison, as everyone hopped out of their vehicles to assess the situation. The energy among our would-be heroes immediately changed.

Brinley and I looked at them like, *Well . . . fix it already!* One of the young men had a lifted vehicle, so he drove up and around our truck–literally hanging by a thread, and got positioned in front of it. Our rescuers attached winches to the front and back end of Cory's truck.

No one joked or laughed–the realization of our perilous situation was palpable. Pulling Cory's truck from one end more than the other risked breaking the tree and putting excessive weight on one of the trucks–which could cause it to slide.

The anchored trucks slowly bounced the big red Ford sideways and back onto the trail. At one point, they had to put their massive 4-wheel drive trucks in reverse and gun their engines to keep them from being pulled forward.

Finally, the entire group let out a big sigh of relief. The beautiful red liability was safely back on the trail. Feeling relieved and triumphant, everyone let out a loud cheer. *Oh, thank you God,* was all I could think.

One of the guys was nice enough to drive the truck (that had given everyone a heart attack) back down the mountain for us. Brinley and I were still physically shaking and stone-sober from our hellacious experience.

The ironic part of this story happened two days later when Brinley was backing out of her garage. Cory was home, and she was returning his truck. As a relieved and thankful Brinley backed out of her garage . . . she tore the side-view mirror completely off. No shit. We had managed to get out of the biggest cluster-fuck of our lives, getting his truck off the mountain without a scratch, not to mention staying alive; and Brinley tore the mirror off, *backing out of her own garage.*

This must have been karma for thinking we had gotten away with something too awful to contemplate. That's the crazy thing about life as a teenager, so many factors (that I was completely unaware of) were determining my future. Every party, every chance encounter. It was like a wild game show where unseen forces played with my destiny.

My stunning friend Linda and I had stayed gal-pals since I met her in my sophomore year and taught her how to tap dance. Being graduated, her circle of people were different than the circle that Brinley and I hung out with.

On a beautiful Saturday in the spring of my senior year, Linda and I drove three hours south to a desert race. Linda was dating one of the racers. Being the super-supportive friend that I was, I happily went along for moral support.

Dressed in appropriate desert wear–string bikini tops and frayed short-shorts, I was beyond excited to experience my first race. I would have been shot if I had tried to leave my house dressed like this. But a quick stop at the outskirts of town (just inside an apple orchard for cover) solved the dilemma of my mother thinking she had any control whatsoever over what I wore. *Ah, bless her heart.*

Linda and I were a fun contrast . . . her long dark brown hair with her light green eyes–and my short blonde hair with my light blue eyes. The smell of Hawaiian Tropic coconut oil lingered in Linda's truck. Planning to get a great start on our summer tans, every square inch of our exposed skin was glistening. The rebelliousness of two small-town girls was out in full force as we happily drank light beer and smoked cigarettes. I could never smoke more than one cigarette without blowing chunks, but I made the most of it–feeling proud to hold my own.

As we got within a mile of the starting point, terror set in as we encountered a roadblock with police cars. Linda and I both started yell-whispering, "Oh-shit! Oh-shit! Oh-shit!" There were empty beer cans all over the floor of the truck. *We're screwed!* Visions of being handcuffed and sitting in the back of a police car started flashing in my mind.

Linda was thinking of a slightly more optimistic outcome. As we pulled up to the roadblock, Linda ran her fingers through her silky hair and adjusted her tiny bikini top. I frantically sprayed perfume into the air while kicking the beer cans under the seat. Linda shoved some gum in her mouth and threw the pack my way to do the same.

Imagine the most beautiful supermodel you can think of . . . multiply it by two, and that was Linda. As we pulled up to the officer, I watched in awe, fascinated as Linda's sexuality went through the roof! The only reason Linda wasn't on every fashion magazine cover in the U.S., was because Linda was from a little town that no one had ever heard of.

I was watching a *master at work.* The police officer nervously and flirtatiously chatted with Linda. I had never seen anything like it. I could have had the head of a unicorn *(neigh!),* and I don't think he would have noticed me. In fact, I'm surprised he didn't give us a police escort!

After the officer told Linda about his hobbies of racing cars and doing every other manly thing he could think of, he gave Linda one of his cards.

"In case you ever find yourself in a bind, it's nice to know someone with authority," he said. *Yeah. Authority . . . Alrighty then.*

"Thank you, officer," she said with a seductive wink as she took the card.

We were both females, but Linda was a completely different species than I was. Compared to her, I had the sexual energy of a nun. My mojo was like a little baby bird. As we pulled away, Linda began singing *Respect* by Aretha Franklin—in an exaggerated, raspy voice. I raised both hands above my head and bowed towards her, repeating, "I'm not worthy, I'm not worthy!" as we laughed. It took a while for my adrenaline to settle, but the lessons weren't lost.

As we arrived at the race, Linda spotted her boyfriend. His name was Vince, and he was beaming—like any man on the planet would be if he had Linda for a girlfriend. Vince grabbed Linda up in his arms and gave her a big kiss, the kind of kiss that declared: *Yeah, boys, that's right, she's taken!*

Vince greeted me with a big smile, "Hey, there's someone I want you to meet," he said. Taking me by the shoulders, we walked over to a friend of his. "This is Bruce," Vince grinned.

"Well, hello," Bruce said enthusiastically. I was utterly taken aback by Bruce's good looks. *Wow, this day just keeps getting better and better!*

Bruce had big, beautiful brown eyes that made me weak in the knees when they locked with mine. He was definitely a man's man, with thick brows and a Tom Selleck mustache that could woo any woman. Bruce could have passed for his younger brother. And even though he was incredibly handsome, a kindness about him stood out to me even more.

After what I had experienced with men like Cory, Bruce had a subtle shyness that made me want to attack him. *Yummy!* And if that wasn't enough, he was also educated. Being six years older than me, he had established his career as an electrical engineer. Everything about him was perfect–*this is the sweetest man I have ever met!* There was never a hint of treating me like I didn't measure up because of my age. Bruce was from a small town like me, so he *got me* better than Cory or his friends had.

We started dating immediately. Every time Bruce picked me up for a date, I wondered, how did I get *so lucky?* After a couple months had passed, Bruce took me to meet his family over dinner. Bruce had two brothers, two sisters, and a mother who had been widowed for twenty years. They were all every bit as kind as Bruce; this was the most loving family I had ever met!

Eight weeks later, after wrestling with the guilt of not dealing with the fact that I had a boyfriend whom I hadn't written in a while, I wrote Byron a "Dear John" letter. It had all the dramatics of an afternoon soap opera. After three pages of bleeding heart, sensational articulation of: "This is the hardest letter I've ever written," "We'll carry on," and "We just weren't meant to be," blah, blah, blah, blah, *blaaaah!* I signed it, "I will love you always, Ramona." *Wow! I need some water. I just threw up in my mouth a little bit.*

After all, back then, I thought I had it all figured out, and anyone who thought differently be damned. What could go wrong when I had true love?

Warrior Wisdom:

It honestly makes me cringe, looking back at my teenage rebel years. But I'm sticking it out for you, my dear reader, who stands to learn from my barf-worthy mistakes. Isn't it insane that my life could have easily been over at seventeen? What the hell were Brinley and I thinking—getting drunk and taking a truck up on the mountain?

Why any thought of caution never entered our minds is just one more fun-filled example of two teenage girls who were never taught about the dangers of alcohol and how it affects decision-making. I was taught to look both ways before I crossed a road—so I didn't get hit by a car. I was also taught to never touch a hot stove—because I would get burned. What's the difference? One would think we would have both learned this lesson via dumb luck and sheer baptism by fire. But that wasn't my experience.

When you have the stigma of sinning or "being bad," it doesn't exactly bring about thinking responsibly. Being rebellious and reckless was a natural response to assuming we were going to hell anyway. And we didn't have anyone older or wiser who thought to tell us any different.

I invite you to ponder what I'm about to say: trying to shame children into doing things our way never works. On the contrary, it brings about reckless behavior when they finally say "fuck it!" because they've had enough. Knowledge is power; how can teenagers know the dangers of alcohol unless they know everything there is to know about alcohol? And not from the standpoint of, "You had better never do this!" They deserve better than that. I sure did. I'm lucky to be alive today.

Learning about what alcohol does to the brain, post-alcohol withdrawal syndrome (PAWS), and the mere fact that alcohol is a depressant are just a few things I can think of off the top of my head that would have been really handy to know while growing up! To stay ignorant about something is not protecting anyone; it's not the answer.

Hear my Warrior roar to save lives: If you're a parent, whether you drink or not, it's your responsibility to teach your children about alcohol. When we stop and get real, we love our children too much to stay ignorant and roll the dice. I know that sometimes terrible things happen to our children, no matter how much we have taught them. But not teaching them only puts them at a higher risk.

It's so unfortunate that Linda and I were able to get past the police officer. The earlier we learn life lessons, the less consequential they tend to be. We don't "get away" with these choices as children and adults. We only postpone learning their consequences until later in life when the stakes are much higher.

That experience taught me that authority is corruptible when you throw sexuality at it. Yuck! As adults, we can fantasize about wanting harsher life lessons at an earlier age because we see their value in shaping who we become. Knowing this, we can see the value of not robbing our children of the opportunity to experience the pain that life brings via their actions.

As a parent, this is so hard! I would die for my children! I would rather spare my child from feeling pain and hardship. And if that tactic actually worked, I would take it all! Bring it on! Unfortunately, this doesn't work; it only postpones the life lesson that would have allowed our child to grow stronger. And consequently, keeps our child in a weak and vulnerable state.

Having unconditional love for our children comes with the heart-wrenching job of allowing them to fail. When we become parents ourselves, that love is finally understood. But when raising our children, that's a cross we have to bear–knowing they will never understand until they have children of their own. OUCH!

CHAPTER 6

Pan? What Pan?

Graduation = Freedom. *Here we come!* Brinley and I wanted to have the experience of living away from home. We found an apartment on a church-owned property within a mile of a church-owned college campus. Truth be told, there weren't any other options in our price range within a hundred miles.

We became roommates with a fourth-year college art major named Shelley, and we couldn't have been more different. The look Brinley and I received from Shelley as we came strolling into our new apartment (wearing our cut-off short shorts and tube tops) was priceless. *Damn . . . this is going to be fun!*

Even though Shelley was a member of the same X-Factor faith, she was the polar opposite of Brinley and me–not that Brinley and I resembled anything close to young ladies raised in our religion. Shelley was a refined artist–now living with Brinley, a beautiful, wild Homecoming Queen who kept up outward appearances. And me, a crazy hottie who didn't really give a shit what people thought. That was us, and it was the makings of a perfect storm.

Getting settled into our new apartment, I quickly realized that I wasn't too fond of keeping any house rules. I ate Shelley's cereal, used her lounge chair when I laid out at the pool, and got under her skin at any given opportunity. It was both sad and pointless when Shelley thought she could intimidate me in any way just because she was older than me.

"Ramona, I realize this is your first time living away from home. So, I'm going to explain how things work. When you have roommates, you need to respect their things. I put my name on my food because it's *my food*!" Shelley huffed–with an angry, red face. I gave her a flat stare as I ate her Captain Crunch cereal.

"Gotcha, sorry about that," I answered as I took another mouthful. I tried to keep my crunching to a minimum as Shelley went on. Her rant turned into *wa wa wa* . . . in my head as I thought, *I hope she plans on shopping today. Her cereal is almost gone.*

I had experienced real battles growing up. *This woman doesn't know who she is dealing with.* I gave Shelley a pitiful little shake of my head as she marched out of the room. *Bless her heart.*

Shelley had even gone as far as marking the milk jug with a permanent marker line every time she had some milk. *Doesn't she realize she's messing up her milk?* I shook my head in disapproval every time I put water in the jug. I had to get the amount up to the fill line again after I poured some on her cereal. *Why doesn't she stop this madness?*

One night, as Brinley and I were eavesdropping on her telephone call, we listened to Shelley venting to her mother.

"I'm so sick of these little seventeen-year-olds! It's like living with juvenile delinquents!" she cried.

"Oh precious, I'm so sorry you have to tolerate that behavior. It's just appalling!" Shelley's mother answered sympathetically.

Brinley and I both covered our mouths to muffle our snickers. *We're more experienced in life's hard knocks than you will ever be. You don't stand a chance, you little pedigree prima donna!* The contrast between Shelley and us begged retaliation. How could we not be as outwardly obnoxious as possible? We were demonstrating freedom, baby!

One weekend, I decided to cook dinner for Bruce. We had been seeing each other for six months now. Shelley and Brinley were out of town for the weekend, so Bruce and I would have the apartment to ourselves. I was going to make a romantic dinner for the two of us. I had never, ever cooked before–but how hard could it be? My older sister Rita had done it all the time. *It's not rocket science, for heaven's sake.* I had planned a fantastic meal: beef stroganoff and Bud Light.

Everything was cooking perfectly in one of Shelley's fancy, non-stick pans she had told us never to use. As I was stirring the boiling concoction, I could feel a budding gourmet chef being born. *I need more mushrooms. Running to the store and back will only take me fifteen minutes. More mushrooms will definitely be better.* I was thrilled with the inspiration coming to me!

Naturally, I left the stove between medium and high to keep cooking my masterpiece while I was gone. This would ensure that dinner was ready by the time Bruce arrived. *Cooking is fun!* I could tell I was a natural. Bruce was going to be so impressed. *I'm going to make such a great wife!*

As I was driving to the store, I fantasized about Bruce coming home after work to our beautiful house with a fabulous meal on the table. Bruce would see the perfect meal and gather me up in his arms. Giving me a warm hug, he would say, "You're amazing," with tears in his eyes.

Yes . . . we were going to have a perfect life. *Whoa! Shit! I just drove right past the grocery store. Get your head back in the game, Ramona!*

When I returned to the apartment twenty-five minutes later, my gourmet meal was anything but. Panic burst inside me as I opened the door to the apartment filled with smoke. *Shit! Shit! Shit!* Stroganoff ala, burnt to a crisp. I turned off the stove and quickly opened the front door and all the windows. I thought for a minute, then I grabbed the Lysol spray from the bathroom and emptied the entire can in the apartment. *That will fix the smoke smell.*

I stared at the charred remains on the stove. *Damn . . . well, so much for that.* Next, I did what any seventeen-year-old (who was never given any responsibilities) would do. I filled Shelley's pan with water–burnt food and all, and promptly hid it under my bed. Voila: Problem solved. *Wow! All that Lysol is a bit strong . . . I think I'm going to be sick!*

I grabbed one of Shelley's clean, folded beach towels and got it wet. I wrung it out and flailed it through the air to capture the Lysol and lingering smoke. As soon as I was satisfied, I stuck the towel under my bed as well. *Okay, I've had just about enough of this cleaning bullshit!*

I put more deodorant and perfume on, fixed my make-up, and shut my bedroom door behind me as I got on with my evening. Discarding the mushrooms I had just purchased without a second thought, I bid adieu to their culinary potential–no use for those things anymore. I wiped off Shelley's signature gourmet cutting knife with a Kleenex and stuck it back in the knife block. A newfound sense of responsibility came over me as I wiped off the kitchen counter with the same dry tissue.

When Bruce arrived, I told him we were skipping the main course and going straight to the beer. "I had a little mishap with dinner," I confessed.

Bruce didn't even ask what had happened . . . I guess he didn't want to hurt my feelings. *How I love this man!* I certainly wasn't going to offer up that information. Instead, I planted a big kiss on his handsome face. I loved the tickle of his mustache, *rawr!*

"How was your day, baby?" I asked, clearly changing the subject.

Bruce chuckled, "You're adorable," he said.

Needless to say, having beer for dinner didn't put a damper on our evening. Bruce and I were still in the euphoric stage of our relationship. *He doesn't even mind that I ruined his dinner! This man is too perfect!* I grabbed Shelley's comforter and oversized pillows off her bed and laid them on the living room floor. Then I popped some of Shelley's popcorn, and we had a perfect evening.

Shelley asked me where her pan was the following week.

"Pan? What pan? I don't cook. I've never cooked," I replied to Shelley.

"My beach towel is missing too," Shelley pointed out.

"It's been cloudy all week. Why would I have taken your beach towel?" I said, with a look that suggested *maybe you should go lie down and get a grip.* I had no shame!

When my room began to stink from the rotting food under my bed, I moved into Brinley's room; problem solved again. *I'll have to remember to spray air freshener when I'm in there changing my clothes to keep the smell down.* I prided myself on thinking so responsibly. *That's just the kind of girl I am.*

It never crossed my mind to try and wash Shelley's pan or towel–not even once. That was still an empty file card in my brain, waiting for the life experience that would allow me to file, "How and when to wash a pan." For now, I felt triumphant–I was avoiding Shelley's wrath, and my way of doing things was working out just fine.

Six weeks passed, and by then, Brinley had been asking me to "deal with the pan issue" for a month. I finally took Shelley's burnt pan–moldy food and all, along with her moldy-smelling towel out from under my bed. *Okie dokie. It's time to act responsible here. I had better be quick before someone gets home.* I beelined it to the back of our building and threw them in the dumpster.

Accountability was not in my brain's bandwidth; conveniently, I can't say brutal honesty was present either. *That's a real shame about Shelley's pan. It looked like a nice one. And that towel would have been great to take to the pool.*

Brinley and I ended up leaving the apartment a few weeks early from the date on our contract. Shelley had ratted us out because she found cigarettes hidden in the potted plants. Brinley and I weren't really smokers, but anything rebellious fit within our protocol at the time.

That's also the reason I dressed in as little clothing as possible. Years of oppression with extreme modesty can do that to a girl.

The nail in the coffin had been the night that Brinley and Cory got engaged. Cory emerged from Brinley's room the next morning after a celebratory all-nighter–and gallantly tipped his hat to Shelley. I'm pretty sure she began seeing a therapist after that incident.

Because our apartment was owned by the church, Brinley and I were expected to conduct ourselves properly, per church standards. Let's just say alcohol, smoking, and sex were frowned upon. And based on the contracts we signed, it warranted evicting our asses.

Brinley and I moved into the house she and Cory would live in once they married. It was a darling little farmhouse that Cory was leasing. Brinley and I painted the walls and made it perfect for the two love birds. It's funny how things work out. I had Bruce now and wouldn't trade him for Cory or anyone else!

Brinley started taking GE classes at the local university, and I started school to become certified in electrolysis. It was a three-month course in permanent hair removal–that I completed in just five months. I should mention . . . just like accountability and brutal honesty, discipline was also missing my brain's bandwidth.

Being accountable, honest, and discipline-handicapped, I conducted myself accordingly. Sale at Forever 21? Skipped school. Craft fair in my hometown? Skipped school. Needed to work on my tan? Skipped school. Fortunately, my instructors' tolerance lasted long enough for me to graduate.

After graduating from electrology school by the skin of my teeth, I enrolled in cosmetology school. The owner/instructor of the cosmetology school liked me, but I wasn't any more disciplined there than I had been in my previous courses. Of all the girls in my class, one would have picked me as "the most likely to fail" if they had looked at my attendance. It took me sixteen months to graduate from the twelve-month course.

Halfway through cosmetology school, Bruce and I were to spend the weekend at a ski resort two weeks before Christmas. I had told my mother

I was going with my friend Jana (who didn't exist) to her family cabin. I suspect my mother knew precisely who I was with, but she certainly couldn't condone that. So we both played the game.

When Bruce and I arrived at the beautiful mountainside resort, I discovered he had planned a treasure hunt for me. He surprised me with the details when we arrived at our room before I even unpacked. Jumping off the elevator at different floors, I felt like Indiana Jones as I followed the clues Bruce had tucked away under garbage cans, plants, and a sofa cushion in the lobby. As my excitement grew, I began to step up the pace with anticipation. *What's waiting for me?*

I finally came to the last note in Bruce's well-planned adventure. It said, "Go back to the room." As I walked into our room, Bruce got on one knee and held out a beautiful diamond ring.

"Ramona," he said shyly, "Will you marry me?"

"Yes!" I cried as I threw my arms around him. It couldn't have been more perfect–it was magical.

We went out for dinner afterward. I couldn't stop staring at the beautiful ring Bruce had given me. Smiling, I kept tilting my hand back and forth in the candlelight at our table to see the marquise-cut diamond sparkle. Everything in my life was working out perfectly.

As we drove home from our perfect weekend, I began to decorate our ideal home in my mind. *Dad sells TVs, so we've got that covered. We'll have it made!* Yup, that was my bar for a comfortable home–a television.

Warrior Wisdom:

How cool would it have been if Shelley had found her pan and towel under my bed, gathered three or four friends, and put the fear of God into me? They could have watched me wash her pan while apologizing profusely–promising to quit acting like such a little punk. Now, that would have made a fantastic story!

And think of the amazing life lesson I would have received. Accountability would have been my new badge of honor! Natural laws and consequences? Those were foreign concepts to me at that point in my life. From an adult perspective, it's fun to fantasize about me stepping into Shelley's body and bringing down the wrath of Ramona–on the Ramona that was such a disrespectful delinquent. I would have scared the shit out of that little wise-ass!

To Shelley, whose life I completely disrupted that summer because of my shenanigans . . . I hope you are living your best life. If I ever track you down, I owe you a pan, towel, cereal, milk, popcorn, and laundry service for your comforter! XOXO

As you've seen in my stories, all this stemmed from having those blank "how-to" cards in my head from childhood. My sister Rita took on Mom's role; I never had to cook, clean, or maturely manage anything. At that point in my life, I had been gifted with the knowledge of one religion. A religion that carried a heavy stigma over my head because I wasn't living it. My mother had managed the best she could. Looking back, I'm sure depression played a significant role in many of her actions.

That's the beautiful thing about learning grace–realizing you did the best you could every day with what you knew. Knowing this, you understand that's precisely how it goes for everyone else. That might be hard to swallow when you think about some people's actions. However, because of my own actions, I know there's absolutely no exception to that rule. You can find understanding through grace, leading to forgiveness, ultimately bringing peace and love.

At eighteen, I was the last of my friends to get married. That's what people did in my small hometown. I thank my lucky stars I didn't have a baby on the way like many of my friends at the beginning of their marriages! I'm also very grateful the man I married was loving and a good provider. This allowed me a few years to grow up. I needed all the time I could get!

CHAPTER 7

Fucking Awesome! Who Knew?

With all unexplained miracles working in my favor, I finally graduated from cosmetology. And even though I graduated last in my class, as my luck would have it, I had a secret weapon. I just happened to have a BFF that sang my praises. As my cosmetology skills increased, Brinley told everyone and anyone that I was "fucking awesome!" And guess what? *I became fucking awesome!* I had developed a true confidence in doing hair.

Brinley's rock-solid belief in me set something in motion; I would never be the same. The gift she gave me by simply *believing* in me changed my life. I now had a path to follow and goals to achieve. Who wouldn't want to do their best to live up to such a profound title? Suddenly, my days of passive existence were over. Not since my dance classes had I felt this epic. I had gotten a tiny taste of success and accomplishment before I even had it. There was no turning back. I would do whatever it took to keep this feeling alive within myself.

I set my eyes on a prestigious salon in the state's second-largest city. Oliver Stein was a well-known photographer who worked with models and pageant queens. Within Oliver's photography studio, there was a full-service salon. He employed top stylists to do hair and make-up for the models he photographed. Oliver's salon was also open to the affluent public it attracted.

I met with Oliver and pitched my idea on how much he could charge per hour for electrolysis in his salon, recognizing the untapped potential in a pre-laser hair removal era–I was hitting the target on a big market. I shared my vision of setting up my machine in the facial room. Oliver immediately liked the idea, his enthusiasm was palpable. Seizing the moment, I disclosed my additional expertise as a cosmetologist.

Oliver then asked me how much experience I had. I watched the look on his face change from happy to concerned when I told him I had just graduated. Ignoring Oliver's look, I kept right on talking, with enough audacity to sell a ketchup popsicle to a man in a white suit; I lied my ass off about how I had graduated top of my class. Why not? I had my secret weapon of being fucking awesome–a title that made me invincible!

Oliver reluctantly agreed to hire me as a cosmetologist as well. He gave me a station in between two seasoned, professional stylists. This was when my *real* education began.

Witnessing firsthand the artistry and professionalism of real pros, I gleaned invaluable insights far beyond the scope of textbook teachings. It was an education I couldn't have received in a million years–while in cosmetology school.

I learned their language and observed their professional report with clients. "Denice! How *are* you?" Looking her client right in the eyes and waiting for her answer. "It's *so great* to see you! Have a seat, my dear. Any problems with your last cut or color? Anything that didn't work for you?"

This allowed the client to discuss her hair without feeling like she was complaining. "You want about two inches trimmed off? Perfect, I can do that. Show me *your* two inches." It was essential to know the client's version of two inches. I learned quickly that "their" reality of two inches might be three and a half inches, or only one inch.

I sat in awe daily, taking in each word my mentors told me. "It's *your job* to suggest new looks to your clients, not theirs. You don't just plan to succeed. You plan not to fail–there's a huge difference." My mentors saw everything, each lesson imparted by them fueled my aspiration for success, and I was eager to absorb every bit of knowledge.

One of my mentors shampooed and conditioned my hair to show me what I should be doing. Holy shit! That experience alone would keep me coming back to a hairdresser. They educated their clients on the products they were using while they were using them. I would watch in amazement as their clients would leave with over $50 worth of products.

Seeing my admiration, one pointed out the obvious, "You can't expect your client to replicate what you did using Aqua-net hairspray. When you go to a doctor, he tells you exactly what medications you need. He doesn't send you out the door and say good luck," she mused.

I wanted to be successful (like my mentors) more than I had ever wanted anything, igniting a fervent desire to emulate their mastery and build a loyal clientele.

One Saturday, I printed up a bunch of fliers to hand out at the local mall. I wanted to duplicate my first freakish success with my dance lessons. I walked right up to strangers who were shopping and said, "I would love to do your hair!" as I handed them a flier and then quickly walked off. I probably handed out over one hundred fliers throughout the day. *My brave act is going to cash in big!*

Believe it or not, over the next month, I received almost zero–okay, *precisely* zero clients from the fliers. In my efforts to build a clientele, I had learned one way *not* to do it. People will not let a stranger touch their hair because they were handed a piece of paper at the mall.

The people I approached had no idea if I was a good stylist or if I sucked. People go to a new hair stylist via referral from someone's hair they have seen. At Oliver's salon, I needed to ensure the walk-in I was given once in a blue moon was blown away and tickled pink. I would do everything in my power to ensure every new client I received left not just satisfied, but utterly enthralled and devoted to me.

With everything I was learning, it was Oliver who had enough courage to be brutally honest with me regarding my clothes (or lack thereof). Thankfully, he was more concerned about the professional appearance of his employees than he was with offending me.

Oliver dealt directly with topics that most people avoided because they were uncomfortable. When he spoke to me, it was with a calm, assertive tone. Executing the conversation with the precision that only a mentor of his caliber could muster.

With a demeanor as composed as a seasoned conductor, Oliver's words resonated with a clarity that left no room for misinterpretation.

"You have to *be* that person before you can *become* that person, not the other way around," Oliver said. "You must embody the role before you can truly inhabit it. There should be a difference between the clothes you wear to the club and the clothes you wear to work. If you want to master your profession, take it seriously, make it the most important thing in your life." Simple. Done.

Gratefully accepting Oliver's guidance, I embarked on a transformation, channeling my focus into crafting a professional persona worthy of the title I aspired to. Armed with a modest yet sophisticated wardrobe, I embraced a newfound sense of self that reverberated in every client interaction.

As I stood before the mirror in my professional attire, Oliver's words echoed in my mind, igniting a spark that transformed my energy and outlook. Each client became not just a customer but a cherished companion, a canvas awaiting my artistic touch.

In the ensuing months, I honed my skills, emulating the prowess of my mentors with a fervor that launched me to greater heights. With each appointment, each snip of the shears, my clientele grew, and my passion for this amazing industry that I was now a part of swelled.

The path to success, paved with Oliver's candid guidance and my unwavering commitment to excellence, unfurled effortlessly before me. The once-daunting obstacles now appeared as mere stepping stones on my journey. I had embodied the essence of being "fucking awesome." What could possibly stand in my way now?

Warrior Wisdom:

All it took was for one person to believe in me. Brinley not only believed in me, she shouted it at the top of her lungs. Brinley was such a rare, beautiful human being. She wanted the very best for me, and most importantly–without a shred of jealousy.

Being placed between two seasoned stylists at Oliver's salon was a perfect example of the law of attraction at work. We create our life based on what we have in our predominant thoughts. Our higher power always says yes . . . putting people and situations in our path to create what we believe. This can work for us–if our thoughts are positive, or against us–if our thoughts are negative. Knowing this, we can understand the importance of keeping our predominant thoughts positive.

I didn't know a single thing about vibrational energy, but because of Brinley, I had the belief and the desire to be fucking awesome. And that's precisely why I landed the job at Oliver's salon–so I could learn what I needed to learn to become exactly that. Energy is always playing out, whether we understand how it works or not.

Being in Oliver's salon with such great mentors was a huge life lesson. When you want to acquire a particular skill set, or level of success, hang with someone who is that person. Real education comes from listening to people and paying attention. That statement holds true to any situation in life.

Oliver's words would stay with me forever; "You have to be that person before you can become that person. You must embody the role before you can truly inhabit it." That simple truth doesn't just apply to how you dress; it applies to every disciplined action you must take to powerfully step into the space of who you want to become.

My success in cosmetology turned into my success in life. The energy field (that I was completely unaware of) in success and abundance was blown wide open. Suddenly, everything was within my reach. The situations in my life were simply a response to the energy I was emitting at that time.

CHAPTER 8

Bring It On, Baby!

Who knew being a grown-up could be so much fun? Bruce and I were living in a nice duplex. I had been so naïve about money before we married; if someone had asked me what a mortgage was, I might have guessed, "A fancy French dish?" I went from having everything taken care of by my mother to having everything taken care of by my husband. Except, my husband was extremely careful with his money, and this was something I wasn't at all used to.

As I got to know my hubby better and better, I realized I never had to worry about anything–he worried more than enough for both of us! Bruce paid the bills and took care of all the finances. I did the grocery shopping and kept our house spotless. Incredibly enough, the girl who couldn't wash a pan had become a clean freak.

Even though I had a fucking awesome shield to wear at work, as soon as I got home, I was forced to put on my immature kid hat. It seemed like Bruce was always stressed about something, but he would never talk to me, so I felt like a little kid who wasn't supposed to try to understand his grown-up world. That being said, we were madly in love, and that trumped everything else.

Cory and Brinley were our best friends. We did everything together. They had moved into the basement of an elderly couple in the small town next to ours so they could help them out and enjoy a reduced rent. It wasn't terrible, but they had actual mushrooms growing in the carpet of their living room . . . and not the fun kind either.

Brinley became pregnant three months after she and Cory were married. She had been a straight-A student from the sixth grade to graduation, but with a baby on the way, college quickly fizzled. I was impressed and happy for her when she got a job as an assistant at a doctor's office. My best friend had the perfect cheery disposition and was incredibly smart.

When Brinley had her baby, she was the most beautiful baby girl I had ever seen. I watched my best friend blossom into a wonderful mother, and for the first time, I was hit with a strong realization of how young we were. Seeing the loss of freedom motherhood brought for Brinley, I wasn't in a hurry to follow suit.

Bruce and I purchased our first home a year and a half into our marriage. It was an older rambler with big windows and wooden shutters. I absolutely fell in love with it–and immediately wanted to put a salon in our walk-out basement. It would be perfect! Clients could come in and out of that entrance like a professional business. I was so excited about the thought of having my very own place!

Bruce burst my over-eager bubble in a matter of seconds: "What if it doesn't work? What if you don't get any clients?"

Excuse me? I thought, stepping back and staring at him. *Don't you know who I am?* "What do you mean? I have a lot of clients," I answered flatly.

"Yeah, at Oliver's salon, thirty minutes away," Bruce replied.

That was the most hurtful thing Bruce had ever said to me. I played it over and over in my mind that night, adding liberties, of course, to make it even more hurtful. *What if you fail? What if you're not good enough? If you move, you won't ever have another client again! Let's be honest . . . you suck, Ramona!* By morning, I felt heartbroken.

I brought the subject up again the following evening–a little more determined. Bruce countered my determination by making it very clear that he would not be investing in building me a salon. I sat in silence while a fiery anger began to replace the hurt. Slowly, that rage took hold and filled me with an immense sense of heated power.

Fuck that! And fuck you! No man is going to tell me what I can and cannot do! If you don't want to be supportive, so be it. I'll do it myself.

I furiously began saving money over the next two years. Although I had a good clientele, Oliver still took 65% of my earnings. I became laser-focused. And I wasn't going to discuss one more thing with Bruce.

I imagined my clients arriving at my house and exiting their cars. So I began my efforts precisely from that point. When Bruce came home to construction men putting in the framework for a sidewalk, he inspected their work for any potential imperfections, even before stepping foot inside the house.

"What the hell Ramona! Why isn't the sidewalk at the edge of our property? You're shortening the property!" Bruce said, fuming.

Matching Bruce's aggression, I announced, "I'm going to put rose bushes on the other side of the sidewalk, with a cement border in front of them and a chain link fence with privacy slats behind them."

"Along the entire walkway? It will take thirty rose bushes to fill up that much space!" Bruce huffed. *Is that the best complaint you have?* I looked at Bruce as if *he* were the little kid now.

"Exactly," I said. With that, Bruce walked out of the room-cursing under his breath.

This little confrontation was an excellent way to break the ice with Bruce regarding my plan. When the noisy cement truck showed up the next day . . . it made the shock of the whole thing a little softer. *If you think I need your permission to do anything, Bruce–think again!*

Every night–after I had worked a long day at Oliver's, I went downstairs and got to work in our basement. If they had made a video game with me as the playable character, it would have been called "The Angry Carpenter." This was partly because Bruce and I had just learned we were expecting our first baby. I was thrilled to be pregnant; it had only taken three months to conceive. However, the hormones that showed up soon after were straight-up venomous. *And you thought I was overbearing before, Bruce? Everyone had better just stay the hell out of my way!*

The actual carpentry was fun. Trips to the local hardware store with helpful men behind the counter were all I needed. They would tell me everything to purchase and explain how to use it. It took forever to scrape the old glue off the floor from the ugly checkered tile that had previously been there. But being pregnant, I didn't want to use solvents–even with a mask.

I learned how to use a miter box and nail punch. I became skilled in laying wallpaper with a perfect, seamless finish. I painted–wearing a gas mask that would have made OSHA proud. My colors were a foam green and dusty peach, with cream-colored ceramic tile and natural pine molding. It was a perfect modern look for the '90s.

In a stroke of serendipity, a local carpenter materialized to fashion a double hair station with a massive mirror extending to the ceiling, illuminating the salon with the glow of globe lights. I knew the benefit of having two stations, so I could work clients between each other while they were processing. A make-up station placed right in the middle optimized the space.

The carpenter also built a side room for electrolysis, and I put a tanning bed in the electrolysis room instead of an electrolysis table. This gave me the maximum use of the room.

When it was time to lay the tile floor, Bruce reluctantly assisted me with laying the tile. I was so grateful! I wouldn't admit it . . . but my back was killing me, and my belly was getting in the way!

Then, just as suddenly, he left me to grapple with grout and aching muscles. *Whatever . . . to hell with you.* Bruce's indifference actually gave me the extra energy I needed. Unleashing my *inner umph* for home improvement–Tim Allen had nothing on me. I created a one-room salon that was every bit as luxurious as Oliver's.

Then, after months of work and nearly two years of saving every penny, I stepped back, took a breath, and in a moment of triumph, reveled in the joy that it was finally done! Everything was perfect! As I looked around the salon, I had never felt so proud. It was beautiful. *I did it! I created every bit of this!*

But as I stood there, an unexpected wave of sadness washed over me. I had no one to celebrate my accomplishment with. My angry determination was gone. I had done exactly what my husband said he would never support–how could Bruce and I possibly celebrate that? The echoes of my husband's disapproval lingered, a bittersweet reminder of sacrifices made in pursuit of a dream that stood tall, yet solitary, in its splendor.

It was a rainy day in February . . . and my last day at Oliver's salon. As Oliver and I sat with our feet up, picking the M&M's out of the trail mix he had on his desk, he asked me all the helpful questions he could.

"Do you have your business license and tax ID number?" Oliver's tone was that of a caring father.

How I adore and appreciate you; you have taught me so much! "Yes," I answered confidently. "I got them both a few weeks ago when you told me to."

"Good girl," Oliver replied proudly. "What are you going to charge?"

"The same price you charge here," I said without hesitation.

Oliver let out a gasp, his face incredulous. "Ramona! No one is going to pay those prices in a home salon! That's crazy!"

I looked at him with raised eyebrows. *Asshole!* Oliver's prediction stung–I had such a great admiration for him!

"We'll see," I replied, trying to mask my hurt feelings. Oliver was a brilliant businessman, but he was dead wrong in this case. *No man is going to tell me what I can or should charge! Remember, you're fucking awesome, Ramona!*

The following week, I was hanging wallpaper in our nursery. Being eight and a half months pregnant–I was never one for getting things done with time to spare. The phone rang, and when I answered, it was a woman from my church. She had heard I opened a salon in my home.

"What do you charge for a perm?" she asked.

I closed my eyes and winced, "$65.00," I responded . . . and waited.

"I'm so glad we *finally* have a good stylist in town!" she gushed. "Now I don't have to drive thirty miles to get my hair done."

Talk about the best first call I could ever get! This was an answer to my prayers–because this woman had never been my client before. *Her conclusion was based on what I charged.* I wanted to kiss her! Suddenly, I knew everything was going to work out. I had never felt such relief, excitement, and gratitude all at once.

Two weeks later, my beautiful, perfect baby girl was born. We named her Jessie. I was in labor for twenty-six hours; even with an epidural, it was so hard. Jessie looked like she had a baseball on the top of her head for the first few hours from how long I had pushed.

But finally, there she was. I was holding my real, live baby girl who had grown inside me. I instantly fell in love with my angelic little Jessie. This most perfect gift from God was now my world. I spent every day rocking my sweet baby, marveling at how gorgeous she was with her big blue eyes.

I had been a mother for a week now, and every day, I felt sadder and sadder. *What the hell is wrong with me? I have a healthy, beautiful, precious baby girl. My salon turned out better than I ever dreamed it could be. Everything is just as I planned. Why am I so sad?* I rocked Jessie as my tears fell on her soft, pink blanket. I felt so overwhelmed . . . but I didn't have the slightest clue as to why.

That afternoon, Rita and my mother paid me a visit, and while I greeted them with a smile, words escaped me. Engaging in conversation took more effort than I had in me. I should have been happy to see both of them–they gushed over how beautiful my little Jessie was. I tried to be gracious, but the heaviness of the state I was in felt suffocating.

After a while, Rita and Mom kissed me goodbye and left. I instantly began to sob. After a minute, I heard the kitchen door open. I looked up to see my mother walking back into the house. She had her purse clutched in both hands with a worried look on her face. This was a look I had only seen a handful of times.

Sensing my apathy, my mother had returned to speak with me. Setting her purse down, she walked over to the rocking chair and touched my shoulder. "You know, Ramona, sometimes after you have a baby, it's natural to feel sad, *my* mother called them the baby blues," Mom said, stroking my hair as I silently wept. "It won't last, but I'll take you to the doctor if it does. It'll be okay, sweetheart."

That was the first time my mother had spoken to me with such an understanding and sympathetic tone. If anyone knew about the effects of having babies, it was her.

I finally managed to reply, "Thanks, Mom . . . I love you."

"I love you too, sweetheart," my mother answered with emotion in her voice.

That simple gesture of having my mother understand and validate what I was feeling, as well as the relief of knowing that I wasn't going crazy, had a profound impact. Understanding this was common felt like a huge weight being lifted from my shoulders.

The gratitude and love I felt for my mother grew immensely that day. Not just her loving gesture to talk to me, but knowing how much I loved my baby girl brought into perspective my mother's love for me.

A mother's love is an innate knowing that I would die or kill for my child. A fierce, protective love that sparked the moment I held Jessie in my arms. This precious baby had become the single most important thing in my life.

My baby blues disappeared completely within a few days after talking to Mom. The knowledge that I wouldn't end up in a padded room was all I needed to feel better and get my power back.

Before I knew it, I was ready to dive into my new business. As I contemplated what that would look like, I knew I had some decisions to make. Staying true to my tendencies of never getting things done ahead of time, I hadn't yet figured out how I was going to manage things.

As I held Jessie, rocking her back and forth and kissing her soft cheeks, I knew that taking my baby to a sitter was out of the question. I had worked too hard to get a salon in my home, and she was far too precious to be away from me.

Oh my gosh! I need a nanny! The solution flowed through me. She could come to my house, and we would all be there together. I instantly thought of the perfect person. Patty was a client of mine with three girls of her own, but they were in school during the day. I knew she was a kind and patient mother. She adored babies and lived just eight blocks from my house!

When Patty took the job, I was ecstatic. *Who says I can't have my cake and eat it too? I can do anything I set my mind to!* Employing Patty made me ultra-focused on getting my books full . . . I had to. Making that bold move reminded me that I was a professional stylist who would never settle for anything below amazing for my clients anyway.

I devoted meticulous attention to each and every client–they left my salon looking fabulous! I began my day at 5:00 a.m. (because I didn't work on

Saturdays). When my darling Jessie woke up, I brought her into the salon. My clients loved feeding my sweet angel her morning bottle. Patty would arrive by 8:00 a.m. And I finished every work day by 3:30 p.m.

Everything fell into perfect harmony–igniting an energy unlike anything I had ever experienced. *Bring it on, baby!* I built a full clientele in my little home salon within six months. Despite the absence of a public listing or an exterior sign, two hundred and fifty clients came religiously every six weeks–all from referrals. It was a career that surpassed my wildest professional expectations.

My mindset was sending clients out of my salon looking noticeably different. Doing a make-up touch-up with every service (no charge) begged the question, "Where have you been?" when people saw them. And there was a tsunami of follow-up referrals.

Moreover, I provided each client with a personalized stack of business cards with their own name on the back. Every card I got back with their name earned them a free full-size product. They were delighted. A single hair appointment for a bank teller led to bookings from her entire circle of colleagues within a few short weeks.

As time passed, I got even more creative and added things like applying a beautiful sunless tanning spray on their arms and neck while processing, or adding false eyelashes to enhance the outer corners of their lash line. I wanted to be the one who made their day.

I loved hearing about my clients' lives because I was their biggest fan. Supporting these beautiful warriors in everything they did or dreamed of doing gave me profound joy. And I would have fought for any of them, defending them against any opposition–because these beautiful, courageous women had become my family.

Warrior Wisdom:

I take pride in knowing I didn't allow Bruce to stop me from getting what I wanted. But I'm sad for the young woman who thought she needed to make her husband the enemy to do so. I still had many painful lessons ahead before I finally learned how to choose peace and see people through an understanding and compassionate lens.

I could have interpreted my husband's behavior in the best possible light and still accomplished everything without the bitter attitude. Everything begins with us. Seeing the world through a lens of positivity, we see things more as they are . . . instead of a knee-jerk reaction–followed by a story we attach to.

I could have answered Bruce's hurtful question with, "You are so sweet; I love you for being concerned about me. This is an opportunity to work from home when we start a family. I've learned so much from the other stylists at Oliver's salon. If I can build a clientele at Oliver's place, I can build one here. It's all right if you don't want to invest any money; you take such good care of me, sweetheart. We have a beautiful home that I'm very grateful for. I will take this challenge on myself." My bitterness and hurt came from me . . . not Bruce.

What a wonderful life lesson that first client call was. If I had let Oliver's reaction influence me and cut my prices, that woman would have continued to drive thirty miles to get her hair done–after hearing my low price. Why do I share this with you? It's a big world out there. We decide what we are worth, and the world responds accordingly.

I didn't give myself any limitations when it came to finding solutions, and that's precisely why I got what I wanted. If I would have thought, "I can't afford a nanny," or "I'll just have to use a sitter at someone else's home," or "My husband won't let me build a salon," that's exactly what I would have gotten.

Remember, we are the ones who either accept or reject limitations.

CHAPTER 9

Therapy and Beauty

It was like a big party at my salon every day! The education I received in human nature was unbelievable. I spent an average of one to two hours with my clients every six weeks. I had entire extended families who were my clients. I became privy to multiple perspectives on the same story, assuming the role of a confidant and therapist. I never repeated a single word I was told. My clients knew this about me because I never had any juicy stories regarding anyone else.

Even Rita had become a loyal client. So it's a good thing I never repeated what my clients told me; Rita might have been arrested! She has graciously given me permission to share this hilarious event.

My sister casually told me one afternoon as I colored her hair–that she had dug up a tree from the entrance of the town cemetery the night before.

"What?" I asked in disbelief.

Rita continued with her *perfectly logical* story. "Well, the city dug up *my* tree when they fixed a water line and refused to replace it."

"So naturally, you dug up a tree from the cemetery," I responded. *Oh my hell! This is getting good!* "How on earth did you get it home?" I chuckled.

"I just tied it to the top of my van," Rita answered matter-of-factly. "That's why I went in the middle of the night."

"Of course, that's the best time to go if you're going to steal a tree," I said, shaking my head and laughing. *Holy shit, Rita! You're my hero!*

Multiply such stories and shenanigans by two hundred and fifty–okay, maybe not *that* extreme, and that was my life. When I had a client in my chair, we talked about *their* lives, heartaches, unimaginable tragedies, triumphs, and the most hilarious stories.

In turn, my clients got to experience many of *my* quirky life experiences of motherhood firsthand. Fortunately for me, they always got a kick out of my kids.

By the time the year 1998 rolled around, Bruce and I had three children. We had settled into the piety of our religious community and attended church regularly with our kids. Jessie was ten, our son Chance was seven, and our youngest son Conner was two and a half.

One afternoon, while engaged in a fascinating conversation with a client about her recent trip to Rome, my sweet Connor walked into the salon. He looked up at me, his tiny hands were clasped together with a very concerned look on his adorable little face.

"Mom, does poop stain cawpet?" he asked me intently.

That question got both me and my client's attention. *Oh damn!* A feeling of dread came over me as I imagined how bad the damage was upstairs.

"Oh no-no-no!" my client laughed, shaking her head. "How can you be mad at a face like that? He's so freaking cute!" Clearly, she was entertained by the situation.

Just then, Patty–our saint of a nanny, came in. As she pushed the blonde strands of hair away from her face, I could see that her light freckles were hidden in her red cheeks. She let us know she had just finished scrubbing the carpet in Conner's room. Patty was in her early thirties; she was beautiful and vibrant. But looking at her right now, she looked like she had just come out of being lost in a desert. Completely defeated.

We were in the process of potty-training my rogue toddler, and he had gone #2 in his pull-ups. After this deed, he went into his room, slid out of his pull-ups, and scooted his little butt from one end of his room to the other on the soft, ivory-colored carpet. Yup, one long skid mark–that was par for the course from my little pint-sized *Dennis The Menace!*

"Oh, Patty!" I said, immediately covering my mouth. This was not the time to laugh, and I did not trust myself. *I should be giving you hazard pay!*

One of the perks to having close relationships with so many clients was the invaluable font of knowledge they provided in an era that predated Google. Through casual salon conversations, I gained insights from corporate professionals, legal and financial experts, real estate mavens, horticulturists, fitness enthusiasts, psychologists, as well as stay-at-home mothers possessing a mountain of knowledge garnered from years of experience raising children and husbands.

One client in particular, a brilliant psychologist named Aleesa Hathaway, had a PhD in marriage and family therapy. A mother of seven, she had given birth to all her children at home. Aleesa was beautiful, slender, and elegant. And she always gave me such good advice. Sometimes, I felt like I should be paying her instead of the other way around.

Aleesa had her work cut out for her with me. I was so intent on being the quintessential mother. When Jessie was little, I painted her tiny nails to match her outfits. Jessie even wore hair extensions in preschool. Once, I picked Jessie up from preschool, and her sweet teacher said, "Some of Jessie's hair fell out during recess, so we just stashed it in her cubby." I don't know how Jessie's teacher kept a straight face since Jessie's hair was bigger than she was.

Aleesa kindly told me, "The more you can allow Jessie to be 'not perfect,' the more likely she will be to engage in social interaction, empathize with others, and form a healthy self-esteem." It made complete sense. I chilled out … a little.

Aleesa also referred me to Jessie's violin instructor. I started Jessie on the violin at three and a half with the Suzuki method. Her daily practice regimen kicked off with a grand total of ninety seconds. The key was unwavering consistency–never skipping a day of practice, gradually increasing the playing time as they learn a song. Once a piece was mastered, it became a daily staple until the entire repertoire was ready for a grand recital performance.

Jessie's violin instructor was a true virtuoso in the art of teaching. She was also a master in passive aggressiveness. I'll never forget the lesson with *the note*. As Jessie played, her instructor praised her for everything she was doing right. At the same time, she was discreetly penning a message that she slyly slipped to me when Jessie wasn't looking. The note said, "Did you even practice this week?"

Ouch! Right to the heart! I bit into my cheek. *Suck it up! Don't cry, don't cry! I'll fix lasagna tonight . . . the vegetable one–so Jessie will eat it.* My inner dialog slowly shifted my focus and brought me back away from the ledge. *Whew, that was close!* There was no crying allowed at violin lessons.

Jessie's teacher forbade any negativity whatsoever toward the student when it came to violin practice or lessons, a philosophy I happened to agree with 100%. *If I get my ass chewed, so be it. I'm willing to take one for the team.*

Naturally, when my second child, Chance, came along, I started him on the viola at three and a half years old. Chance was my alpha male–strong as an ox and *loud*. The viola idea with him lasted about five weeks. He was more interested in using the bow for a sword. It humbled me to realize an important fact of life: my children were born with their *own* ideas of what they liked to do.

Regarding obsessive behavior, my little Jessie had her own OCD traits. *Is it any wonder? I mean . . . come on!* One evening, I saw Jessie's Flintstones multi-vitamin on the kitchen table; she had forgotten to take it before bed. I picked up "Fred" from the counter and walked into Jessie's room. Seeing the vitamin in my hand, she quickly scolded me. "Mom! I said no food in my room!"

Don't react, don't react! I've got this, smile and nod. Thinking about my recent conversation with Aleesa, I went into chill mode. "Sorry, sweetheart, I wasn't thinking. You can come take your vitamin in the kitchen," I answered casually. I didn't show the slightest resistance towards Jessie's neurotic behavior. Therefore, Jessie didn't need to hold on to it quite so tight–I wasn't trying to make her change it.

And just like Aleesa said, Jessie outgrew her ultra-neurotic behaviors within a year. Why wasn't a warning pamphlet attached to the little suction bulb they sent you home with when you left the hospital with your new baby? Would it kill them to mention a few things? Maybe something along the lines of . . . "Your kid is going to do some freaky shit. Start practicing your poker faces right away." Or better yet, "Your kids will make *you* do some freaky shit. Start expanding what you consider normal. You have no idea what's coming."

Once every blue moon, I would dedicate a couple of hours on a Saturday for a client on her wedding day. On this particular Saturday, Bruce was off at wrestling practice with Chance, Jessie was at a sleep-over, and I had Conner wandering around the salon while I was doing an elegant updo for my radiant client on her special day.

Conner had just turned three and was so curious. He loved to explore and eventually wandered into Chance's room. A minute later, he came out so happy with himself and the new toy he had found–Chance's pocket knife. Beaming with pride, Conner held it out to show me with a big smile. I promptly took the knife away and said, "I'm sorry, buddy, this can cut you, and that would hurt. You can't play with it."

Conner looked up at me with surprise and hurt; taking the knife away was the ultimate betrayal. So, he did what any three-year-old would do–he pitched a fit. Furious with me for ruining his fun, he hit my backside with his little fists, screaming over the unjust situation that was a complete travesty in his eyes.

Why didn't I send him with Bruce? At first, I tried sitting him on a chair with some toys, then I offered him some snacks, but Conner wasn't having it.

I mused that I couldn't beat him, and my poor bride couldn't be late for her own wedding. *I've got it!* I grabbed a chair from the laundry room and set it in the salon doorway–so I could still see my sweet little *devil child*. I sat Conner in the chair and duct-taped his little body to the chair. Then I calmly turned up the radio to try and drown out his melt-down and got back to work.

When Bruce got home ten minutes later, he entered the salon and looked at Conner. Without a word, he picked up the chair–with a furious Conner still duck-taped to it, and walked out.

A few minutes later, Conner marched in with an angry face. "I'm sowy!" he shouted. Then, he made an about-face and stomped back out of the salon.

"Thanks, buddy!" I said to Conner, trying to keep a straight face as I witnessed his little clenched fists. My bride had her face in a towel so he wouldn't see her laughing.

Every kid came with a different set of challenges. After hearing a weird popping noise one morning . . . *What the hell? That doesn't sound good.* I hurried into the kitchen. There was Chance, shooting his BB gun at a spider as it walked up the kitchen cabinet.

"Chance! You don't shoot your BB gun in the house!" I yelled. *Oh my hell!*

"So, you think it's okay to have dangerous spiders in the house?" he answered in a condescending nine-year-old voice.

Son of a bitch! Argh! My cool, calm, and collected was nowhere in sight.

"Chance, take that gun outside, now!"

As crazy as my kids made me feel at times, I still felt like I had control for the most part. Then, in the fall of Conner's first-grade year, I hit a wall I had no idea how to overcome. Conner started praying . . . everywhere. If we were at the baseball park and Conner heard someone say a bad word, he would drop to his knees right on the spot and say a prayer.

I was trying to be the mother who would never judge or make my child wrong for doing something, so I said nothing.

Then, Conner's teacher called me one afternoon and told me he had been asking to be excused to go to the bathroom every day, but he wouldn't return for fifteen minutes. She finally decided to send Principal Smith in to check on him, and he had come out shaking his head. Conner had been praying silently next to the bathroom sink.

As I listened to Conner's teacher, I felt sick. *This is not normal! Is someone abusing him?*

I carefully asked Conner about it that evening after dinner. We sat on his bed, ready to read some of his favorite Dr. Seuss books. "What's going on, bud? Why do you want to say your prayers all the time?"

Conner didn't make a peep. Through the almost white wisps of his blonde hair, he gave me a stone-cold look. As I lovingly moved his hair away from his face, his big brown eyes showed no emotion.

If someone has hurt you, I thought, *I'm going to kill them. What can I say to get you to talk?*

Out loud, I said, "We're so safe, buddy. No one can hurt anyone in our family. If someone has told you they will hurt us, you can tell me. Me and Dad are tougher and stronger than everyone. If someone is hurting you, we will make them stop."

Still, not a peep. I was beginning to feel desperate. I got up from the bed to quickly wipe away the tears overflowing onto my cheeks. "I'm going to make us some popcorn, and then we can read," I said as I left the room. *What the hell is happening to my little boy?*

Bruce and I took the kids on a boat trip to Lake Powell the following weekend. Conner ran into the cuddy cabin to pray for me as I took off my oversized T-shirt (I had on a bikini underneath, planning to work on my tan). I had to wear that big T-shirt the entire trip! In the evening, when we returned to camp, Conner would be praying on top of the red rock. "Here comes Moses," Chance said under his breath as Conner descended from the sandstone mountain.

The next time I did Aleesa's hair, I spoke to her about Conner's behavior. She pondered over my words for a moment before she replied. "Why don't you try telling Conner that Heavenly Father has spoken to you? Tell him how happy Heavenly Father is with him; tell him he told you what a good boy Conner has been and how proud he is of him."

I like that idea. It feels right inside. "I'll try anything, thank you!" I told Aleesa as I began to think about what I would say to Conner.

When Conner came home from school that day, I excitedly took him by the hand and walked into my bedroom. "Guess what? I talked to Heavenly Father today!" I said excitedly.

"You did?" he said, as his worried expression changed to surprise, and his eyes widened. I had his full attention.

"Yes," I told him, "Heavenly Father came to talk to me about you, Conner. He told me what a good boy you are and how proud he is of you! Heavenly Father wants you to know how happy he is because you're such a good boy!"

Conner put his face in his little hands and began to sob. I immediately started to cry as I knelt down and hugged my sweet boy.

"I love you so much, Conner, and Heavenly Father loves you so much!" I rocked side to side with him in my arms.

As Conner and I cried and hugged each other, he finally looked up at me and gave me a huge smile. The look of relief on his sweet face made me feel like a hundred pounds had been lifted from my shoulders. Conner didn't have a reason he could articulate for wanting to pray all the time, but after that day, it was over. *Aleesa is a rock star!*

Several years later, when Conner was old enough to understand what he went through, we talked about his "little phase that scared the shit out of me."

Conner told me how that phase of his had unfolded.

I had been helping little six-year-old Conner clean his room. He had picked up a picture of Jesus that his teacher had given him at church. The picture had been underneath his racetrack and was torn halfway through. "What should I do with this, Mom?" he asked.

I was in my "let's get-r-done" mode—and absentmindedly answered, "Just chuck it, buddy. It's ruined."

Conner's first-grade mind was so shocked that I would tell him to throw away a picture of Jesus! He told me at the time he thought I must be an imposter, or at the very least, on "Satan's side."

"Are you shitting me?" I answered, aghast at his story.

"Yup," Conner laughed, "I thought you were an evil little scallywag!"

The crazy thing about this story is that I had never taught my kids the concept of Satan or good versus evil. Instead, I had sent my kiddos to their church classes, completely trusting what they would be taught. I had no idea if "Sister wound-up-to-the-coo-coo-hour" was choosing to embellish her lesson or not. I learned the hard way that children believe everything they hear. Thank God, Conner believed I had talked to God just as easily.

Warrior Wisdom:

Being a mother is hard, but as cliché as this sounds, it's the most important job there is.

A small child actively absorbs and shapes their very identity through the interactions with those around them on a daily basis. These are beliefs about themselves they can hold on to for a lifetime.

Paying close attention to who our children are being influenced by is so important. If I could do it all again, I would have talked to my children more and listened more, being interested to hear about their day. I would have given them the opportunity to recall things. Aside from difficult conversations that could arise, there are great opportunities to teach our children the value of seeing all the wonderful things that happen every day. I continue to be very grateful for Patty and the daily love and patience she gave my kids. And yes, we had our share of shit shows . . . usually in the evening hours . . . but what family doesn't?

Looking back, I was in the beginning stages of full-on pageant-mom-bullshit! When I watch our old family videos, it reminds me of a spoof movie, where they exaggerate things to the point of being ridiculous–that's what makes it so funny. Except our family videos are for real! Jessie's hair . . . seriously, what the hell was I thinking?

Did my little Jessie care if her nails matched her dress? Did she care how full her hair was? I don't think so. I did those things for me *and me alone–so I would feel more confident, knowing that I was caring for my daughter in a way I never was.*

How often do we find ourselves parenting to the opposite extreme from how we were raised? When we get extreme with anything, we can stop and ask ourselves, "Why do I feel this way?" Understanding the root of what it is that's driving us to behave a certain way can be the beginning of making peace with what we yearned for as a child. Identifying this can allow us to see things objectively and not over-correct to the extreme with our own children. Balance . . . it's a beautiful thing!

I will be forever grateful for the excellent advice my beautiful client, Aleesa, gave me. Little did she know what a positive impact her words had with assisting me in navigating my way through motherhood. Giving my children the freedom to be who they wanted to be in their little quirky phases was brilliant.

With my first child, I tried out all the prototypes of parenting, eventually finding my stride with the invaluable guidance from Aleesa. When my second child came along, he couldn't have been more different. What works for one kid can be entirely wrong for another. Learn to celebrate your child's individuality; it will benefit them for the rest of their lives.

As we contemplate what brings us joy, it becomes easier to create that scenario for our children. Consider this: envision an entire community celebrating and acknowledging who you are as a person–how would that influence your perspective on life? This analogy encapsulates the essence of our children's reality, particularly when they are young. You, dear Mama, are their community; you are their world.

Whenever we try to mold our children into who "we" think they should be–a dancer, gymnast, violinist, football player, etc. . . if it doesn't resonate with them, there will be pushback at best. At worst, we create a scenario where our children perceive themselves as falling short.

Of course, we're going to shape their lives. Jessie became an accomplished violinist because playing that instrument resonated with her.

Shaping our children's lives while allowing their personalities to grow is a delicate dance. Believe me–I get this! Chance did not resonate with the viola in any way. I'm surprised we made it three weeks without him chucking his pint-sized instrument into the fireplace!

However, he became an accomplished firefighter and commercial pilot– this is who Chance was right out of the gate. His loud, opinionated, alpha personality is precisely what made him such a powerful creator as an adult. I can think of so many instances where I could have celebrated that more in my son when he was growing up.

I didn't always get it right. I just want to say how grateful I am that my children still speak to me!

When Chance was in his late teens, I sent him a text asking him to love on Mocha and Jerry (our two pups), because I would be gone for most of the evening.

Chance answered my text by saying:

I don't love creatures who destroy my sandals.

I answered with the following:

You destroyed a lot more than sandals when you were little, and I still love you.

Touché, *he answered.*

It's the simplest things in life that make my heart smile—every time.

So celebrate those moments with your children, big and small, life-changing or just plain silly. Give them space to speak up and make sure you're ready to listen—no matter how exhausted by life or work you may be. And I challenge you to redefine your idea of what a "normal" kid looks like. It doesn't matter what the world thinks of our babies . . . it only matters what we give them as a foundation of love, support, and acceptance.

CHAPTER 10

Excess and Utter Impulse

Excess is the birth of ridiculousness. Didn't someone say that? If they didn't, then it's mine. When my children started getting older, I loved using the barter system with many of my clients.

One of my clients was a professional seamstress, so I traded to have massive balloon curtains made for Jessie's room. The materials were pink floral and pinstripe. The curtains were big enough to fit in a wedding venue.

As eleven-year-old Jessie walked in, I saw her eyes go big as she saw the billowing floral print overflowing into her room. She could have easily taken a running jump and completely disappeared inside her new curtains.

"What do you think, sweetie? Aren't they so beautiful?" I exclaimed–in a voice that was five octaves higher than normal.

"Yeah," Jessie answered with an unsure chuckle–trying to follow my lead for being ecstatic about the ninety yards of audacious fabric that was the literal elephant in her room. "They're so pretty," she managed, with a stamped smile on her face.

Good girl! One more project to check off my list.

I also traded with a family who owned a massive greenhouse chain. I was absolutely giddy loading up all the beautiful flowers and bushes I wanted. When I finished planting, my home looked like the home on the movie, *Christmas Vacation*, when Chevy Chase put up his Christmas lights. Except at my house, it was flowers! Excess and variation like you wouldn't believe! It was a botanical Noah's ark.

Bruce was building exquisite jaw muscles from clenching his teeth so much. By this time, Bruce knew I took action on every whim of thought. It was easier to ask for forgiveness than permission. And I had learned that it was foolish to wait for a pat on the back from him. I was utterly addicted to the validation and admiration I received from the powerful women who were my clients.

One of these powerful women just happened to work in the judicial system. Terry had been with me since the very beginning of my career.

When Bruce put in for a lottery on "the hunt of a lifetime," as he called it, I made a little wish for him to draw out. *Come on . . . please!* When he drew for the hunt, we were both ecstatic! But for slightly different reasons.

My wicked sense of humor had been waiting for this scenario forever. I asked Terry if she could send Bruce an official (fake) notice calling him in for jury duty exactly when his life-changing hunt was supposed to be.

"Some men would call this sadistic," Terry said with a smile.

"I know!" I said–with a devilish snicker, completely pleased with myself.

I was tossed into four feet of snow for that little prank–even though Bruce only had to suffer for about ten minutes before the jig was up.

Was it worth it? Oh yes! Definitely!

One afternoon, as I admired the newly installed French doors in my living room, Rita dropped by to pick up some hair products from my salon.

"Those look beautiful!" Rita exclaimed, showing genuine admiration as she gazed at my latest upgrade.

"Thanks!" I answered. Rita and I had a shared love–remodeling.

"Now I've got to get rid of my old sliding glass doors," I sighed.

"I'll take them!" Rita said enthusiastically.

"Perfect! They're all yours," I replied happily. *Yay! One less thing to do.*

With that, Rita and I put the doors in her minivan, and she was off.

I visited Rita the next day; the doors were already perfectly installed in her outer kitchen wall. It had only been fifteen hours! I was dumbfounded–her husband worked away and wouldn't be home until the weekend. I listened in awe as Rita nonchalantly detailed how she solo installed those sizable doors on her own. She explained it as if it had been a piece of cake.

"I marked in pencil on the kitchen wall where I wanted the sliding doors. Then I just fired up my chainsaw," Rita exclaimed proudly. She hadn't thought twice as she cut a big hole in the back of her house. Even I wasn't that daring!

"How did you figure out where the electric cables were?" I asked.

Rita paused for a moment, then her expression transformed as if a light had suddenly switched on in her mind. "Oh . . . I didn't think about that. Oh well, I didn't hit anything," she said matter-of-factly.

"Indeed . . . holy shit, Rita!" I laughed with relief. *And here I was feeling sorry for Bruce . . . I didn't hold a candle to Rita's impulsiveness.*

In the midst of my sister's antics and the party going on in my salon every day, I firmly held the belief that, "You can never have too much of a good thing." One summer, Brinley and I decided we would get a Bunco group together. Bunco is a simple dice game, akin to bridge or poker, it served as the perfect excuse to get together with fun ladies every month. I rounded up ten of my clients from the same graduating class–what a crew!

Each Bunco night left my stomach hurting for days after from laughing so hard. And we had that much fun without a single drop of alcohol! What does a group of religious ladies do for entertainment, you ask? Let me give you a little example.

During the summer of 2001, we were forced to take action one evening at Bunco. We learned of a woman in town who had said something deeply insulting to one of our beloved Bunco girls–and hurt her feelings. *Oh no she didn't!*

"And I will strike down upon thee with great vengeance and furious anger those who attempt to poison and destroy my ~~brothers~~–I mean sisters!" *Regulators! Mount up! This bitch has messed with the wrong woman!*

We pulled out a box of Halloween costumes at Katie's house–the woman hosting Bunco that month. All twelve of us chose a costume to wear as a disguise. I snagged the butterfly costume. I got the antennas and wings situated just right, then I tucked the little skirt into the front of my jeans–since it was a costume for a toddler.

We set out on a daring mission to the local grocery store, where two members of our outlaw gang went in and purchased every plastic fork they had on the shelves. Watching our two comrades check out inside the grocery store was a spectacle in itself. They sported dark sunglasses and baseball caps belonging to Katie's husband–guilt permeated them, making the clerk wide-eyed and uneasy.

I'm sure the police would have been called if they had purchased garbage sacks, rope, or duct tape. But I personally couldn't think of any crime you could commit with plastic forks.

Our little sorority drove to the said bitch's house and parked a block away. Then, twelve housewives from hell–clad in children's Halloween costumes, stealthy approached the house like swat sisters' in action–and executed a Pearl Harbor on the woman's lawn with 2,400 forks sticking in her grass.

Having completed our mission, we stood in pride, admiring our handiwork. Then, in unison, we whispered, "Fork You!" before executing our triumphant escape, laughing and utterly thrilled with our joint retaliation.

We were *so hilarious*; all you had to do was ask us how funny we were. We would laugh our asses off about a woman in the congregation earning her "Silver Beaver" award in the Boy Scouts. Our rebel group was worse than a bunch of fourteen-year-old boys–laughing at anything that could be construed as remotely sexual. Outrageous was our motto!

Warrior Wisdom:

Everything in my life at that time could have been viewed as ridiculous. Jessie's curtains, my yard, Bruce's fake call to jury duty, Bunco night–it was all outrageous and so much fun! As ridiculous as it all was, I was having a great time!

Joy and excitement are contagious. A joyous state brings more things into our life to be joyous about . . . it has to. Like energies attract–this is our strongest, most basic law of nature. If you are emitting an energy of joy, you are attracting more things to be joyous about.

Rita . . . what she did with those sliding glass doors was one of a hundred things that made me shake my head in awe. My sister was and is a total badass. If I had held onto our petty childhood drama that raged between us for years, I would have been robbed of knowing and adoring a sister with a unique and beautiful soul . . . with an energy every bit as crazy as mine.

Our little Bunco group was a space in time where we could take our focus off daily living and turn "on" our inner child. In short, we could all act like idiots and have the time of our lives! This is an activity I highly recommend. There's something about laughing so hard you have to cross your legs so you don't pee your pants–that is so cleansing! I personally think it's one of the healthiest things you can do for yourself.

CHAPTER 11

Parade of Fools

E mbracing my ethos of asking forgiveness rather than permission, I learned early on with my salon–if I wanted something done, I did it myself.

Observing Bruce's indecisive nature made me feel akin to a human volcano. If I wanted to do something, I did it. If I did it wrong, then I did it again. *Repeat until finished!* It wasn't in my thought process to complain or nag at him–that was a waste of my time.

In response to my impulsive and brazen attitude, Bruce began incessantly criticizing my actions. I mowed the lawn too often and planted the flowers too close–okay, I'll give him that one. He found faults in everything I did, right down to buying the wrong size of toothpaste. It was always something. I felt like I was walking on eggshells around him.

Bruce began a relentless cycle of unloading his grievances on me. I had no idea he carried a PhD in the art of finding fault. After the boiling point was reached, and his lecture was delivered–he felt better, almost on a high. I, however, felt like digging a hole and jumping in. He put some serious cracks in the "Fucking Awesome" label I bore so proudly.

Twelve years into our marriage, Bruce and I got into a terrible argument over Labor Day weekend. Our home, located along the parade route, was the traditional gathering spot for an elaborate breakfast that I hosted, attended by my family, as well as Patty's and Brinley's, to enjoy a feast and watch the celebration together.

The night before my big event, Bruce and I were returning from the carnival with our kids and Brinley's family. As we arrived home, I noticed unfamiliar lawn chairs sitting in front of my house, claiming our epic spot for the parade. *What the hell?* I wasn't going to allow some stranger to block out space for the parade in front of my own house. Brinley and her husband were also baffled–they had followed us home to drop their boys off for a sleepover.

This is bullshit. I've got thirty-five people coming tomorrow. I promptly took the chairs and put them in front of my next-door neighbor's house in a neat, respectful line. They were out of town anyway, and the view was equally as good. However, my husband suddenly got a surge of righteousness flowing through him regarding property rights.

"You can't just move a stranger's chairs if they have put them here! That's not your property!" Bruce huffed, scolding me in front of Brinley, her husband, and all the kids. He was never comfortable regarding my big fanfare with the parade anyway; his discomfort over my enthusiasm was palpable. I watched incredulous, as he collected the mysterious chairs–handling them with the greatest care, and returning them to their original place.

Really? I thought. "Are you having a stroke? Or are you stoned?" I asked Bruce.

If he didn't mind chastising me in front of everyone, I certainly didn't mind answering him in front of the same audience. "This is our property. I have better things to do, Bruce!" I shouted as I collected the chairs a second time to move them back in front of the neighbors.

Ignoring me entirely now, Bruce defiantly collected the royal chairs again and put them back where they had originally been placed. *Are we really doing this? You wouldn't like me when I'm angry.* I glared at my husband while visions of a large, green, beastly hulk–chucking my human Bruce into the neighbor's yard flashed in my mind.

Now, I was past the point of being angry with my husband, not to mention that hulk green was a terrible color on me–it wasn't even in my color wheel! Forget that he didn't help me in any way for our breakfast event; Bruce was actually trying to put a damper on all of my hard work . . . purposefully!

"You *know* my family comes up every year!" I said, this time much louder. "Strangers aren't going to care if they are sitting in front of our house or the fucking neighbors!"

We had this little tiff right in front of Brinley, her husband, and all the kids. It's a good thing my brother Kyle wasn't on call that evening as a police officer. He would have been called to my home for a domestic disturbance.

In a battle of the wills, Bruce and I went back and forth, moving the chairs across the three car lengths of space for ten minutes. There was no way I was giving in to his idiocy. I would have my way! No quarter! The absurdity of the spectacle we were causing belonged in a slapstick comedy–except I wasn't laughing.

Why can't he support me just one fucking time? Why is he taking the side of a complete stranger over his own wife? That particularly hurtful thought pinged my heart, causing a lump in my throat. I bit into my cheek to stop the tears that were building.

After we demonstrated stupidity at its finest, Bruce finally got in his truck and left in a huff. I just shook my head as I watched him go. *What–the–hell? That's just great!* My children looked at me with sad eyes.

"Don't worry guys. Dad just needs a time out," I explained with a tight-lipped smile.

The plot thickened when I discovered the origins of the presumptuous chairs. The following day, as we sat down for pancakes, Rita casually revealed that she had dropped off the chairs while we were at the carnival, helping to secure a prime spot for the entire family. I managed to muster a "Good idea" in response, trying to mask my surprise at her proactive planning.

Holy shit! I thought as I pictured the scene that Bruce and I had displayed in front of everyone the night before. *They were Rita's chairs.*

"Where's Bruce?" everyone kept asking.

"He had to take his truck in to have it worked on," I lied. I didn't want anyone to know what a ridiculous shit-show our marriage was at times. I was humiliated that my own husband was absent from my parade breakfast, which had become an event that everyone looked forward to.

Bruce didn't return until later that day after everyone had left. When I tried to talk to him, he still defended his actions. *Unbelievable.* I immediately shut it down entirely and quit speaking to him. It was done and over. Bruce never apologized, and I added some height to the wall that had come between us.

Every time I tried to do something special for Easter, Christmas, or even Valentine's, Bruce found a way to blow it up with unnecessary drama. His behavior ranged from overreacting because he thought I was putting too many lights on the tree–okay, I'll give him that one, to pitching a fit during the kids' Easter egg hunt, an event for which I had prepared tirelessly through the night–because the dog had pooped in the living room.

Eventually, I started tuning Bruce out. I mentally hit the mute button. Doing this wasn't always easy, but selective deafness was the only way I could tolerate my marriage.

The positive vibes I got with my children, my clients, and Brinley were the polar opposite of the unsolicited opinions I was now constantly receiving from my husband. I turned up my energy and never slowed down for a second–masterfully bobbing and weaving like a nimble ninja at Bruce's attempts to grab my attention.

It's interesting how clearly I could see things with other people's relationships, just not my own. My oldest daughter, Jessie, had a best friend named Ally. They were both twelve at the time, and she lived just down the block.

We had always kept a close eye on our *Ally-girl* because she had a physically abusive father. He had a name, but to me–he was *Dickhead (DH)*.

On one occasion, to really set terror into his children's hearts, DH killed their small dog with a pitchfork right in front of them. They hadn't tied it up, and it was barking at their horse. It was his way of controlling those precious young souls through violence and horror. Knowing this, we had Ally at our house as often as possible.

On a picturesque Saturday in January, I promised Jessie and Ally a day of skiing. The recent snowstorm had blanketed the ski resorts with six inches of fresh powder, and the girls were eligible for discounted tickets due to their outstanding academic performance–both girls were 4.0 perfectionists. They were excited to go skiing as a reward for their dedication in school.

We arrived at Ally's house that morning to find her devastated–sitting in the kitchen all by herself. DH had hidden Ally's skis. I wasn't surprised; that's just the kind of thing he did.

Still, Ally's mother, Janet, had told her she could go skiing with us before she left the house that morning, so I didn't let his antics ruin our day. I told Ally not to worry; I would rent her a pair of skis. *I'm not going to give that two-year-old little piss-ant any power. It's bad enough that Janet won't stand up to him.* I wanted to show Ally something different.

The girls had a wonderful day. They talked non-stop, sharing their adventures of skiing the slopes all the way home. Their newfound sense of independence and spirit for adventure was evident. It warmed my heart to see Jessie have such a kind friend.

As I dropped Ally off at her home early that evening, I had an uncomfortable ping in my gut that lasted for a split second, leaving my stomach feeling momentarily sick. I watched Ally walk down her driveway and into the house. Backing out of her driveway, however, my thoughts returned to motherhood and what I would do for dinner. *Pizza,* I decided. *I'm bone-tired.*

We received a phone call thirty minutes later . . . it was Ally, and she was sobbing. DH had beat her up for going skiing. I saw red.

"I'll be right there," I said, trying to hide my anger. "Sweetheart? Listen to me. Go lock yourself in the bathroom, and don't come out until I get you." I hung up the phone as a big lump formed in my throat. *Why didn't I listen to my gut feeling? I should have gone inside with her . . . this is my fault!*

As I drove back to Ally's house, images of her being hit by that monster flashed through my mind. *That spineless son of a bitch!* My hands were shaking as I rang the doorbell. Janet answered the door, sobbing helplessly.

"Where is he?" I demanded with a scathing voice.

"He's in the bedroom," Janet cried softly–pointing to a room with an open door. Without hesitating, I stalked right past her and into their bedroom. *It's about time someone takes a stand against this unbelievable prick!*

DH was lying on the bed watching TV. I walked in front of the screen and glared at him. Pointing my finger straight out, I yelled, "If you *ever* touch Ally again, you're going to be sorry!"

DH picked up the TV remote and turned the volume up as high as it would go.

Even better . . . fuck verbal resolution! I turned around, grabbed the TV cord, and yanked it from the wall. I was there for battle.

In an instant, he jumped off the bed and put his fingers on my shoulders. "You need to go," he said, pushing me back toward the bedroom door.

The rage of everything I knew he had done to terrorize and inflict pain on his family came to a boiling point. I shoved him back with all my might. "Get your fucking hands off me! You fuck!" I screamed. The sound that came out of me was a noise I had never heard before. A guttural, savage scream that spent all my energy to get it out. I could feel a deep sting in my throat.

DH stood there in silence, hate searing from his eyes. Shaking, I stared back at him defiantly.

In a quavering voice, I choked, "You're not so tough without your pitchfork, you son of a bitch!" Trying to hold in my fear, I could feel the tears coming to the brim of my eyes. "Come on, Janet. Let's get the hell out of here," I said, efforting to keep it together while my entire body shook. I felt like an electric charge was buzzing within me.

Ally's father did nothing to stop us, as Janet, Ally, and her two older brothers left with me. When we got home, Bruce looked at me pointedly. He said nothing, and I offered no explanation.

After getting the kids settled at my house, I drove Janet to the police station to file a restraining order against her husband–for beating up their twelve-year-old daughter. Janet and her children lived with us until he was removed from their house so they could return home.

During the weeks the restraining order was in place, DH slipped Janet a letter. He begged her not to leave him, saying things like, "Please don't break up our family that has been blessed by God." I saw this man as a ruthless coward, hiding behind a peaceful religion to keep his family from leaving after all the terror and abuse he had put them through.

Religious ties ran deep in our community; the family unit was very important–rightly so. But even more prevalent with many women in our community was the belief, "I can't make it on my own." I was completely unaware that I held this belief myself.

Six weeks later, Janet reconciled with her husband. Witnessing their family's struggle, I felt a deep sadness and helplessness. The betrayal Ally felt toward her mother was palpable. I kept an even closer watch on our beloved Ally. The entire town knew about my confrontation with DH. That was one piece of information I wasn't about to keep quiet in the salon. He kept a rather low profile after that.

Warrior Wisdom:

I wish I could say I realized that Bruce's dissatisfaction was about Bruce, but that would be bullshit. It took me a long time to know the truth.

Regrets? Absolutely! Whatever we put our time and energy into grows. Because my marriage didn't fall in line easily like everything else had, I chose to ignore it rather than work on it. I was so determined to give my children a wonderful life. But what about providing them with a healthy example of parents who figure things out together? That was something neither Bruce nor I had an example of growing up.

Resentment, stubbornness, and sarcasm are choices. I wonder what kind of marriage I would have had if I had put in even half the energy I put into my clients toward my husband.

If I could go back to that time, I would tell Bruce what a great husband and father he was. I would tell him how incredibly grateful and proud I was to have married an educated man who could provide for his family so well. These are true statements; that was how I really felt. But neither of us had the tools to navigate through our lives with the challenges that we presented for each other.

I had been able to grow and expand via the praise and support I received from Linda, Brinley, and my clients. Bruce didn't have an opportunity for any of that. I could have been his biggest fan. I could have shouted to the entire planet that my husband was "fucking awesome!" If only I would have known the importance of doing so. One would think it should have been obvious because of my own experience. But unfortunately, it wasn't. I'm also not blind to the fact that Bruce's careful planning with his money made it very easy to be so cavalier with mine.

Many people (including myself) can relate to lost time in their lives, time that can never be recovered. We don't get to rewind the clock. People can spend a lifetime wanting and waiting for someone to be different. I did it with Bruce for years. I'm not saying he was bad or violent toward me or our children. He wasn't–that wouldn't have ended well. He was a very good man.

However, continuous negative verbal exchanges can get into your psyche and stay there. Although I was very good at tuning Bruce out, not knowing what would be around the corner if I left kept me stuck for years. As strong as I was, it felt safer to live in denial.

To move forward in life, I needed to look at my situation exactly the way it was. I needed to quit arguing with reality, thinking I could change it. All it takes is a simple question: Does this situation "right now" work for me? Yes or no?

It was so easy to see the obvious in Janet's life. I had tried to empower Janet when she and her children lived at my home. She did finally leave her husband–twenty-five years later. When I think about the incident with DH, it wasn't the smartest idea for me to try and fix violence with more violence. However, me standing up to him made him not quite so scary to his family. I'm very lucky; that situation could have turned out so differently.

CHAPTER 12

Baggies and Girdles

L ife refused to slow down, and I might have just been that continual instigator. The busier I stayed, the more in control I felt. I didn't need idle time to sit and think about what wasn't working.

One day in the salon, a client told me about a new diet regime she was taking. "It's called Fen-Phen," she said. "It's Fenfluramine and Phentermine. This little drug combination is the best thing since Diet Coke! I'm never hungry, and I have so much energy."

"Really?" I asked excitedly, stopping for the first time that day to take in what she had said. *This is definitely something I'm going to have to check out!* My answer to controlling my weight had been bulimia in my younger years, and then I went straight into not eating to get my weight off once I started having babies. The underlying fear of following my mother's path of obesity was always present, not only for me but for Rita as well.

When I told Rita about this new wonder regime, she joined me, and we drove over an hour to my client's doctor–she had told me he would give a prescription to anyone. As we entered the clinic lobby, I was shocked to see at least fifteen other women waiting to see him. Many were standing because there weren't enough chairs. I observed a mixed bag of every size and age as I looked around.

When I finally made it into the doctor's office, I was surprised; it looked more like a study than a medical office. I sat in a big leather-bound chair in front of a large oak desk. There was freeze-dried noodle soup displayed along the desk–three different flavors. *He can't possibly be promoting this crap . . . the Styrofoam cup is more nutritious than the soup!*

Dr. Taylor entered the room and sat down behind his desk. I noticed his tacky, black pleather vest as he introduced himself. He opened my chart and quickly glanced over it.

"Five feet, seven inches, one hundred and thirteen pounds," he paused for thought. "You should probably stay above a hundred and five pounds, Ramona. If you drop below that, be sure you put some weight in your shoes or pockets if you ever get weighed," he said matter-of-factly, without looking up.

Oh my hell, you're going to end up on 20/20. This is embarrassing. Can't you at least pretend to be professional?

"Here are some soups I recommend for a low-calorie diet," he said, gesturing at the little display on his desk. *Holy shit! He "is" pushing the soup. This is funny.*

"Sounds great," I replied flatly. *I'd rather eat the container.*

Then, Dr. Taylor reached across his desk . . . and handed me my golden ticket. "I'm giving you three months," he said with a smile. My judgment toward him quickly dissipated as I took the prescription. *You know absolutely nothing about health–but you're still my hero.*

I was giddy with excitement as Rita and I walked up to the pharmacy counter–conveniently just across the street. *I have my prescription. Yay me!* The technician eyed me up and down as she read my script. *Bite me, lady!* I thought as I felt the judgment through her gaze.

"It'll be twenty minutes," she announced curtly.

We popped the first two pills on our way home. I chased them with my Diet Coke. Rita took a healthier approach with her water–she didn't drink soda of any kind. "My client wasn't wrong. This stuff feels fantastic!" I exclaimed in a state of exuberance. Rita agreed wholeheartedly and enthusiastically!

I was like the Energizer bunny on steroids that night and every day moving forward. When I mowed my lawn, as I finished, I kept right on trucking over the sidewalk–to start cutting our neighbor's lawn. She was a widow, and her grandson didn't always get to her lawn as frequently as she liked. But I did.

Overachieving felt amazing, especially with a husband whose second job was to criticize. *Look at everything I can do, Bruce! This is a piece of cake! In-your-face, you little buzz-kill!* Only now, Bruce made it a point to ignore me whenever I was in power mode. Not that I cared. Who needs a husband? I had more energy than I knew what to do with.

Six months later–on a typical weeknight, as I prepared dinner in the kitchen, I could hear the evening news on the television in the living room. It caught my attention when the news anchor said, "A diet combination called Fen/Phen."

What about Fen/Phen? I quickly walked into the living room to listen.

"The miraculous wonder drug called Fen/Phen is under serious scrutiny. People who have been taking this diet regimen are showing signs of serious heart damage," the reporter stated.

Shit! That's just great. I hope Bruce didn't hear that. I quickly put in a Disney movie; this was more suited to my taste anyway. *Screw that!* I thought as I went back to fixing dinner.

I felt like a female Hercules–a perfect specimen of unadulterated brawn-ess. But just to be on the safe side, I went in for a free ultrasound of my heart. Of course, I didn't stop taking the pills; this was just a little speed bump I needed to handle. The only difficult part of the visit was sitting still for the five-minute procedure.

As the radiologist finished, she smiled at me and said, "You're fit as a fiddle."

"Great!" I said with relief. "Then I can keep taking it, right?"

She shook her head vehemently. "No, this medication is no longer available," stating the obvious.

I just looked at her. *Shit! Shit! Shit! I need this! I'm focused and balanced! I will not go back to being resentful and chubby!* I felt like a mighty Gladiator who had just been hurled into the dust with a powerful blow–from a wicked opponent who wanted all women to be docile and bloated.

The radiologist continued cautiously. "You look very thin; you don't want to take something that could be damaging," she said sympathetically.

On my last visit to Dr. Taylor, I had weighed in at one hundred and three pounds. "Well, it looks like you're going to have to get some weights, young lady," he said–as he wrote out my prescription refill.

I looked at the radiologist with an emotionless stare. *You don't get it. Away with you!* I was devastated.

As I drove home from the radiology appointment that afternoon, my brain was scrambling. I only had nineteen days left . . . tucked safely away in my purse–it suddenly became my most prized possession. I had to find a way to remedy my little dilemma. One of my clients had told me about pharmacies in Mexico where you could get almost anything. *That's it! I'll just go to Mexico!* Suddenly, there was a glimmer of hope for my situation.

Within two weeks, I had a plan mapped out to the minute. It was a Tuesday, and Bruce left for work at 5:00 a.m. (he commuted an hour and a half to and from work every day). When the coast was clear, my co-conspirator showed up to watch my sleeping kiddos. Having no time to waste, I jumped in the car and raced to the airport. If everything went to schedule, I'd be back in the kitchen with dinner on the table come evening.

My plane landed in San Diego, and I promptly jumped on a trolley that went into Tijuana. Walking down the dusty, narrow streets by myself was nerve-wracking, to say the least. Having never been south of California, it was like being on another planet. The barefooted children and dogs so skinny their ribs were showing was a culture shock I wasn't prepared for.

Focus! I kept telling myself as my heart pounded in my chest. There were dozens of pharmacies that lined the streets. I chose a big one on the corner–it looked clean, with tall windows and a white-tiled floor. As I walked in, the Mexican man behind the counter met me with a smile.

I asked the kind man if they had Fenfluramine and Phentermine.

"Yes," he answered. "How much do you want?"

Triumph! "How much is it?" I asked.

"Twelve U.S. dollars," he replied, pointing to the first bottle. "Eight U.S. dollars," he added, pointing to the second bottle.

Oh my gosh–that's so cheap! God Bless America! I was ecstatic! "I want twenty-four bottles of each one," I said matter-of-factly, grinning from ear to ear.

"Ah, okay, okay. I will get this for you," he answered. Rubbing his chin, he spoke Spanish to his assistant, who quickly exited the pharmacy.

The pharmacist then said, "You can't take this much into U.S.; I will help you." He took a big empty vitamin bottle and filled it with Phentermine pills. Then he put super glue around the rim of the bottle and stuck on an old, used-looking seal.

Shit, that looks ridiculous! "That's okay, I'm staying here for a while," I lied.

Now, he gave me a puzzled look. "Okay . . ." he said, shrugging his shoulders.

Within ten minutes, the pharmacist's assistant returned with the rest of my order. As I watched them put the vitamin bottle and all the boxes in two over-sized white shopping bags, I could hardly contain my excitement–holding back my urge to break out in spontaneous dance around the pharmacy.

"Thank you very much!" I said, blissfully smiling like a Cheshire cat as I waved goodbye to my newfound heroes. Walking back out onto the street, however, it didn't take long for my joy to turn into panic and fear. I was being stared at by the men and women I passed. I had to find a restaurant–and quick, so I could get on with my plan.

I found a place that looked inviting. It had a small courtyard displaying beautiful succulents in Talavera pots. A tall bird bath stood in the corner, with a gentle waterspout bubbling in the center. Upon entering the restaurant, I was quickly seated. I ordered a Diet Coke and the first thing I saw on the menu. Then, I asked the waitress where their restroom was. The woman smiled and pointed toward the back of the restaurant.

I took all my bags and went inside the single-room restroom. Locking the door behind me, I immediately pulled the large zip-lock freezer bags I'd been toting around out of my purse. Then I began to tear into the boxes of pills I had just purchased, ripping them open and dumping the bottles of medications into the zip-lock bags.

Now came the ingenious part that I'd come up with all on my own . . . even though it had made my flight over a bit uncomfortable.

I took the belt off the loose maternity dress I was wearing. When a bag was about three-quarters full of my drug of choice, I zipped it up and shoved it into the full-length girdle I had on. With the last pack of pills in my girdle, I looked like I was at least seven months pregnant. *Voila! Perfect!*

I quickly shoved the bags, empty boxes, and bottles into the bathroom garbage, feeling grateful it was a tall canister with a lid on it. After guzzling down the Diet Coke, I took a few bites of my meal while messing up the food to make it look like I had eaten more than I had. Then I quickly paid, leaving a big tip.

Waddling down the street looking pregnant–instead of loaded, made me feel just as vulnerable, but in a different way. I couldn't get back to the trolley fast enough. *Thank God it's a different driver!* I thought as I stepped on and took a seat.

As we pulled into the San Diego airport ninety minutes later, I was beyond frazzled. *I'm actually going to smuggle drugs on an airplane! Fuck! Okay . . . get your shit together, Ramona! It's game time. Calm . . . be calm!*

Fortunately for me, in 1997, the airport protocol wasn't a big production. But I was still scared shitless! As I went through security, I swallowed hard and found the temerity within me. Letting out a little sigh, I arched my back, putting one hand on my lumbar and the other on my belly. I needed a reason as to why I looked so distressed. The woman at the checkpoint gave me a sympathetic smile.

God bless you for not arresting me!

During the flight back home, I thought, *So this is what PTSD feels like?* I couldn't shake the terrified feeling I had experienced more than once that day. I found it ironic that my older brother Kyle was actually an undercover narcotics officer now. *Thank God I wasn't busted, that would have made family dinners so awkward.*

My plane finally landed, and I made it back to my car. *I'm okay, everything's good.* Within seconds, my head snapped back in the game. I had to get my ass home before Bruce walked in from work! Then everything would go back to normal in my happy life.

As Bruce walked through the door that evening, I was cooking dinner, as usual, in my sweats. The mere fact that I had pulled it off and succeeded with my plan put me in a very good mood. Thinking about the course of events that had taken place that day, my heart welled up with gratitude for the helpful pharmacist. *It's too bad I can't send them a big gift basket to say thank you.*

This little stash of mine would secure my way of life for two years before I'd needed to stock up again. Not having to worry about my dilemma anymore, I was going full steam ahead. As time passed, leaving the mute button on Bruce only added to his anxiety–but thankfully reduced mine. I had joy in my life through my four beautiful children, my work, and my best friend Brinley. Life was easy–predictable.

Brinley and I had a McDonald's date once a week with our kids. Every Wednesday, I took a break from 11:45 a.m. until 1:30 p.m. We ordered chicken nuggets for our kiddos and then scooted them out to the playland so we could talk. The two of us were closer than sisters; we were more like identical twins.

This weekly date was our therapy time. We would vent out every single frustration that had occurred during the week with our husbands. Man-bashing was our way of coping with life.

Both Brinley and I had four children each. With the exception of our firstborn, we had planned out having our other three children together. Our husbands had no say in the matter, which was rightly so; we were doing all the work of raising our kids anyway. By then, Brinley had been through one divorce and married her sophomore high school sweetheart.

One particular Wednesday, as we watched a storm come in, the kids played happily inside the playland. Brinley looked at me cautiously.

"Romer," she said slowly, "Umm, I need to talk to you about something."

"What is it, sweetie?" I said, suddenly concerned. She had my full attention.

"I'm getting so tired of working in a doctor's office. I love seeing the freedom you have in your schedule and the financial stability you've created with having a salon in your home. I thought I might want to go to cosmetology school–so I could do what you do. What do you think?"

As I absorbed Brinley's words, a surge of excitement welled up within me. This extraordinary woman had believed in me and given me unwavering, enthusiastic support when I was in school. Having her in my corner had always been empowering–she was still in my corner to this day. *I wouldn't be where I am today if I hadn't had you. You gave me my "Fucking Awesome" badge of courage!* Would I support her?

"Hell, yes!" I shouted–in the middle of Mickey-Dee's, startling a few people nearby. I was thrilled! The thought that Brinley lived only two blocks from me didn't make me hesitate–not for one split second.

I jumped on the bandwagon and proclaimed, "I'm here for you, girl. We're going to have so much fun!"

"I'm so happy you're cool with this," Brinley said with relief.

"Are you kidding? You just made my day! Don't you know how good this is going to feel to pay you back for always believing in me? My career could have turned out so differently. I love you, Brin! I'm so excited!" I cheered with a tearful, heartfelt hug.

I was fifteen years into my career; my clients were family, and I had absolutely no fear of losing them. The cosmetology business was either feast or famine–fortunately, I had fallen into a career where I thrived. I was happy to support Brinley in achieving that life too.

Brinley enrolled in cosmetology school immediately, and her family started living as frugally as possible. They ate "Helper" for dinner–not "Hamburger Helper," just "Helper." I took Brinley's kids, who were like my own, every day after school until her husband picked them up at 5:00 p.m.

Brinley's little Porter, at seven years old, was a mini guru with an old-soul wisdom. He came up to me one afternoon with a concerned face. "Wamona," he began thoughtfully, with that same "W" for "R" that I'd struggled with as a kid. "How do you do it? You got da house to clean, da bills to pay, all dees kids wunnin' awound . . . suntines, don't you jus' feel like goin' in on yo bed and ballin'?"

Oh my heart! I love this kid! "Yes, Porter," I said with a chuckle. "Yes I do." Smiling at his insight as I handed him his PB&J. I watched my little

Socrates go with his sandwich in hand, walking a slow stroll–like he was deep in a vortex of thoughts. I couldn't wait to hear what he came up with next.

Empowering Brinley in her pursuit of a new career became a transformative experience for all involved. While the goal was Brinley's, I found myself just as exhilarated to be a part of her journey. The anticipation of a remarkable new adventure hung in the air. With my reserve of Mexican energy and sanity stowed safely under my mattress, I was ready to take on anything.

Warrior Wisdom:

Writing about my little drug run was hard. My life could have crashed and burned so many times. What the hell was I thinking? But that's the insidious power of addiction–it clouds all sound judgment. My sole focus was obtaining the drug I "thought" was making my world work. That innocuous diet regimen started an addiction that lasted for years and years. Addiction to anything that changes your natural state begins when you don't–or feel like you can't, deal with something in your life.

It's crucial to remember that just because a medication is prescribed by a doctor does not mean it's safe or good for you. The physician who fed into my body image issues so he could write out his prescriptions allowed me to become so much worse. It was the perfect storm. While I do recognize the existence of exceptional doctors, I now meticulously research the potential side effects of any prescribed medication–perhaps even more thoroughly than the prescribing physician.

I thought it was too much to deal with the stress that my marriage was causing. But when I look at the span of my life and what substance abuse led to (including emasculating my husband), dealing with my marriage head-on would have been a piece of cake compared to the alternative.

Supporting Brinley going to school was one of my proudest moments. Having a friend to talk to about my troubles with Bruce was a Godsend. On the other hand, I can see that it slowed me from wanting to take any type of action toward my marriage. When you have a girlfriend who you constantly vent to, what good is that doing? It may offer temporary relief, but nothing changes. How empowering is that? If I had done less venting to Brinley and more communicating with Bruce, it certainly wouldn't have hurt.

Burying our deepest hurts or unhappiness behind certain coping mechanisms could be as simple as having a girlfriend who supports a victim stance by listening to the never-ending woes of a broken marriage, or as damaging as a heart-stopping, addictive medication. Coping with anything in unhealthy ways can change the trajectory of your life. I beg you, don't do it my friend.

Don't push the mute button on your husband. And while we're at it, smuggling discontinued drugs over the border was "one" of the many stupidest things I have ever done! Facing the music, however hard, will be infinitely better than the dark alternatives. I didn't face any of my demons back then . . . and you'll see how detrimental that was for me.

I didn't realize the collision course I was on at the time. Brinley and I were rapidly approaching the end of an era–the simplicity of our lives would never be the same. The innocence we carried from being a couple of small-town girls–albeit with adventurous spirits–was about to change.

CHAPTER 13

If I Jump Off This Mountain . . .

Brinley was attending a trendy, cutting-edge cosmetology school, rubbing shoulders with revered stylists who were renowned for their exceptional skills as platform artists. It was an absolute gift to hear about the wealth of knowledge she was acquiring. As she shared the latest products and advanced styling techniques with me, it added another layer to our conversations and provided us with yet another shared interest to bond over. I was already loving having her in the business.

When Brinley's cosmetology school took a field trip to California for a hair show–I went right along with them. It was like Brinley and I were back in high school. We hit the nightclubs with two of the instructors and had the time of our lives!

Despite all of us being married and sharing the same faith, we reveled in the joy of our freedom for the night, doing tequila shots and dancing our asses off. I hadn't imbibed in alcohol for years; it was part of my "be a perfect mother, wife, and business owner routine." Brinley was the only one who knew my marriage with Bruce was mismatched mayhem.

Our party drank and danced for most of the night, creating an atmosphere that brought about an unparalleled sense of euphoria. It was a profound awakening for me, breathing life into a part of myself that had long been dormant. I had shut down my sexuality, putting it on permanent lockdown. I was too resentful to feel sexy. Instead, my energies were channeled into the things that brought me joy and a sense of fulfillment–my children and my business.

When we had to leave *Fantasy Island* and fly home, I couldn't wait to go back!

Brinley's cosmetology school attended two more hair shows while she was in school. I eagerly jumped back on the attendance list–the apocalypse couldn't have kept me from going! Being admired on the dance floor and feeling sexy was like a drug in itself. We never broke any chastity rules, only the hard and fast rule the X-Factor religion had against alcohol.

Brinley finished in record time; unlike me, she hadn't missed a single day of school. Her family had been living on "Helper" for far too long, and she wasn't messing around. In addition to the student loan, Brinley also took out a small business loan and built a salon in her basement.

I was thrilled to see Brinley realize her dream of having her own salon. I eagerly shared every bit of knowledge I had acquired from my time at Oliver's salon, as well as the insights gained from my own professional journey. I had every confidence that Brinley was destined for success–she was going to crush it!

As the weeks and months went by, however, Brinley did not have the same experience I had in building a clientele. It came as a surprise to me; she had always been much more outgoing than I was. Brinley possessed an exceptional ability to connect with people, being genuinely kind to everyone she encountered.

I couldn't understand why I hadn't been able to empower her the way she had been able to empower me. I wanted her success just as badly as she did, maybe even more, because I knew what it felt like. I had sung her praises– loud! But it just wasn't happening for her. I'm sure this had to feel frustrat- ing–and defeating. She had sacrificed and worked so hard; her dedication to school put my own to shame.

A year and a half into Brinley's career, she acquired a new client who had just moved into town with his family. At first, he seemed pretty impressive–a big talker. He told Brinley, "Open a cosmetology school! That's where the money is. I can help you get funding. That's the easy part."

When Brinley approached me with the idea of opening a school together, it was honestly quite intriguing. *Maybe this is the next step for me.* I had been doing hair in my home for over eighteen years. I pictured the trendy school that Brinley had graduated from two years before; the students we had gone to the hair shows with had been so much fun. I imagined myself on the stage, inspiring wanna-be cosmetology students. The idea became more and more appealing.

Despite the allure of this new venture, I was hesitant. Brinley's client, at times, seemed to be a master of illusions. I suggested we bring in a third partner, a gorgeous client of mine who looked so impressive. Her name was Melanie, and she had just recently graduated from cosmetology school herself.

Melanie had initially asked if I could bring her into my salon and do an apprenticeship. However, I already had a system and a rhythm that worked flawlessly. I didn't have the time or desire to change it in any way. But nevertheless, we had a natural rapport.

When Brinley and I approached Melanie with the idea of opening a school, she jumped at the opportunity. We were all so excited, and the scenario with the three of us felt right. We immediately began to look at buildings for our school.

With the sweet smell of something new in the air came a bittersweet fact–diving into this new venture meant I couldn't keep running my successful salon. There was no way I could launch into the education world and keep my clients, even with all the Fen/Phen in the world.

A second trip to Mexico had only given me half of my secret combination. Fenfluramine was no longer available, even in Mexico. So I only had the stimulant, but not the mood evening drug that made me feel so focused. This left me feeling edgy all the time.

Everything had come so easy for me when I opened my home salon, so I expected this venture to go off without a hitch. Not long after that, Brinley's client, who had initially championed the idea of a school, showed his true colors, and we all saw what a complete fraud he was. It was his wife and her parents that had the business sense–and the money. Now, the three of us girls found ourselves entirely on our own in navigating our new adventure.

The sudden shift in circumstances left me feeling ill-prepared for the business side of our endeavor, as my expertise had been confined to the operations of my salon. The closest I came to business affairs was getting writer's cramp from signing my client's checks for deposit at the end of the week–that was it!

Suddenly, the idea of opening a school became very intimidating. Putting on a brave face, I forged ahead. With my best friend in the world and our trustworthy partner, we could figure it out. I found myself feeling a heavy responsibility. After all, neither Brin nor Melanie had the expertise and longevity I had. It felt like the success of the business fell squarely on my shoulders.

It didn't take long for my lack of business acumen to get us pointed in the wrong direction. I determined that establishing a school in a town devoid of other cosmetology institutions would provide a promising starting point. After securing a building, we all put in $20k and took the leap.

Now came the part I had been dreading–breaking the news to my clients. Two hundred and fifty clients whom I considered family. How was I going to tell everyone I had just pulled the rug out from under them? After nineteen years, I would no longer be doing their hair.

My party place turned into a funeral home overnight. The once vibrant atmosphere of my salon became laden with sadness. Every day was full of tearful goodbyes. These were people I had seen every six weeks for almost two decades. The gravity of my decision only fully dawned on me as I walked upstairs at the end of each day, filled with lingering doubts and a sense of profound loss. *What have I done?* I never realized the entirety of what I had created until I was in the process of giving it up.

The only thing to do now was suck it up and move forward. We had three months to turn our building from a soup and salad restaurant into a unique, appealing cosmetology school.

My new partners and I transformed the space, converting the salad bar into double-sided hair stations and adding a classroom with a stage in the basement. We painted the interior and created a jungle-themed decor. I thought it would be cool to build a waterfall–I didn't know shit about building waterfalls . . . *but how hard can it be?*

I went through a cement phase in my living room. *Nope, well . . . that's "one" way not to do it.* It finally evolved into creating a base out of cardboard boxes, pizza boxes, and anything from the trash I could nail or staple to the wall to form the base. Spraying insulation foam over all the boxes–once dried, could be cut into the shape of rocks.

I applied a water-proof tar adhesive over the foam, with sand and small rocks rubbed into the tar, creating the texture of an actual rock surface. As the final step, I started painting and adding layers of color, moss, and texture.

One evening, as I worked through the night, I could tell I was getting high from the paint fumes. I was beyond exhausted. As I stood up to stretch my back and arms, I noticed an open box of assorted nuts we had been given as a gift–wishing us well on our new venture.

My hands were covered in paint and moss. So I shuffled over to the box, dropped my head, and began grazing on the delicious nuts. Devouring every nut I could get in my mouth, nothing had ever tasted so delicious!

I basically lived at the soon-to-be academy as the project consumed my days and nights. I would pick my kids up from school, grab a pizza, then we headed back to the work site so we could be together while I stapled vinyl tile on the wall, nailed bamboo beneath the stations, and wrapped rope around all the exposed pipes in the basement. Our list of things to get done was endless.

At bedtime, I took my children home, tucked them in, and headed back to the school. I would work until 3:00 or 4:00 a.m. before heading home to sleep for a few hours until I began my day all over again.

It didn't take me long to learn that Brinley's work ethic was completely normal–at least in the beginning. At 6:00 p.m., she went home. It didn't matter how much we had to do or how big of an undertaking we had jumped into. Melanie had a husband who was a great handyman and loved doing whatever she needed–at home. So she wasn't the type of gal to jump in and get things done at any cost either. Brinley and Melanie were both so great . . . and completely normal.

Soon, I found I was the odd woman out in our trio. I didn't have the typical, sensible way of seeing things. I was that manic woman who got things done– and made up for lack of energy with my trusty pills. The transition left me feeling isolated and anxious, grappling with the weight of the sacrifices I had made.

Brinley's seemingly cavalier attitude made me want to strangle her. And Melanie was as non-confrontational and passive as a human could possibly be. A permanent fixture had settled in my thoughts during the ten weeks since I'd flipped my life upside down. *What the hell have I gotten myself into?*

I quit sleeping altogether. I was freaking out . . . my kids were freaking out. The safe, stable home with us all being together was over. Patty, our dear nanny, would arrive in the morning, and we would all cry as I left the house.

I found myself in a state of crisis, overwhelmed by fear and uncertainty. Stopping at the liquor store to buy vodka to pour in my coffee while I shoveled in Phentermine pills became my morning ritual. I hoped the vodka would take the edge off of being so terrified. Partying at the hair show had been the first time I ever drank hard liquor. I was shooting for anything even remotely close to that blissful feeling.

As I kept tackling my new nightmare, Bruce became increasingly critical.

"Who was that man who just left?" Bruce asked one evening as he came walking into the school out of the blue.

"Hello to you too," I said. "That was Jim Reynolds, the director for the Technical College; he stopped by to wish us well."

"Why would he do that?" Bruce asked accusingly.

"I don't know Bruce, probably because he's a nice person," I answered. I could feel another argument coming on. I had stopped going anywhere alone with Bruce because the evening would turn into one, big, long catharsis secession. Now, he was showing up at the school.

"So, you're telling me the director of a college just happened to stop by?" Bruce said mockingly.

"Are you really going to punish me because a man whom I've never met before, stopped by to introduce himself and wish us well?" I asked in utter contempt. "Give me a fucking break Bruce!"

This was my new reality; the resentment I felt toward my husband had gone to a new depth. I could handle getting no support from him–I was used to that. However, his verbal outbursts were now breaking me down. My fucking awesome shield was gone. I was no longer the powerhouse crushing it every day. I was the woman who had become scared shitless because I didn't know what the hell I was doing. I was terrified.

Averaging less than three hours of sleep every night; the overwhelming, frantic feeling that we weren't getting things finished fast enough, and wouldn't be ready before we were scheduled to open was suffocating.

It wasn't long before a final shift occurred. I still remember it like it was yesterday. Bruce and I were in the kitchen, I had just gotten the kids settled in bed and was gearing up to head back to the school for a long night of work. Bruce made a snide comment about me never being home–it was par for the course, just another evening. But *that* particular evening, I snapped. I went from feeling numb, to truly hating him.

The man I had once adored, now made my skin crawl. To make matters worse, it wasn't until I emotionally checked out that Bruce wanted to see a counselor. Thinking back on all the heart-wrenching fights we had experienced and the numerous times I had implored Bruce to seek counseling together–it felt like a slap in the face.

The day of our magnificent school's grand opening finally arrived. We ran a big ad in the local paper and decorated with balloons for an open house to meet as many people as possible. By the end of the day, our grand opening had produced a total of three new students. And so began our new endeavor of operating a cosmetology school.

As the three owners, we tried our hand at everything: instructor, office work, recruiter. I grabbed the janitor position because it drove me crazy if things weren't done *my way*. I went through a major identity crisis. I was used to being everyone's favorite person. I made hundreds of women beautiful! Now, I was having a hard time keeping my students' attention. I felt like screaming, "Don't you know who I am?"

More often than not, I would go off on some tangent, trying to give these teenage girls–looking at me with emotionless stares, just one spark of passion. One spark of anything! As time passed, my spark was slowly dying.

Melanie was a natural teacher. She had it dialed in from the beginning. Her persona was cool, calm, and collected. Watching Melanie teach, one would think she had been doing it for years. I was happy and relieved to have such a strong asset in our newly budding school. But if I'm being honest, Melanie's rock-star teaching abilities only added to my insecurity of not knowing what the hell I was doing. My fame was dead and buried.

Brinley discovered right out of the gate that she did not like to teach; she would be the office manager. Among us, she was the best suited for operating a school; she had just been in school herself, she also had excellent PR skills, and was incredibly smart.

For me and Brinley, the days of singing each other's praises went out the window when we opened the academy. We were all trying to find our way in this new, terrifying world we had created, navigating the challenges of our fledgling institution.

I'll go ahead and point out the twenty-twenty hindsight I acquired within the first six months of starting our academy. College students want to have a college experience; they want to be in a college town—not a Podunk town with absolutely nothing going on. It was a stark reality: our location did not offer the college experience sought by our target demographic. *Demographic analysis? What the hell is a demographic analysis?*

I became so restless! I was used to putting the pedal to the metal five days a week, with my weekends off. Now, I didn't even know what to do with myself, and I had to work on Saturdays! I was also making a pittance that we paid ourselves, and I didn't even feel the pride of earning it. I had given up a perfect life—earning $150k per year, to jump into a living hell!

The creative, high energy I had carried for so many years was gone—and I had no clue what to do about it. I just knew that I used to feel empowered and joyous every day. Now, I felt fear, loss, pain, and regret.

Warrior Wisdom:

I was not equipped to handle what was happening to me. I had been living inside a Neverland Bubble for almost twenty years. At the time, I thought the vodka was helping me cope. In reality, that was like me saying: "If I jump off this mountain, I will fly." In addition to the diet pills, I was adding a new and more destructive layer–alcohol. I began to operate at a different level, slowly withdrawing from life.

With alcohol, it's so easy to tell ourselves, "I'll stop drinking so much when my crisis is over." What I failed to recognize is that alcohol does not give you one fucking thing *to help you get yourself out of your crisis. If anything, it keeps you weak and guarantees you will stay right where you are.*

If I could go back and talk to my younger self . . . well, I could write an entire book on that alone! But one of the things I would have said is this: When you think about it rationally, Ramona, would you rather numb out and stay in your shithole? Or would you rather confront 100% of the pain and terror, and eventually climb out of that hole? Emerging profoundly stronger and resilient for having gotten through your crisis. We don't dodge anything by numbing out; we only prolong it.

In addition, I could have written a highly educational book titled, Everything Not to do in a Business, because I did them all!

Numero uno would be: Partnerships don't work; there has to be a boss. I had no idea how it would be working with Brinley and Melanie until after we had made the plunge and started a business together. When you hire an employee, and things don't work out, you let them go. When things don't go as planned with a partner (or partners), it's not so easy. I couldn't have been more opposite from Brinley and Melanie if I had tried.

In my humble opinion, venturing into business with a family member or close friend is incredibly risky. If things go south, you have put your relationship at risk. Family and cherished friendships are too important to gamble on with a business.

Peace comes from aligning within ourselves and realizing it's not our business what others think of us. Letting go of what others think is pure freedom, baby! Live your life through the beauty of peacefulness. The example you will provide by simply being happy will be your greatest shield from ever feeling judged or misunderstood.

The shift I had with Bruce was heartbreaking for everyone. It wasn't until I lost my love for him that he wanted to change. I didn't do myself or Bruce any favors by tolerating a marriage that didn't work for me. Having self-love is the only answer. It forces us to find solutions for our best interests. If you think ignoring a situation will eventually work itself out, I can tell you through personal experience–it won't.

When I opened my salon, I had been working with masters of the trade for over two years. Why I thought I could just hop into something I knew nothing about still baffles me. If you have an interest in something, seek out people who have mastered this particular thing. We should have found a successful school in another state and learned everything we could before we ever thought about a location. I would have saved myself so much time if I had remembered the value of mentorship before *becoming a school owner.*

Furthermore, be willing to pay for this knowledge you would have otherwise taken years to learn on your own! As cliché as this sounds–you don't know what you don't know. One of my dear friends worked for me as an instructor for over a year and then opened a cosmetology school herself in the college town eighteen miles away. I still love her and hold absolutely no grudge. However, if I would have had the slightest business acumen, a non-compete clause would have been in my employees' contracts.

Looking back, I'm sure the constant state of hyperness I was in did not allow an opportunity for me to ponder over how I should go about doing anything.

CHAPTER 14

Free-Fall

Four months after our academy opened, Brinley, Melanie, and I embarked on a trip to Las Vegas to attend a seminar, marking the beginning of our training process for becoming an accredited school. At that point, I was completely unfamiliar with accreditation, Title IV funding/student loans, or any other matter that bore no relation to my success as a cosmetologist. Going to Vegas had felt daunting. Grappling with a profound yearning for familiarity, I missed being at home and the beautiful life I once had.

I had always known how much I loved to stay busy, but I had never realized that it was next to impossible for me to sit still, especially for hours on end. The three of us sat in the seminar and I was in a state of complete torment. As I drew a picture of me hanging from a rope, I had never felt more discombobulated in my entire life. Next, I drew a picture of me with a gun to my head, another picture of me holding a lit bomb . . . you get the picture.

And then out of nowhere, the heavens parted . . . and mercifully, they quit talking. The relief in the room was palpable. *Thank you, dear Lord! At least we can go out for the evening.*

Having returned to our rooms and now being dressed in appropriate Vegas attire, the three of us descended floors in the hotel elevator with a family man who had stepped in with his little boy. As we all stood there, the man whispered to his son, "Just don't look at them." We all turned and snickered. That was the first time I had chuckled in months!

I guess you could say we all held our own, but Melanie got stares from people across the street and in all directions–she was beyond stunning. She had short, white spiked hair with piercing, almond-shaped, ice-blue eyes and perfect, full lips. Her bone structure was also exceptional . . . high cheekbones, a long neck, and a figure that made everyone do a double-take. Brinley and I loved to give Melanie a hard time, stating that we would take on the role of being her bodyguards from the *stan club* that seemed to gather wherever we went.

Our first night in Vegas, we went to a club in Caesar's Palace called the Blue Ocean. When we arrived at the club, we got in line behind everyone else. Three naïve little hotties from a town no one had ever heard of. After a minute, one of the large men at the door shook his head; then, he left his post and started walking toward us! *Oh shit . . . maybe this is a private club. How embarrassing!*

As he approached us, he said impatiently, "You don't wait in line; you walk into the club." He motioned in an *after-you* gesture and said, "This way, ladies."

Wait, what? Why? This isn't fair.

One of the other men at the entrance opened the side partition and escorted us in. "Enjoy yourselves, ladies," he said with a smile as he turned to go back out to the entrance.

With that, Melanie let out a little giggle and was out on the floor dancing. She was the most incredible dancer I had ever seen! Melanie could move her body in directions that weren't humanly possible for most people. I was in awe!

As Brinley and I stood there–coveting Melanie's curvy body and the way she could move it, a tall, beautiful man with chiseled features and dark hair approached me and asked, "Can I buy you a drink?"

His name was Arash. He was half-Iranian but had grown up in England. I couldn't take my eyes off his full lips and thick eyelashes. Me and my homies nicknamed him Jafar from the Disney movie *Aladdin*, even though he looked nothing like the character. Being from the incredibly non-diverse area I was raised in, Arash was mystifying.

His charm sparked an engaging conversation, I was undeniably drawn to his enigmatic persona–and completely smitten with his beautiful English accent. Being in his company reminded me what happiness felt like. I had been in fear and isolation for so many months.

As the evening went on, Arash and I got into a fun facts conversation with each other.

He said, "I've slept with nineteen women." *Of course you have; you look like an Arabian James Bond!*

I said, "I can count on one finger the number of men I've slept with."

Arash answered, "Don't you mean one hand, darling?"

I answered back, "No, I mean one finger."

Arash's eyes widened–truly surprised. "Oh my dear, are you serious?" he marveled.

"Yes, I was married at eighteen and just got divorced a few months ago," I lied–just about the being divorced part. In my mind, X-Factor sex in high school didn't count. Arash was completely perplexed by my answer. We danced and talked for the rest of the night.

Before I left, Arash kissed me. After our kiss, he kept me close in his arms and whispered, "I've never wanted to be second so bad in my entire life."

I instantly became weak in the knees. I was overcome with equal parts fear and emotion. *This is getting way too real!* After I left, the guilt I felt for kissing another man quickly dissipated, and I couldn't wait to see him again.

Picture a big, crocheted Afghan blanket . . . a crazy little creature has just grabbed onto the yarn at the end, and now it's running . . . unraveling. That blanket was me, and that was precisely how I felt. Finding myself in a place like Vegas, meeting a man like Arash, waking up that passion within my heart that was completely dead, and ultimately having that feeling completely overpower my sense of right and wrong.

I had given Arash my number before we left the club, so the following evening, I was elated when he called and proposed meeting at the Blue Ocean again. We spent half the night making out in the corner and then parted ways a second time.

The third and final day of the conference was torture. The neverending lectures were almost more than I could bear. All I could think about was Arash. When they finally concluded, we got our workbooks stamped and bolted for the door.

As we were getting ready to go out that night, my anxiety began to rise. It was after 7:00 p.m., and Arash hadn't called. I was sipping on a big cup of vodka and slipping into the total mercy of my emotions. I kept popping Phentermine pills to keep myself from getting too drunk.

I felt disconnected from everything I held dear. I had four children whom I would die or kill for. I had a husband at home, whom I resented with every fiber of my being–but nevertheless, he was still my husband. And there I was, getting heartsick over a man I had seen only twice.

What the fuck happened to me? I had been a strong woman who controlled everything in her world. And now I found myself in a world that made no sense, in which I was powerless. I had jumped off a cliff . . . free falling, with absolutely nothing to grab onto.

"Are you okay, Romer?" Brinley asked as the three of us were seated at a little Italian restaurant, just a stone throw from the club we had been at the two previous evenings.

"What's wrong, sweetie?" Melanie added before I could answer.

"I'm good," was all I managed to say.

Arash finally called me at 9:45 p.m. Pushing down the red flag of being an afterthought, I couldn't get to the Blue Ocean fast enough. When I finally arrived at the club, I was pretty intoxicated–and very wired.

We stayed at the club for less than an hour. Within two hours, we were in Arash's room. Within four hours, I had committed adultery.

I woke up around 4:00 a.m. As I snuck out of Arash's room, the self-loathing I felt was almost unbearable. *I'm now a person who has cheated on her husband. It will never be the same again. I can never undo this.*

As I got back to our hotel room, Melanie woke up. "Where have you been?" she said. "We had no idea what happened to you." I was trying my hardest not to burst into tears.

"I'm an adult, Melanie. I don't need to check in, and you don't need to worry about me." My tone was harsher than intended. Without waiting for a response, I found quick refuge in the bathroom. Succumbing to sobs, I undressed and climbed in the shower.

Throughout the long drive back home, I wept in silence, concealing the reason from Brinley and Melanie. Deleting Arash's number, I tried to convince myself that it had never happened. By the time I reached home, I felt numb and utterly detached.

Bruce knew I was miserable, but when he saw me as I walked into our house that evening, for the first time, he backed off for the moment. I saw a look in his eyes that I'd never seen before. It was a frightened look that left him with no words. The guilt and remorse I felt was paralyzing. *What am I going to do?*

As the shock subsided over the following days, the remorse and guilt gradually transformed into a desperate need to speak with Arash and hear his voice again. For a moment I was panic-stricken–I had deleted his number! But then I realized it would be on our phone bill. Relief washed over me and I was instantly grateful my cell phone was a company phone–Bruce would never see the bill. It would be over two weeks before it arrived, and my stomach was in knots!

I no longer found a shred of normalcy in my life. A cruel twist had upended my reality; everything I had been good at was gone. How could I be this stressed and still be bored to death at the same time? My work day had been over at 3:30 p.m. when I worked at home. Now with the school, I didn't get home until 5:30 or 6:00 p.m. And finally . . . *this man*–had turned my life inside out and upside down.

I brought this on myself. How could I have been so foolish?

Finally, the anticipated moment arrived as I pored over the mail. Now holding what I had so anxiously been waiting for–my hands were shaking as I tore open the envelope . . . and there it was, Arash's number. That evening, I went to my backyard and dialed him–but Arash didn't pick up. My mind told me Arash was busy at work, so I left a short message saying hi.

The same outcome ensued the following day, shattering my emotions. The utter desperation I felt longing to speak with him left an ache in my chest that never subsided. Somehow, I had to let Arash know how I felt. I spent that entire night composing my thoughts and preparing what I would say when his phone inevitably went to voicemail again.

The following morning, I was ready to call Arash. I stopped at the park on my way to work. Sitting on the park bench, it took every ounce of courage I had to call his number. It predictably led to voicemail.

In a shaky voice, I bared my heart. Admitting I was married, I told him I had no intention of divorcing my children's father, but I needed a lover. As I approached the end of my message, my voice wavered.

"Anyway . . . thank you, beautiful man, for our time together. You take my breath away." I clicked off the phone and began to sob.

After composing myself ten minutes later, I ripped up my letter, threw it in the dumpster, and returned to my car. Even if Arash never called me back, I felt better for having said it. I could finally breathe again. It was the first time I had come to terms with my feelings in a long time. Everything I grew up believing to be right and wrong had gone right out the window. I felt exposed and raw, like a newborn deer trying to find its footing for the first time.

Later that day, Brinley answered the phone at our school. It was Arash! He told her he would call me back the next day at 2:00 p.m.

Sitting in Brinley's office chair the next day, I was silently freaking out. At 2:02, the phone rang. I jerked it off the receiver on the first ring.

"Hello?" I said in a shaky voice.

Then I heard Arash's beautiful English voice say, "Hello."

"Hello!" I cried back at him, three octives higher than normal. "It's so good to hear your voice!"

Arash told me my message had made him cry; he told me he was also married but felt the same way I did. I had never heard so many words that made me ecstatic in one conversation! We quickly made a plan for me to fly over to Denver and spend a weekend together the following month.

Completely checked out from my world as I knew it, I was mentally back in Vegas with Arash. I had been a good mother, yet within two years, I had become a completely different person. I was miserable. Arash was like a new drug in my system; he was all I ever thought about.

I was elated when we were together . . . and completely miserable when we weren't. Even our conversations were painful because I missed him. I was sad on my youngest daughter, Noel's first day of school. I was sad on Christmas. I was in a deep shithole and had no idea how to get out.

After five months, Arash lost interest and broke my heart. As painful as that was, it was less painful than the roller coaster I had been on while we were seeing each other. I was still miserable, but the heart-wrenching desperation slowly dissipated with time.

In the past, I had always doubled down and made myself crazy busy to cope when I was hurting. But now, there was nothing to get busy with. I was like a fish out of water. The morose state that had become my normal was a new form of torture. Within the following year, Brinley, Melanie, and I had built up our student base to around thirty students and were cash rich . . . for about five minutes. Being the *super smart* business owners we were, we naturally figured our hard times were over, and things would start looking up.

We were back in Vegas for another conference regarding our accreditation. After a long day of lectures, the three of us got ready and headed back to the Blue Ocean at Caesar's Palace.

I still felt the sting of my memory with Arash. As I was standing there with Brinley and Melanie, a huge man in a suit approached me and said, "Adam Hoffman, the owner of the Blue Ocean, would like to meet you."

I was taken aback for a second, then I shrugged my shoulders at my homies and turned to follow Adam Hoffman's bodyguard to his table.

"You call us, Romer!" Melanie said in her stern, motherish voice.

"Love you!" I said as I blew them both a kiss.

Adam was a handsome man who looked like he belonged to the Italian mafia. It was like meeting a sexy villain. We talked for the rest of the night at Adam's private table; he was fascinated with my story.

Adam lived on the top floor of Caesar's Palace. He told me he had once been an attorney but then became a club owner. "There's more money in it," he said. His place had ceiling-to-floor glass, with a bird's-eye view of the Las Vegas Strip. I had never seen anything so luxurious in my entire life.

Adam liked me; he called me his "little X-Factor." After we met, he started flying me out every other weekend to stay with him. This experience was different than Arash; I was drawn to the power Adam exuded. Everything in Vegas was at his fingertips.

I didn't even try to be convincing with the excuses I gave Bruce for being gone anymore. At this point, I was doing everything in my power to make Bruce leave me. In efforts to revive our marriage again, he had even built a new home. I had purchased the property ten years prior and begged Bruce to build a new home–but for that entire decade, he wouldn't budge.

Now, he had built it, and I didn't want to be there. That was just one more thing, eating me alive with resentment. When we moved in, I slept on the floor in the living room–in front of the fireplace.

I tried to be a more present mother on the weekends I stayed home. Jessie and Chance were in their teens; Conner was nine, and Noel was six. I would do anything with them that was out of the house–away from Bruce.

Adam's world was a life of total disconnect from reality and humanity. On my first trip out, he introduced me to cocaine and ecstasy. This lifestyle triggered every addicted part of my body and psyche. The bodyguards, Adam's black Porsche, the money, the drugs, walking right into any restaurant on the strip, sitting ringside at the big fights . . . the list of perks was endless. It was all an escape from a life I no longer recognized or controlled at home.

Adam doted on me like no other; shopping trips were his therapy–spending thousands every time. But he had absolutely no tolerance for other people or kids. Adam once told me he had only killed two people, but they both deserved it. *What the fuck, man?*

On one of my trips, we were in the elevator–on our way to Adam's private cabana to soak up some sun, when a woman stepped on with her two small children. They were all dressed in swimming suits, and the mom was carrying a giant, inflated donut.

"Oh my God," Adam said under his breath, acting put out that we had to share the elevator.

I elbowed Adam to show him my disapproval. "That looks like fun!" I said with a smile, gesturing towards the floating device.

"That looks like my cock ring," Adam muttered under his breath with a little chuckle.

You want to be a smart ass? Okay, game on!

I turned to the young boy and girl. "You guys have so much fun today! If you get bored or hungry, come on over to our cabana! This is Adam . . . he loves kids!" I said, with all the enthusiasm of a kindergarten teacher.

Adam looked at me like I was insane. "Are you high?" he asked sincerely.

I gave the mother a smile with a look that said, *I'm sorry he's such an ass!* She smiled back, and I knew she understood. A wave of emotion washed over me. *I miss my kids!* I blinked away my watery eyes and swallowed down the lump in my throat.

Our affair lasted four months. When Adam matter-of-factly told me he had a new girlfriend, I had a come-a-part. No more celebrity status, no more drugs, no more luxury. It all ended as promptly as it had begun.

Just three years before, I had taken a leadership role teaching children in our X-Factor congregation. And now? I was the freshly dumped girlfriend of a high-power club owner who was tied to the drug cartel.

I had such a fake high, phony status, bogus importance, and demeaning self-worth. The rest of my world now seemed void of color, joy, and life. At the time, my self-worth was based on how thin I was, how blonde I could get my hair, how big my boobs were, how tan I was, and how white I could get my teeth. I had been comparing myself to the high-end call girls Adam had walking through his club every night.

When Adam dumped me, my sick brain took a look at myself to assess what wasn't good enough. Then I promptly flew to a doctor in California and had him tighten my va-jay-jay back to its virginal state–and then some. This was the best I could do to make my oh-so-sick self, better.

Warrior Wisdom:

Cross my heart, hand to God, I was so naïve. I had broken free of the bubble and fell flat on my ass–with no tools or knowledge to help myself stand up again. My situation was a perfect example of the consequences from growing up with the mindset of having just "one way," religious or not religious–take your pick. I wouldn't learn about our level of vibration as human beings and how energy works for a few more years.

There's a sea of knowledge out there, my dear readers. I challenge you to always seek out something to learn–outside of your beliefs. This doesn't have to make you feel insecure about your faith; it simply makes you a more educated person.

During my free fall, every single thing I did, thinking I was improving my outer self, only confirmed to my psyche and soul that I had fallen so far–my looks were the only thing I had left to offer. Turning me into a mentally unstable shell of my former self. I'm so thankful I made it out of Vegas alive!

After that tidal wave, I made attempts to regain some semblance of my former self. I even sought solace from a spiritual healer–which (for me and with this particular person) made zero difference. At this point in my life, I hadn't yet fallen far enough to want to seek forgiveness from those I had hurt, or redemption for that matter. That's where the real *healing would have occurred.*

But that's the ironic nature of life–it will let us fall as far as we need to in order to humble us.

I did one of the most hurtful things you can do to a human being with Bruce. I caused so much pain. Would I take it back if I could? Abso-fucking-lutely! *I was so lost. There wasn't a single good thing that came from me cheating on my husband.*

I kept myself in the weakest state possible with drugs and alcohol–I was such a coward. In doing this, I caused so much heartache to Bruce and my children. Did I experience profound heartache in my marriage? Of course I did. But two wrongs do not make a right!

Having an affair is never *the solution. If you find yourself in a marriage that isn't working, have the courage and integrity to seek peace on the other side with a separation. The first time I broke my vows, it gutted me, despite how much I loathed my husband at the time. However, after that . . . it became inconsequential. I never sought redemption, and that piece of my humanity was torn from my soul.*

*If you are one of the fortunate few who has never experienced this, I'm telling you–*don't ever go down that rabbit hole. *It took me so many years to straighten my course. Having courage is hard, but as you will see in my upcoming chapters, dealing with the aftermath of being a coward is so much harder.*

CHAPTER 15

The Perfect Storm

T hree months after Adam and I broke up, I was existing—drinking to cope and popping Phentermine pills to keep from getting sloppy.

One weekend, I met a man who was about to change my life forever. I went to a Cinco De Mayo party with a friend whom I had known from high school, and we were going to the home of a friend of his. This home was a mansion at the top of a famous ski resort. That evening at the party, I met the homeowner. His name was Curtis Arnoult.

Curtis had changed the world as we knew it in the fields of botanical medicines and nutritional supplements; just his presence exuded an energy that permeated the room–it was palpable. His larger-than-life aura commanded attention.

My friend and I drank and drank that evening. At one point, he told me people were skinny dipping in the hot tub. He was like a girlfriend–I had immediately put him in the friend zone back in high school, and that's where he had stayed. So, I had no issues losing my clothes in front of him. We both got naked, grabbed some towels, and headed out.

However, as we approached the hot tub, I noticed a small problem: no one else was naked. The women in the hot tub looked at me like . . . *You slut!* I met their stares with a coy smile. *Bitches, if this shocks you, try surviving Vegas.* Curtis was also in the hot tub. The woman he was sitting next to acted exactly how I would have acted if I were in her position–she simply pretended I wasn't there.

Curtis got the scoop on me the next day from my friend. I wasn't divorced, still living in the same house with my husband, and slept on the living room floor in front of the fireplace. Curtis called me the following week. He asked if I wanted to meet him for dinner at one of his other homes–located in a beautiful canyon. This place literally blew my mind! Even Adam's place didn't hold a candle to this mansion!

The two of us enjoyed a fabulous dinner, all set up in the middle of a bridge–that went over a deep river through his backyard. It was like meeting the president.

Curtis was strong as an ox, very good-looking, powerful, immensely wealthy, and he had accomplished the impossible. There was also a wiseness about him . . . his piercing light blue eyes looked like they held a million stories. His voice matched his persona, it was a deep voice that demanded respect when he spoke.

There wasn't another man on the planet who could have stood outside Curtis's shadow. I slept with Curtis on our first date–I wanted to seal the deal. *I have the body, I have the boobs, I have blonde hair, and I have the new va-jay-jay. I'm going to win!*

The only problem was, given that Curtis had twenty-two years and a lifetime more experience in relationships than I did, we didn't exactly see eye to eye. I was completely intimidated by someone like Curtis.

When I first met Adam in Vegas, I became acutely aware of my limited vocabulary–I didn't like this about myself. So, I purchased a book called *Word Smart* by Adam Robinson and Julian Fleisher. It focused on building a more educated vocabulary.

When I began dating Curtis, he noticed I always carried this book. I loved to quiz him on difficult words. Curtis could spell any word correctly and tell me the definition of the word and the root of where it came from. There was nothing that didn't impress me about this man.

As much fun as Curtis and I had together, I had just come out of a relationship with a drug lord from Vegas–how could he possibly take me seriously? At the time, I believed my biggest asset was my looks. However, it didn't take Curtis long to learn there was more to me than met the eye. To my surprise and delight, we started seeing each other all the time. With renewed confidence, I finally said the word 'divorce' to Bruce.

Even with my blatant cheating, Bruce wanted nothing to do with a divorce. He just shut down, refusing to speak, and wouldn't budge. I had gone through so many stages. At first, I suggested moving into the basement to keep the family together. Then, I thought maybe we could trade off every week; Bruce would live in our house for a week, and then I would live there for a week. This way, our kids wouldn't have to be disrupted.

Bruce wasn't having any of it. I wasn't going to leave this marriage peacefully. Instead, it was ugly and traumatic. This war lasted almost two years. As time passed, there was nothing Bruce and I wouldn't do to hurt each other. My dear mother was brokenhearted, but she was my mother–I had her unconditional love and support no matter what.

Curtis and I began to have our own drama. He had told me he was far from being ready or even wanting to become exclusive. *Wait, what?* My little baby psyche couldn't even comprehend what Curtis was saying. *Why are you helping me get divorced if you don't want to be exclusive? If we are having sex, how dare you have sex with other women!*

I couldn't emotionally handle it. So I drank, and found an ecstasy supplier so I could appear to be okay. Curtis and I traveled all over the world, but inside, I was slowly losing my sanity.

During this crazy time in my life, I met my earth angel, a remarkable individual. Her name was Melissa Osanaka. She and her husband were dear friends of Curtis's. She knew so much about energy and how life worked. Curtis asked Melissa if she would meet with me because he knew how much

I was struggling. Melissa's compassion was profound, and her ability to resonate with my feelings was remarkable.

Melissa gave me a book. The name of the book was, *The Secret,* by Rhonda Byrne. I learned for the first time about energy and how we, as humans, are capable of changing our lives. While the basic concept of this book is a universal law, like the law of gravity, it didn't begin to cover enough information to give a newbie like myself the knowledge to put it to good use. It was like telling someone who has never seen water before that "water is wet," right before they jump into the deep end of a swimming pool.

This book gave me a new hope for my own life. It basically said that all we had to do was want and wish for something, and it could be ours. At this point, I would have tried anything! And that little baby spark set something in motion.

My children were so very unhappy–they were suffering more than any child should ever have to suffer. I remember thinking, *this is not my life.*

As luck would have it, the very next day, I was called in for a special meeting with Conner's third-grade teacher. Connor kept his sad eyes on the floor as the teacher proceeded to tell me, "If Connor could just learn to focus better, he could pick things up like all the other kids."

As I listened to this woman's self-righteous speech, everything slowed way, way down. When she finally quit talking, I thanked her, promptly got up, and left with Connor.

When we got in the car, I looked at my sweet son and said, "You know what, Conner? Fuck her! She doesn't have the slightest clue what she's talking about! You're an amazing kid! And you don't *ever* have to go to that school again!"

That was the first smile I had seen on my precious son's face in a long time. That day with Connor's teacher, I got a tiny little spark of my former badass self. And it caused me to wake up.

For the first time, I noticed what a low energy level I had been operating on. It was a level that said: "To hell with everyone else and look at me because I'm a victim and I can make an excuse for every single thing I've done." I felt like there was hope for the first time in such a long time. I couldn't wait to make things better.

I began to research schools. I found a school thirty minutes away that fit Connor perfectly called the Wessington School of Liberal Arts. I spoke privately with the principal and explained my situation with Conner. The compassionate woman listened to me, then pondered for a moment. Finally, she looked at me and said, "We would be happy to have him." I cried right there in her office. My pride was gone as the tears streamed down my face. *Connor will be seen and understood here.*

The students at Wessington called the teachers by their first names. Instead of traditional desks, they had beanbags and couches to sit on, with lap desks to write on. Each student decided what they wanted to learn about–every hour of every day. Then, it would be offered to them through various learning styles.

This school couldn't have been more perfect for my sweet boy. The following school year, Chance and Noel also decided to attend there as well.

With momentum building, I thought about what I would want my life to be like if I could have anything I asked for. *What would make my children happy again?* When I had a plan, I called Bruce. After almost two years of fighting in court, I asked him if we could meet for breakfast at the local diner the following morning–just the two of us.

It was a Saturday, and Bruce showed up genuinely perplexed. After all, he was used to both of us being at each other's throats. So, I laid it out.

"I don't want to fight anymore, Bruce. I'm so grateful for the four children we have; it breaks my heart to see them suffering so much." I paused, my voice full of emotion. "I'm truly sorry for hurting you. Let's figure this out."

I didn't need or expect an apology in return. This was me seeing a faint light at the very top and desperately trying to climb out of my shit hole. "We don't need to fight over custody; the kids shouldn't have to pay the price for what's happening between us."

Bruce looked at me with a hopeless sigh. "What do you suggest?" he asked quietly.

"We're the parents; we can make the rules. The courts don't know what's best for our kids; we do! Why can't we let them hang out with you when they want to be with you, and let them hang out with me when they want to be with me? Our children love us both, and they still need a loving family whether we are in the same house or not."

Bruce smiled. With tears in his eyes, he said, "I like that." And in that moment, we were on the same side again.

When I told Bruce he could decide what our home was worth, he raised a brow. "No, seriously, I will trust you to be fair and accept your decision–and be just fine with splitting it down the middle."

I told him I wouldn't touch his retirement, and he could leave my school alone. We both knew the actual value of each. But I wasn't going to spend one more red cent paying attorneys to get rich off of both of us.

"You can keep the boat, the motorcycles, and four-wheelers; they're all yours," I said. In addition, I told him he could keep all the furniture because I wanted him to have the house. I wanted this action to allow Bruce's ego, heart, and soul to heal. I knew I had hurt this man who I once loved. I wanted him to know that I cared about his happiness. I felt invincible as I looked at the humbled man sitting across from me. It brought about a sense of liberation and contentment that had long eluded me.

After that day, my children told me every time they saw me for months, "Mom, thanks so much for getting along with Dad . . . it's so much better!" And Bruce was very fair with the amount he paid me for my equity in the house.

I realized in the ensuing months just how lucky I was. Bruce could've refused to meet with me, he could've been an asshole, he could have wanted to keep on fighting. But when I swallowed my pride, apologized, and quit acting like a freaking idiot–so did he. I felt free and happy for the first time in years.

The following day, when I told Curtis what I had done, he asked me, "Where are you going to live?"

Without hesitation, I said, "with you." He was speechless.

Warrior Wisdom:

When I look back on my relationship with Curtis, I see things so differently. I had the emotional maturity of a thirteen-year-old. Curtis was just trying to live his life unapologetically. He was helping me get divorced because he was a generous man. No one had a gun to my head.

At this point in life, still having absolutely no coping skills with relationships, I chose to once again numb out to my situation. By the grace of God, my ecstasy supplier was arrested seven months after I found her–it unnerved me enough that I never found another one.

Melissa was literally my saving angel. After everything I had experienced and as far as I had fallen, all it took was one glimpse of light to spark hope in me again. The incident with Conner's teacher was a big turning point. First, if I had sided with Conner's teacher that day, it would have been a nail in the coffin to stamping my approval on giving my son the label that he didn't measure up to everyone else.

I put my faith squarely in my boy . . . and stood up for him–confirming to and reminding Conner that he was an amazing human being. He went on to thrive at Wessington Academy, learning that you do not have to wear the negative labels that authoritative figures try to place on you.

Secondly, that was the first time I had made the right decision in such a long time. It was so empowering to get that tiny little taste of my old, empowered, badass self. And it was a catalyst for greater change.

When I made peace with Bruce, I broke "all the rules" of divorce court protocol. It was the first time I didn't need to or care about being "right." Obviously, when I quit fighting, so did he. I had to lose all pride and finally be accountable for my part. I had zero interest in getting an apology from him–that was his business.

Expecting an apology from Bruce would have left me at the mercy of his actions and kept me in the space of being a complete victim. Knowing I was just fine, whether he apologized or not, was very empowering. It's not other people's actions that trip us up or set us free–whether we realize it or not, it's our own.

Having the itsy bitsy introduction to the Law of Energy allowed me to recognize that fighting over every petty little thing with Bruce emitted an energy of "lack of" or "not enough." I chose to look at my situation in a space of complete abundance. I knew one truth that was burning in my gut; it was important for Bruce and I to have peaceful feelings toward each other for the sake of our children.

If I can give one piece of advice regarding divorce that my readers will remember, it's this: When you criticize your spouse in front of your children, you might as well be criticizing them directly–because they are a part of your spouse. It would be like someone coming up to your face and openly criticizing your child to you. Oh–hell no!

Just remember . . . that's the kind of anger and hurt you are causing for your child when you do this. What's worse . . . your child has to keep it bottled in. Because, after all, they can't tell you to watch your mouth before they bitch slap you–can they?

There are no limits as to what can be accomplished when we put aside our egos and dare to dream–without the fear.

It's both plausible and practical for the greater good to seek a more positive outcome for ourselves and our families. When we shift our energy by focusing on what we want, rather than what we don't want, this is where miracles unfold!

CHAPTER 16

I've Jumped! Now What?

Now, although Curtis didn't say, "No way, get away from me, you fruitcake!" it didn't magically turn him into a man who wanted to be in a committed relationship. I had just told the *Master of The Universe* I was moving into his home. Curtis said absolutely nothing about the issue. The wheels in his brain were turning . . . playing out every possible scenario.

Within a week, I was settled in–along with Chance, Conner, and Noel. Jessie stayed at Bruce's house full-time because we saw each other daily at the school. She had just enrolled in my academy for her senior year. Obviously, now living together, we did become much closer. We began fun outings just like a normal family. Water parks, movies, out to dinner.

Curtis had orchestrated singles' trips to the lake, and rock climbing in his Hummer's. Now that we were living together, the trips consisted of all the adults–and my kids. No one ever complained; on the contrary, they all became quite attached to my kids. How could they not? I had amazing children!

I was so determined to make the relationship I had with Curtis work. I became obsessed with trying to make myself *enough* to be worthy of a committed relationship. *If I can just be a little better, he'll want me and only me. I can do this!*

In doing so, I became jealous of the entire female race. If I was in a grocery store and passed a beautiful woman, she would get a scathing look from me. I was no longer sociable. I wasn't even fun to be around anymore. I was an insecure, blonde bitch. Okay, maybe I'm exaggerating . . . I wasn't *really* blonde.

I can't, for the life of me, understand why Curtis won't put a ring on this bony little finger of mine! That was sarcasm, people–with a capital S!

Six months went by, and for the most part, Curtis and I got along great. He had an energy about him that was so strong–it was palpable. His goal was to solve, assist, and create. Everything he did was about making the world a better place. With Curtis–anything was possible. My creative thought process went into high gear, and Curtis supported every bit of it. He put me in touch with his patent attorney and would file for patents as fast as I could come up with ideas.

The creative part of my life was wonderful with Curtis. But then I would get that punched-in-the-gut feeling of Curtis being "off." He was the most meticulous man I had ever met. Doing everything the exact same way every day–his routine never swayed. So when Curtis's routine changed for a single day, and his powerful energy was different, it created a complete axis shift.

In turn, I responded by turning into *that* fruitcake, taking on the role of a PI to validate what I was feeling–and what Curtis didn't want to discuss.

One day, my ever-so-desperate mind came up with an ever-so-desperate plan. *Threesomes . . . Yes! A ménage à trois is not something many women will do, but I will–for him. I'll show him I've set aside all jealousy.*

It worked like a charm . . . I had him hooked! *Why didn't I think of this a long time ago?* Everything became so great! Curtis treated me better than he ever had before. For four months, life was wonderful. So when I felt that axis shift from Curtis again, it pierced straight through my fragile heart. Because *this time* I knew exactly who he was spending his time with . . . I had met most of them personally!

What the fuck am I going to do now? I really had a come-apart this time. We're talking full-on fruitcake. I began to drink every night. When we took a trip to Hawaii with Curtis's family and my kids, not knowing if I would have access to any liquor stores–I packed more vodka than I did clothes. Not only liquor bottles, I also filled hairspray bottles of every shape and size with vodka. This way, I could put them in my purse when we were out and about with no one noticing–the actual liquor, that is. I smelled like a distillery. Trying to mask the alcohol that reeked from my every pore, I was constantly spraying perfume from head to toe with mints in my mouth.

Curtis did finally break up with me five months later. *I was so close!* I "thought" I was making my dream come true–and now it was gone. *Fuck! That Rhonda Byrne is full of shit!* Curtis gave me fifteen thousand dollars and told me I had to move out. It was a nightmare I couldn't wake up from.

Hearing about our break-up, my mother tried to convince me to come home. Rita had even painted my room for me, trying to make everything okay. *How I loved her for that!* But I just couldn't.

I decided to move into my academy . . . it was the only thing I had left. I could take sponge baths at the shampoo bowls. Frankly, it was the only place that gave me any sense of security whatsoever. Walking into the school that Sunday, I had never felt more alone. Standing there, looking at all the hair stations, I was a stranger in my own life.

I flipped on the lights as I walked down the stairs to my office. Sitting in the chair that used to be Brinley's, I looked around the room. *I can't believe this is my life. What the fuck?*

I had finally quit shaking . . . when Curtis broke up with me, I quit drinking immediately. Detoxing from alcohol was a special kind of hell; I had no idea how dangerous it was. I spent fifteen hours–alone in a hotel room I had checked into, feeling like I would have a heart attack any minute. It came in big, giant waves–over and over. When the wave would temporarily subside, I would shake violently, feeling like my skin was crawling. I should have gone to the hospital, but I was too ashamed.

I numbly thought about the course of events that had taken place since we started the academy. We had all jumped . . . thinking we could run a school. *We didn't know a single thing about running a school.*

Less than two years into our academy adventure, it became too much stress for Melanie. She asked Brinley and I to buy her out, which we promptly did. Six months after that, we ran out of money. Brinley hadn't seen it coming, and we didn't know how to fix it.

I spoke to Brinley about getting someone in the office who knew more about business management. Offended, she dug her heels in. "No," she said, giving me a hurt look. "This is my job."

I felt like I was being held hostage with no control whatsoever. Curtis had already assisted us plenty; we needed to figure this out. I chose my regular path of *baptism by fire* and took a giant leap of faith–by putting $115k into our academy. It was all the money Bruce had given me for my interest in our house. Brinley and I couldn't fail, not with this courageous move.

Four months after I put the money in, I could see that all it did was buy us a little more time, and Brinley still adamantly refused to let anyone else in her office. Some mornings, when I woke up, I would forget about the nightmare I was living for a couple seconds. And then my reality would come rushing in, and I would have to sit with the fact that it wasn't a bad dream . . . this was real. Those "couple of seconds" were my only relief before the sick feeling returned to my stomach.

I finally got to the point that I couldn't take it one more day. Brinley had made it impossible for me to do anything–except put in money. It had been torturous. It wasn't her $115k that had been slowly draining with no solution in sight. After everything I had been through and given up, my brain finally said, *Fuck it!* And *Fuck you, Brinley!* It was my first hostile takeover.

I told Brinley I was the company's president, and she was fired! I had (by a freak of luck) taken the title of president when we set up our S Corp. I screamed at my best friend, "If you come back on this property, I'll have you arrested!"

I would have scared any human being on the planet at that point. I had given up my life! While putting every penny I had to my name into this fucking academy! I was not going to let it fail!

I just lost my best friend.

That had been just three weeks ago. Now, lying on the floor of my office . . . the horror of being so alone went to a new level. I had been so entangled in Curtis's life that any of "my people" were also "Curtis's people" long before they met me. So when Curtis and I broke up, I felt like I had no one.

The most heartbreaking part of leaving Curtis's house was that I no longer had a home for my kids. Until I found a permanent place to move, they would be at Bruce's house full-time. This is when I began to weep; I wailed until there was nothing left.

When I finally got up, it was after 10:00 p.m. I locked up the school, got in my car, and returned to a home that was no longer mine. Curtis had gone to one of his other homes to give me time to move out. Jessie would be coming up to help me move the following day. The thought of everything was unbearable. I felt like I was being squeezed to the point where I could barely stand it. Sitting on Curtis's bed, I broke–sobbing again.

Two days later, I was all moved in. It was a Tuesday, and the first night I was going to sleep at the school. I had been busy all day; the word had gotten around with my students, and I was trying to keep a stiff upper lip about my unconventional new dwelling.

I looked up from my desk . . . and there stood my precious twelve-year-old Connor–with his sleeping bag. Tears immediately filled my eyes as my sweet son came over and gave me a long hug.

"I love you so much, Conner!" I cried quietly. And for that moment, everything was okay in the world.

Connor did not allow me to spend one night there alone–I will cherish those days until the day I die. Every night, he and I rolled the TV from the classroom into my office–transforming it into a makeshift haven. We watched *That 70's Show* reruns in our sleeping bags, on the carpet of my office floor, eating pizza and reveling in the happiness of being together.

When Conner was asleep at night, I would pop some Phentermine pills and spend most of the night reading everything I could get my hands on. If my school went under, I would have absolutely nothing left. My predicament kept me from drinking anything whatsoever. I studied the policies and procedures for being an accredited school and the mind-boggling rules of Title IV funding–both of which Brinley had acquired for us before I kicked her out.

To give Brinley credit, she really did try. But she didn't know any more than I did (at the time) when it came to running a school. There wasn't a chance in hell we would have passed our first NACCAS review. I learned about all the policies (as ridiculous as they were) we *didn't* have in place, and an entire book of procedures we *weren't* doing. I even found a student who Brinley had overlooked entirely. She was set to graduate within a month, and we had yet to collect one red cent. The gravity of the situation weighed heavy on me. I was dying inside.

Our academy would have lost our government funding for student loans as fast as we had acquired it. And it wasn't fast. It had taken us three years to acquire something we should have had in two. So, here's another fun fact I would list in my book titled, *Everything Not to do in a Business*. "Never hire someone you can't fire." Brinley went out in explosive fashion, because I hadn't succeeded in dealing with the problem in the first place.

My oldest daughter, Jessie, came to me one afternoon, a student herself– she saw my apparent stress. Cautiously, she said, "Mom, I'm worried about you. All this stress isn't good for you. You've got to have a release."

Jessie gave me the number of one of her friends who sold magic mushrooms. His name was Tagger. I met up with Tagger that afternoon and purchased a zip-lock sandwich bag full of shrooms.

That evening, after Conner fell asleep, I ate a couple of mushrooms. As my psychedelic snack kicked in, I watched in amazement as the vines on my waterfall upstairs twisted and grew. I walked into the big classroom and stood on the stage in front of the full-length mirror. I stared at myself . . . and watched in awe as I changed from a woman with dark circles under her eyes, into a beautiful, peaceful human being.

I sobbed, hugging myself and saying, "I love you," over and over. It felt so good to release part of that woman I had so much shame for and give myself the love I so desperately needed at the time.

The next day, I felt lighter, like a huge weight had been taken off my shoulders.

After Conner went to sleep that evening, I was ready for the same beautiful, cleansing experience again. But rather than taking the same amount I had taken the night before, I ate at least four times more.

Let's just say the experience the second night was somewhat different. As Jessie arrived at the school the following morning–seeing all the hydraulic chairs pushed up against the front entrance, she came down to see what was up.

"Don't ask," I told her. I had thrown the rest of the bag into the dumpster, vowing never to take mushrooms again. One of the unfortunate things about, well . . . "me" was my tendency to overdo things. *If one is good, then ten are better.*

I clung to the positive experience I'd had with my first trip: deep underneath the layers of terror that I felt with being completely on my own, was a peaceful creature who didn't have to be afraid. I wanted to dig her out and let her shine like she deserved.

Warrior Wisdom:

Have you ever felt like you met someone before you came to this earth and made an agreement with that person for them to be your greatest teacher? This is precisely who Curtis has been for me . . . and at this point, we're just getting started.

Reflecting back on that crazy time in my life, knowing what I know now, here's how I would have handled my situation with Curtis:

"It's okay if you choose to be polyamorous," I would have told him, "that can be awesome! And fun! I'm sorry I made you out to be the villain for just being you. I appreciate everything you've done for me, but this relationship no longer works for me . . . I wish you the very best. Thank you–I'm a better, wiser person for knowing you." No blame, guilt, shame, or ultimatums. Nothing but peace.

Whose idea was the threesome thing? Mine. Who tried to manipulate and control? That would be me. Who turned into a fruitcake every time she didn't get her way? Me again. Who tried to shame and vilify? Me! The minute we take on the role of "victim" in a situation, we have lost. When I thought, "he is doing this to me," I should have been thinking, "I am doing this to me." I had the power to walk away the entire time. But instead, I chose to give all my power away and take on the role of a pathetic victim.

True love has to come from within. As long as we are looking outward– wanting someone else to make us feel loved and valued, we can lose it within the span of one phone call. Having self-love is the single greatest thing we can acquire for ourselves. It allows us to experience self-worth, whether we are in a relationship or not. It also allows us to leave a relationship that isn't good for us–even if we are in love.

Surgeries and adventurous sex didn't do one thing to give me a happily ever after; neither of those things make a relationship. They are a fleeting fix. After the rush was gone, I was left feeling even more empty than before.

Just so I'm clear, I'm not against plastic surgery. I would invite anyone considering any procedure to ask yourself, "Who am I doing this for?" Do whatever you do for you, and you only. Surgeries for the right reason can be a bonus, but should never be viewed as the bullseye.

Losing my best friend of twenty-five years because we went into business together was a heartbreaking tragedy. I still miss Brinley to this day. I sent her a message about a year before I wrote this book. I told her I was sorry for the pain I had caused her and that I wished I had found a better way. I wished her well and told her I hoped she was living her best life.

Brinley responded very kindly. Although that chapter is closed for both of us, it still needed to be said. We should never leave things unfinished; it's the only way I know how to live in peace and contentment. That brief connection meant the world to me.

Here's the silver lining to me being homeless. If I hadn't moved into my academy and spent every night studying at my desk, I would never have learned what I needed to know about my school. When you focus on creating something, it doesn't just magically appear. However, the energy I emitted in wanting my school to stay afloat brought forth the opportunity *for me to make it so. Painful as it was–that's where I found out what I was made of.*

CHAPTER 17

Clash of the Titans

I finally chose a brand-new condo thirty minutes from my academy to be my new home. It was located at the base of a canyon, and riding my mountain bike six miles up to the waterfalls became my daily addiction. These moments of solitude were my sanctuary. Taking that time for myself was as important as learning how to operate my school. With an office manager now in place, I was out the door of my academy every day by 4:30 p.m. And by 5:00 p.m., I was on my bike.

As I began my ride, I knew exactly where I would smell the honeysuckle cornering the bank of the narrow river. When I reached the falls, the smell was so intoxicating as mist permeated through the air via the thundering water crash–hitting massive granite boulders at the bottom. This was my happy place. It was a time for reflection, which, more often than not, brought about a few tears.

I headed back just as the sun was starting to go down. It always got a little chilly as I made my way down the canyon. But as soon as I came to the section of trail that went through the red rock cliffs, which had been soaking up the sun all day, I felt a rush of heat coming from the rocks as I flew by on my bike. That daily ride was a balm for my soul!

Being settled in my new home, and having the privilege of seeing Curtis on national TV when he attended televised sports with other women instead of me–I had pretty much given up on the two of us ever getting back together.

How am I ever going to move on? Who the hell is going to hold a candle to Curtis? One afternoon, I finally mustered the courage to call a man I had met at his company event the year before. His name was Dillon. I remembered how kind his blue eyes appeared when we spoke. He had jokingly asked Curtis if I had a twin when we were introduced.

Dillon was a handsome, successful businessman. I called his company and asked to speak to him; the receptionist transferred me to his office phone, and I left a short, shaky message.

To my delight, Dillon called me back the next day, and we spoke for over an hour. It felt so good to communicate with another man and have no drama involved. Dillon and I spoke several times within the following weeks. I finally drove to Dillon's house one night to see him; he was so kind! I loved his confidence with women; he could look me straight in the eyes and tell me how beautiful I was. I felt myself blush more than once.

I had been in such a constant state of offense/defense with Curtis; it was never-ending. Although Curtis had a lion's heart and was the most generous man I had ever met, one might say he had difficulty expressing his feelings. Even when we were together, Curtis's emotional distance had made me feel very alone.

Growing up, I had never heard the words, "I love you," from my mother. I just knew she loved me. When it came to saying, "I love you," Curtis not only didn't do it, he wasn't having it. I was so desperate to hear those words! I would mentally beat Curtis over the head, "Tell me you love me! Tell me you love me!" Curtis mentally fought back like a stubborn teenager. "No, I won't! I won't! You can't make me!" Instead, Curtis's love language had been providing me with a very lavish lifestyle.

Being in Dillon's arms and talking comfortably was a welcome change, a rest for my psyche and soul. It didn't take us long to become completely enamored with each other.

What I didn't expect was Curtis stopping by my office a couple weeks later. *What do you want?* I wondered. Something was off. I didn't know it at the time, but Curtis had heard about my call to Dillon (men do gossip).

As Curtis made small talk, I noticed his defense was completely down; he was almost humble. *Ahh, I get it . . . I've become interesting to you again.* I hadn't been interesting when I was the pathetic woman living in my school like a hermit. But now that I was consorting with another powerful business-man, I was appealing again.

Curtis was the type of man who lived for the conquest, the hunt, the next kill. It wasn't all bad; this was also the type of man you wanted to know if the end of the world happened. He would most definitely have a plan for himself and everyone he knew. The aftermath of destruction was still heavy on my heart when I looked at Curtis. *So you "are" capable of being tender. What the hell do you want from me?*

I'd experienced a tie with Curtis that went all the way through to my very identity, and now that spell was broken. My different energy was palpable and very disturbing to my former lover. I didn't know how to react to this new version that stood before me.

It had been easy to fall for Dillon; he had mojo baby! But as hard as I fought to have a relationship with him, we never stood a chance. Curtis wanted me and my kids back.

So let me clarify; if Dillon had taken a badass approach, he would have told Curtis to "Go fuck yourself" when he started telling Dillon's business partners that "Dillon was fucking his girlfriend." Even though Curtis had been openly dating for months.

But Dillon said nothing. So, when Curtis began to invest in businesses that Dillon was also invested in, he exited and broke my heart.

Thus began a ten-year cyclical relationship with Curtis.

We were a power couple, to say the least. Curtis and I lived large, and we broke up even larger! Round and round we went. With our drama came drinking again, but I was too busy to let it consume me. It became an animal I was trying to manage without being destroyed.

I grew my academy steadily over the next eight years, eventually reaching ninety-eight students. And one by one, I took over three other office spaces attached to mine. Free gym memberships were included in our tuition. The hour at the gym counted as part of their eight-hour day. I had always valued the importance of students feeling good about themselves.

I added a nail course, a permanent cosmetic course, a professional make-up artistry course, and a full-size photography studio. I also expanded with night school and a floating class time–being open thirteen hours a day. I tried to see every obstacle through the eyes of my students. Like my early mentors had taught me, I asked myself . . . *How can I plan not to fail?*

As my academy evolved, I began to attract a lot of single mothers–who weren't looking for the college scene. I researched why daycare assistance via the Department of Education (DOE) wasn't offered in cosmetology, even though it was offered in other fields. I was told cosmetology wasn't in demand and would never be eligible for daycare assistance. The feeling I was left with was one of being dismissed. *Well, shit . . . I guess I'll just handle this myself.*

I dove into my favorite brainstorming scenario with the least amount of headache or opposition. This meeting included me, myself, and I. When I was finished, after making a quick change to my school contract, free daycare was added on our campus for all my mothers.

I personally knew how good it felt to have my children close.

It was an *in-your-face* to DOE. The rebellious, *I can't stand you guys* relationship I had developed with agencies like DOE and NACCAS was something I needed to remedy. As soon as I could afford it, I hired a firm to handle reports–so we could stay in compliance with the mind fuck of both agencies.

My youngest daughter Noel–who was ten, organized and ran the daycare. Some people might think that was crazy, but anyone who knew Noel knew she could handle anything. Her natural aptitude for leadership was evident early on. When she was seven, I found a contract she had written. It said, "If you are my worker no crying is allowed." Noel had put a line for herself to sign, "Boss," and a line for the "Worker" to sign as well. Noel created a highly organized, ship-shape daycare–eager to report how things were going at the end of every day.

I had fifteen full-time employees, and finally felt I had accomplished something to be proud of again. My oldest daughter, Jessie, was an amazing instructor. Chance and Conner worked for me at the front desk and in the dispensary after school. All of my kids were crushing it—life felt right again. And if I thought my salon seemed like a party every day, ninety-eight students were like, "Spring Break!" every day.

We were all a little irreverent, but when it came to my students with their clients, they had the lingo and the ultimate respect of any seasoned stylist. I was so freaking proud! The cherry on top was hiring my earth angel, Melissa, to work with every new class for one week before they began learning cosmetology. Melissa was a healer; she assisted my students in dropping the beliefs that did not serve them.

Before I began this program, it would take months for students in a new class to bond with other classmates. After a week with Melissa, they were all best friends.

The first process Melissa facilitated was having our new class of ten to twelve students stand and form a circle facing in. Then, I entered the classroom and joined them as the school owner. Melissa explained the rules: "If I say a statement that is true for any of you, please step forward, and then step back into your place."

Melissa would then begin the silent process. "Are you a middle child? Were you raised by a single parent?" Gradually, the questions became more personal. "Have you ever been cheated on? Have you ever cheated? Were you abused as a child in any way? Have you ever struggled with addiction? Have you ever been bullied?" Surprising my students, I stepped forward and back as Melissa read each question. We had purposefully chosen the questions so every single one would be true for me. Slowly, I could feel the energy of the room change.

By the end of the process, my students felt connected to me and to each other, and I felt connected to them. They discovered we were all the same. I didn't lose my students' respect by doing this–I gained their trust. And they dropped the belief that any of their painful experiences had made them a freak. There would be no judgment here. They were under my watch now.

I wanted my students to feel confident, intelligent, and professional. Every day, I wrote a new vocabulary word on the whiteboard; I explained the definition and used the word in a sentence. For the rest of the day, my students tried to use the word as often as possible when speaking with their clients.

We never had a boring day. My academy could have been a hit reality show . . . you couldn't make this stuff up! For example, I had one student in particular who initiated *holy shit* moments on a daily basis. Her name was Shadow. I will always remember Shadow, and the colorful way she saw the world.

When my students first went out on the floor with their stations, they would tape pictures of their families on the mirrors to personalize their space. I walked past Shadow's station one day and did a double-take. *What the hell?* She had taped a picture of her sister on her mirror, wearing a negligée, with her nipple showing. I was immediately grateful that Shadow didn't have a client at the time.

As Shadow sat across from me in my office, explaining how tastefully the picture of her sister had been done, she couldn't understand why she had been asked to take the picture down. *Seriously? I feel like I'm in the Twilight Zone!*

"It's a stunning portrait, Shadow," I agreed. "However, with our clients, we need to be able to connect with a broad range of personalities. That picture of your beautiful sister might offend some of those clients."

Disappointed, Shadow took my counsel and didn't argue.

A few weeks later, I walked past Shadow–giving a manicure to her client. The scene left me so dumbfounded I just stood there for a couple seconds with my mouth dropped–wide open.

Shadow's distressed client was stretched away from the manicure table as far as she could go, with her head looking off to the other side (which meant she was staring at the wall). I noticed that Shadow had a massive wad of chewing tobacco in her cheek. Finally, I saw the best part; Shadow was spitting into an old coffee can on the floor . . . while she was doing her client's nails.

The floor instructor, noticing the scene seconds after I did, quickly picked up the can and apologized to Shadow's client. "I'm so sorry to interrupt your manicure. I need Shadow for a second; she'll be right back."

"That's just fine," the client said with relief, seeing the chew can in the instructor's hand.

As Shadow once again sat across from me in my office at the end of the day, she immediately began her explanation.

"You told us in theory class it was unprofessional to smell like cigarette smoke," Shadow said, making her case.

"That I did," I answered.

"So now I don't smell like cigarette smoke anymore!" Shadow stated triumphantly.

This girl is killing me!

The shock factor was becoming less and less, I began to take our little incidents as the norm. Just another day at the office, like the time two students took their permanent make-up machines home, got drunk, and tattooed each other's eyebrows on. They were, hands down, the scariest eyebrows I'd ever seen. Two beautiful girls, standing there, looking like Groucho Marx. Although it took everything I had not to laugh as I refused to scar them for life, one thing was certain–we were all set with models for our permanent cosmetics class regarding tattoo removal!

By the time my students were a few weeks in, they knew I didn't put up with bullies and that I was not someone to mess with. I protected them like my own, but the wrath of Ramona was real if I heard of anyone being disrespectful to another.

We had an interesting event happen at the school one morning. I had a suggestion box for my students on how we might improve our school. I read the suggestions out loud to the class once a week, and we would discuss solutions. They were usually things like, "Can we have a day to play country music in the salon?" Or something equally as important.

On one particular beautiful fall day, I picked up a note and read, "Ramona should quit spending so much money on plastic surgery and spend more money on this school." I was totally taken off guard . . . all of a sudden, it felt like I was back in the sixth grade reading the mean note about my mother.

My brain was scrambling. *Buck-up Ramona! Get a hold of yourself!* But there was no use, as much as I tried to keep it together–the tears came. Instantly, students flooded the stage. They were hugging me, saying things like, "We love you, Ramona! Don't listen to that little bitch!" One girl said, "If I find out who wrote that note, I'm going to kick her ass!" My sweet, beloved students, whom I protected, had turned into fierce momma bears, protecting me.

After the traumatic morning, I sat in my office and thought about the student who had written the note. Fortunately for me, her handwriting was a dead giveaway.

Her name was Susanne. Outwardly, Susanne looked like an innocent little X-Factor girl. But clearly, she carried strong feelings toward women's sexuality and plastic surgery. That afternoon I called Susanne into my office. When she entered, the look on her face was both terrified and defiant. I was sure

Susanne intended to deny her note to the bitter end. I bypassed the small talk and cut right to the chase.

"Susanne," I said, looking her straight in the eyes with a calm, assertive smile. "I want you to know that I am your friend. I think you're going to make an amazing cosmetologist someday, and I'm really happy you're here at my school. If there's anything I can do for you, please let me know. I care about every single one of my students, and it's important to me that you have a good experience here."

Susanne thanked me and quickly left my office. Sitting there, I was left with an ache in my chest, wondering what else I could do to find a commonality with this student. The next time I taught a class, I was elated when Susanne approached me afterward and said, "That was a really good lesson, Ramona."

"Thank you, Susanne, that's really kind of you to say," I answered. *Yay!* I thought, *I could just hug you right now!*

I wanted the very best for my students. They had no idea how much I cared about their success and happiness in life.

Warrior Wisdom:

I recognize the significance of needing to do things on my own to create what I had envisioned. After the terrible shock of firing Brinley, it was all on me. The energy of being on my own was completely different—there was no one left to judge how or why I did what I did. This put my head in a different space, and my creative thought process slowly began to gain momentum again.

Working with teenagers evolved into a completely new way of communicating. It was so different from seeing clients at their best because they were excited to be at my salon to get their hair done. I saw my students daily, with rules and consequences when the rules weren't followed. The early visions I once had of being up on the stage doing hair, with all the glory of being admired, had evolved into getting inside the psyche of my students. Getting into their invisible–to find out what made them tick.

I came to realize that every human being on this planet needs to feel like they belong. As I experienced in my youth–and frankly, when the three of us opened the academy–indifference from others towards me felt every bit as painful as judgment. So my mantra became the complete opposite: "Seek to understand."

I think we've all had times when we've been embarrassed or ashamed by how we've had a knee-jerk reaction to certain situations. And though we're all human, we can remember to take a moment and choose to breathe and make a shift. We can choose to seek to understand those around us better.

When we can be aware of those around us, and their unspoken challenges, we walk away from judgment and step into an energy of acceptance. This is a beautiful space to be in.

CHAPTER 18

Fucking Regulators

If you're unsure from the chapter title regarding how I feel about regulating agencies, I will be happy to explain. Regulating agencies can literally do whatever they want, whether it's right or wrong. Shortly after taking over my academy and buying out Brinley (which took me six months to settle in court), I received a notification from DOE.

The letter stated I would need to put $85k into an account and leave it there for at least a year; this action would show the strength of my academy. *What the hell?* I was still doing a skip and a jump every time we could make payroll! There wasn't a single person I spoke to in the cosmetology industry who had ever heard of such a thing.

What am I going to do?

Curtis and I were on one of our quarterly break-ups, but I still asked to meet him for breakfast. As I walked into the restaurant and saw Curtis sitting there, I was immediately comforted. One thing Curtis knew was business, and he wouldn't stand for *anyone* getting picked on . . . ever. When I told him about the letter, he looked at me and simply said, "Okay." He picked up his phone, called his assistant, and told her to prepare a wire for $85k. It wasn't followed with any conditions or manipulative tactics.

Curtis always cheered for the underdog; whether we were together or not, he was still in my court. It was a maturity I had a hard time coping with at times. I was in love with him, so my emotions were always in play. I was always seeking what I couldn't have with this man who was so good to me.

It was over a year–a full eighteen months, in fact–before I received a letter from DOE stating the money could be released. I was doing everything humanly possible to ensure my students had a successful career. DOE was trying to weed me out because they didn't like that I could legally offer them free daycare and gym memberships.

I had owned my academy for nine and a half years and finally made it over the hump. It had been such a hard climb! With running a school, there were always new issues that came up–almost on a daily basis. It was a process of learning how *not* to do things. I never, ever nailed something perfect on the first try. I was finally moving into a space where things weren't quite so hard all the time.

I was sitting in my office one afternoon; I had just returned from a dive trip in Micronesia with Curtis. We had been in Chuuk, exploring the sunken ships from WWII.

I sipped on my coffee as I caught up on the weekly reports. Looking up from my desk, Bonnie–my financial aid officer, had walked into my office. The color was literally drained from her face as she handed me a letter. I noticed it was from DOE. *Oh great! What now?*

I began to read; DOE was going to audit my academy. But this wasn't just any audit–they were withholding funds. I would have to support my school for five months with no money coming in from Title IV student loans. This meant I had to cover living expenses for all ninety-eight of my students. I also had to cover payroll for fifteen employees, and the cost of operations–for five months.

BOOM!

It was two weeks before Thanksgiving. I thought about all the students and instructors who depended on me for their way of life. I thought about our little sweethearts in the daycare . . . including three-year-old Ivan, who sometimes struggled and needed extra loves. He often sat on my lap with his blanket while I worked in the office, happily watching SpongeBob on my computer screen until his momma was finished with her client or classwork.

DOE stated that as soon as the audit was finished, I would receive the money owed to me during the five-month audit. I was so tired of the drama. These weren't just bumps in the road; they were nuclear explosions! *This is what happens when you get a group of people who don't know jack-shit about the dynamic of single mothers. And quite frankly, don't care!* They had no idea the lengths I had gone to ensure my students' success.

That afternoon, I went to my bank and applied for a short-term floating loan. Naturally, the bank asked for documentation of DOE's notification informing me of their intent to audit my academy. I sent the bank the top portion of the letter because that was the portion regarding the audit. In doing so, I added a sentence to close the letter. I also sent a copy of the loan application to DOE as well, telling them I would be proceeding as usual. *Those fuckers aren't going to destroy what I have here!*

A week later, the bank informed me they had denied my loan. I wanted to scream! I had been a loyal customer of this bank for almost ten years. So once again, Curtis stepped in and ultimately carried my academy for five and a half months to see me through the audit.

And once again, I found myself literally living at my school for three months, copying every student file to send in for the audit. I insisted on doing one hundred percent of it myself; I had to know that absolutely nothing would be overlooked or missed. At least this time, I had an upstairs office with a couch, a big window to see outside, and a shower in my bathroom.

As I dissected every student file, my heart ached for the time in my life when everything had made sense. I was caught up in a life that had opposition around every corner. Finally complete, I sent in the required documents just under the deadline; the massive box weighed over fifty pounds.

Two and a half months later, I received the letter for which I had been holding my breath. DOE reported having found no discrepancies and had "no suggestions" for my operations. **In almost ten years, that was the first audit I had ever received without a single limitation.**

But as I read on, my heart completely sank. DOE also reported that I would not be eligible for Title IV funding the following year. *No more student loans means no more academy.* The reason they gave put me in complete shock.

DOE stated I had changed an official government document. I had sent only a portion of their letter to the bank when I applied for a loan and added a sentence to close the letter. This is true; that's precisely what I did. But this action did not benefit me in any way. I was simply sending my bank the portion of the letter from DOE regarding their intent to audit and what that would entail. The rest of the letter contained information regarding the status I would hold with NACCAS during the audit. This portion was not pertinent to my bank's request.

If I had consulted with my firm *before* sending the letter to the bank and DOE, they would have told me, "You can't do that, Ramona," but I didn't. I had been in panic mode, trying to deal with DOE's latest attack. I didn't realize there was anything to even question. If I thought I had done anything wrong, why would I ever have sent a copy of the letter to DOE? They didn't even ask for it!

But, when they couldn't find anything to shut me down for in my audit, that action gave them the ammunition they needed. DOE knew about the letter the second I sent it to them; they had been sitting on it for months. But they didn't use it–not until that was all they had left to work with. The sole purpose of this entire charade had been to shut me down. Discontinuing my Title IV funding was the death knell for my business, comprised of impoverished students.

With all of the outside agencies I had put into place to handle NACCAS and DOE, I thought I had made myself untouchable. But I wasn't.

Curtis found me a D.C. attorney who had spent a portion of his career working in the DOE sector. After hearing my case, he was confident I would win on appeal; we both worked tirelessly for almost four months, appealing DOE's ridiculous decision.

When the letter came, I got in my car and drove home. At the time, I lived in a beautiful home in the river bottoms–just down the canyon from Curtis's house. I walked into my bedroom and shut the door. Shaking, I opened the letter. As I read that DOE would not overturn their decision, I fell to my knees–and wept.

How is everyone going to survive? My students . . . what's going to happen with their little ones? The gut-wrenching pain of no longer being able to have my children close when I opened the school came flooding back. *I've failed them all. I gave them something wonderful, only to have it ripped away.*

As I told Curtis, the totality of what was happening hit me. "I don't think I can handle this. I can't believe this happened," I quietly sobbed.

"Security is an illusion, Ramona," Curtis said, with a strong yet comforting demeanor. "Don't let your setbacks define who you are . . . I've failed more times than I've succeeded."

I was so grateful to Curtis in that moment. He was my only tie to anything that was even remotely stable. His comforting words literally held my sanity together–he became my rock.

Armed with Curtis's support and wisdom, I forged ahead. NACCAS regulations made it impossible to sell my academy because I was now in a school category that had lost its Title IV funding.

My employees lost their jobs–ten of whom were single mothers. It took almost a year for DOE to send me the money I had earned during the audit. For my students who transferred to another school, DOE sent their entire quarterly payment to the new school instead of calculating which portion went to me and which portion went to the new school–something they'd promised would not happen. Curtis had put in well over $200k, but we only received $176k back.

Don't misunderstand; Curtis could have gone to war with DOE and eventually won to get the rest of his money back. But in Curtis's world, that would have been like paying attention to a little brat when they throw a temper tantrum. He had better and more productive things to do with his time and energy.

I had climbed over so many hurdles connecting to my students–we didn't leave *anyone* behind. Anything had been possible at my academy. Cosmetology was actually secondary to the life skills my students had learned. And most importantly, they had learned to love and respect themselves.

When it came time to break the news to my students, I tried to put on a brave face. I tried to be the comfort that Curtis had been for me. A considerable portion of my students were young, single mothers. Remember when I said, "Students want to have a college experience when they go to college. They want to live on a college campus"?

That's true . . . unless you're a single mother. If you're a single mother, you don't move into an apartment with other college students. And because my students couldn't get government assistance for daycare, I had carved out a niche in the world that was tailor-made for them.

Mine was the only academy I had ever heard of (anywhere) that offered free daycare. The good friend of mine, who had once worked for me and now owned her own academy, decided to provide this service and made it possible for many of my students to finish. I will always love her for the care she gave my students.

It took months to do student transfers, and liquidate everything in my academy. Trying to explain exactly what had happened to my mother was torture. She looked so devastated; I felt awful putting that burden of worry on her. As I walked through my empty academy for the last time, I thought about everything that had transpired, and said goodbye to something that would have a part of my heart and soul forever.

Warrior Wisdom:

It was a long time before I made peace with what had happened. Life is hard, but we never know what's intended for us if we quit moving forward. I needed to experience the things I have experienced to acquire the knowledge I have gained along the way. It's as simple as that.

The decade I spent with the school allowed me to learn so much about life. Much of it was agonizing and painful. But it was an invitation to prevail by not giving up. I truly believe that everything is in Divine Order. I never, ever would have walked away from my academy. But my life was destined for other things. I had to accept that fact . . . this particular chapter of my life was finished.

The loss of a business can gut someone to the core. I invite anyone who has experienced failure to recognize that knowing failure is a part of success. I had failures with everything I tried at my school. But learning what didn't work taught me how to finally figure out what did work. And even though my academy was eventually closed, the triumphs I experienced with my students were extraordinary. And those *victories will live on for generations to come!*

DOE sought to shut down my academy because I did things my own way after recognizing what actually made a difference. Just because it's a government-run operation does not mean that it's honest or fair. Harsh, but true.

Losing my academy, while immensely heartbreaking, also set me free. I realized something crucial; I do not like to be told what to do–by anyone. I'm not saying this is good or bad, right or wrong. Accepting this about myself allowed me to move my path in a direction that brought about the freedom to follow my bliss.

Some serious shit hit the fan during this decade of my life. I certainly didn't come out of it triumphant, but the lessons I learned were priceless! Be open to what failure can teach you, my dear reader. There are valuable things to learn about falling down that make us stronger as we stand back up.

CHAPTER 19

A Time for Growth

For the second time in my life, my identity was completely stripped from me. Suddenly, anything associated with cosmetology made me want to say the word "fuck" a lot, and also vomit. I had a blank canvas; what I did with that was now entirely up to me.

Curtis had five homes, so I dove into remodeling like my life depended on it. Anything to stay busy. By this time, YouTube was in full swing. Anything I wanted to learn was now at my fingertips via this fantastic search tool. I discovered what a creative outlet carpentry could be—it became the thing I poured all my energy into.

Power tools became my new obsession . . . as I lay new tile around tubs, travertine on floors, and hardwood in the north wing of Curtis's primary residence. This particular property was an old-world, castle-style home—turrets and all!

My favorite residence to visit was Curtis's adobe-style home. It was located within a fly-in community, four hours away from his main residence. The red rock desert, and the smell of artemisia sage after a heavy rainfall created a peaceful haven. I had spent more time in this home than my own residence in the three years since my academy had closed.

I spent most of my time there without Curtis, just working on the house. My kids would often come down to join me for the weekend.

As I got further into remodeling this home, I decided a major change was needed. Standing at the house's main entrance, I felt like I was in the old television series *Bonanza*. The big, rough ponderosa pines with bark did not match the home's decor or the area like they could.

I had become more lax with drinking again. Red wine became my go-to every day. Looking at the logs throughout the home, I wanted to get the bark off to see the wood's beautiful grain underneath.

One night, with Merlot coursing through my bloodstream, I tore into a log right in the middle of the entryway–with an electric meat cutter. It was the only decent tool I could find on the property, and I was too impatient to wait until morning when the hardware store opened.

Curtis and his son Cameron wouldn't be flying in until the next day for a visit, so I could be as noisy as I wanted. It got very noisy . . . and eventually smokey! The kitchen appliance did surprisingly well before it burned up and quit working entirely. But it had served its purpose until I could purchase something meant for the job.

The next day, I was happily sanding away on the log I had attacked the night before. The electric sander I purchased that morning revealed the wood's gorgeous grain. Cameron approached me with a concerned look on his face. "Ramona, I don't know if changing the logs is going to be a good idea; there's seventeen of them–that's going to take you forever." Cameron knew I was as impulsive as they come.

"It'll be great!" I said enthusiastically. "Trust me!" Thus began the three-month-long hell of working on the logs. I convinced Jessie, now twenty-four, and her boyfriend Max to join me on the project. Conner, seventeen, joined us eventually as well. Chance was twenty, and this particular summer, he was off fire fighting to pay for his flight school. My youngest, Noel, was fourteen and enjoying her summer break with her father.

Max began, using an electric grinder with a six-inch steel wheel. He was a gifted artist–grinding out beautiful curvatures and accentuating the knots in the logs by carving out the wood around them and exposing the beautiful grain. The rest of us would follow behind with electric sanders, smoothing and accentuating the pattern he had made.

In spot-on Ramona fashion, I playfully wrote, "Sanding is fun!" in the endless inches of sawdust. Seeing this, my co-workers wrote, "Fuck this!" right under it.

At the end of the day, we all scattered and chose our own kitchen and section of the compound to have some alone, quiet time–away from everyone else. My hands would be completely numb from the vibration of the sander I had been using all day. In fact, the muscles in my hands were so over-vibrated I couldn't even make a fist–leaving my hands completely useless.

Therefore, I began every evening by using my wrists to pick up the opened wine bottle in the cupboard (ready and waiting) and guzzling at least half the bottle in one go. I had become what you would call a high-functioning alcoholic. Drinking was something I now did every single day.

Shuffling over to the fridge, I opened it with my toe and grabbed a potato with my wrists. I sat the potato in the sink and stabbed it with a big butcher knife I held with my wrists. This way, it wouldn't explode in the microwave.

I finished off the rest of the wine while my dinner was cooking. When the timer dinged, I rolled the potato onto my plate, along with the salt and pepper, and shuffled into the master bath to fill up the tub.

While the tub was filling, I shed my clothes and climbed in. As the water poured in, I used my inventive wrist action to shake salt and pepper onto the plate sitting next to the tub. Then I picked up the potato with my wrists and stuck it under the running water to get it wet. Putting it back on the plate, I rolled it around so the salt and pepper would stick to it. Finally, I ate the potato, skin and all, bite by bite, until it was gone. If my kids were ever looking for the salt and pepper in my kitchen area, they knew they would find it next to the tub.

After three long months, we finished the project. It was beautiful . . . but I had pushed myself to the extreme–sacrificing my body and joints day after day. I was hoping it would be triumphant. But it wasn't. Curtis was at his other home, living his life and taking care of himself–just like I should have been doing!

As Curtis and I progressed past our tenth year, we began to date other people; even though I still worked for him–remodeling his homes, airplane hangars, and warehouses. Wait, let me rephrase that . . . I began to date other people, and Curtis *continued* to date other people. The only problem with dating was how much I hated it. It was like trying to find someone as impressive as the president.

Dating gave me anxiety. But the pain regarding my relationship with Curtis was a thing of the past. I had gained a peaceful understanding. Melissa, my earth angel and healer, had given me an audiobook called *Loving What Is* by Byron Katie.

Whenever I listened to Katie process people in her audiobook, it took away my pain. I wanted this belief system more than anything. It was totally foreign to me at that point. I completely related to one of the women in Katie's book; I had shown up like a complete victim regarding Curtis, a hostage in my own life.

Yes, I also had a stubbornness like no other, and I was fearless. The combination of all that made *me*. Undoing my core belief, "I'm a victim," wasn't as easy as you would think. But listening to that audiobook was my joy–it became my bible.

I listened to random sections of this book every day for over two years. Doing so brought about healing from the tumultuous road I had been on for so long. Having lived with so much drama in my world, discovering peace now made the slightest hint of drama so offensive. Byron Katie shared a way to live in joy and peace.

I learned that sometimes a person identifies with their suffering so much it becomes who they are–it becomes their identity. I had become a victim; that's who I identified as. One would think that someone would want to get rid of that feeling. But giving up the identity of who you are, even if it's negative, can leave you feeling very vulnerable and with a temporary lost sense of purpose. And that's exactly what had kept me stuck.

If you're thinking, "Two years of listening to one audiobook is crazy!" I agree. However, that's just how long it took.

It wasn't long before I decided I would rather be at home with my pups than listening to some guy from a dating site trying to impress me. At that particular point in my life, I enjoyed my dogs' company more than anyone else's.

We loved and adored dogs in my family. My children had a golden retriever growing up that we all loved. But I never really bonded with a dog until I rescued my first one, little Sophie; I took her out of a situation where she was severely neglected. Sophie was a Maltese/Pomeranian mix and was so grateful to be with me. I had met her once, and when I returned to take her home with me, she literally ran up my body and into my arms. From that time forward, I felt a bond with every dog I encountered.

Eventually, even though I was peaceful and joyous, I decided I wanted love in my life. Having this desire in my heart, I came across an audiobook called *Follow Your Passion, Find Your Power* by Bob Doyle.

Bob had written this book to further explain how energy works. When Rhonda Byrne's book, *The Secret*, was published in 2006, it became a worldwide bestseller. However, Rhonda's book only skimmed the surface of how energy works. This ended up creating chaos with some newbies like myself, who had never learned about energy in this particular sense, or how energy and manifesting work.

Thanks to Bob's book, I began daily journaling. Every night, I wrote how grateful I was to have a man who adored and cherished me. At first, they were just words since I wasn't in a relationship with anyone. But after a while, my sheer desire of wanting this to be so allowed me to feel the gratitude and realness behind it. This was a writing ritual I did for over a year.

Even the practice of writing those words every night made me feel loved. I could picture a man holding me and telling me how much he loved me. It was interesting because I had no hang-ups with this man being "perfect." He was so very handsome, even though I never visualized his face completely. I focused my energy on feeling gratitude for a man who *truly* loved and cherished me.

In the fall of 2017, my interest was piqued as I noticed a Facebook request from a beautiful surfer. He was a successful businessman with an MBA. His name was Keith Carrington. Keith reminded me of an actor or someone very familiar, but I couldn't quite place him. His blond hair, square jawline, and perfectly muscular tanned chest in his surfing photos made him very intriguing. I accepted his request and spent half an hour creeping on his posts. *Can he really be this great?*

A month later, I missed a call from Keith. When I listened to his message, his enthusiastic voice said he was in town for the weekend and asked if I would like to have dinner with him. Something was happening. I could feel it.

I met Keith the following evening at a sushi restaurant. I just sat there wide-eyed as I listened to the most interesting, unique man I had ever met. Keith started talking and did not stop for two hours. It was like four Red Bulls instead of just a cup of coffee. *Holy shit!*

I purposely had learned quite a bit about Keith before our first date. He and I had a common friend whom I knew well. When I asked her about Keith, she got very excited–she had known his family growing up. She recalled knowing Keith back in the day; he had scored thirty-five out of thirty-six on his ACT test and was offered a full-ride scholarship to Harvard. But instead, he chose the church college his mother wanted for him. Knowing this about him, it was very endearing to listen to him talk all night.

Keith never brought up his financial planning firm or his accomplishments. Instead, he talked about things that would impress a fifteen-year-old, like his favorite surf spot or where he liked to ride his dirt bike. His animated hand gestures and enthusiasm as he spoke took up all of his space–and half of mine.

At one point, he took a piece of rolled-up tissue out of his pocket and showed me the cool bumble bee he had found dead by the vent at his friend's condo that morning. I couldn't help but chuckle. *You're adorable!*

Everything surrounding us was fascinating to Keith. He certainly wasn't shy. He spoke to the couple seated next to us about what they had ordered and if they were happy with their choice. You could almost take his behavior as obnoxious, but his demeanor was so childlike. *And* he was incredibly handsome! Keith looked into my eyes towards the end of the evening and said, "Ramona . . . you're so beautiful!" An incredible warmth flowed through me, realizing he had no inhibitions whatsoever, yet no strange motives, either.

As we said goodbye that night, Keith apologized, saying he had a slight head cold from standing out in the freezing cold at a football game the day before. And he didn't have as much energy as usual.

This is you not feeling 100% energy? It was hard to imagine what this guy would be like when he felt great. I had been around enough people on drugs to know when someone was high. That was not Keith! He had the eyes of an excited child on Christmas morning . . . the entire evening.

We began seeing each other, and Keith swept me off my feet.

I wrote in my journal just a few weeks after that night:

> I've never known anyone with a bigger love for life. Keith sees every single day like it's the first time he's ever seen it. He doesn't just see the world through rose-colored lenses; they're more like neon, hot-pink lenses!

Even though Keith was twelve years older than me, I felt like we were a couple of teenagers every time we were together. For some reason, he loved to crash weddings; by the end of the evening, I knew why. Within a few hours, he knew more about the people we had met than they knew about each other. Keith had perfect recall, so it didn't take him long to connect complete strangers with people he knew–and all for everyone's greatest benefit.

I couldn't believe it when I learned my most perfect boyfriend had heart disease. With seventeen stents in his heart, he ran circles around everyone. Keith actually met one of his heart doctors by walking onto the wrong house-boat and asking, "Is this where the party is?" He became a solid friend to every person he met. I marveled at the unbridled joy and enthusiasm he had every single day.

Keith had spent two years in Spain and spoke fluent Spanish; Baja was his favorite place. We golfed at Baja Mar and rode four-wheelers further south on the endless beaches. But he also took me to places like the opening day at the horse races in Del Mar. I loved dressing up and wearing a big fancy hat; everything was so posh!

I marveled that the man who could easily camp out with me on the beach felt equally at home at the races. Keith was addicted to life and the excitement he found in everything. Oh, my goodness. I was falling . . . *hard*.

By this time, Curtis had turned into my extremely overprotective father. When I first began dating Keith, Curtis had a full report for me within two weeks–not at my request, mind you.

"You need to stay away from this guy, Ramona," he warned me. "He's a total player."

Wow, really? I just smiled . . . *If that isn't the pot calling the kettle black!*

Now that I was no longer in a romantic relationship with Curtis, he had taken the position that he was going to protect me from everyone out there *who was just like him!* Nothing ironic there.

I had to realize that over thirteen years, I had become an essential part of Curtis's world. Not only had I remodeled all of Curtis's homes and organized his warehouses and airplane hangars, I gave him advice about women, bought gifts or flowers that I would hand to him on his way out the door and say, "Yes, you need to give these to her!"

I always ran my fingers through his hair to get it just right before he went out. I told him what to wear, cut his hair, kept his home organized, managed house cleaners, and did all his grocery shopping. And apparently, I was also the only person on the planet who could fix a proper PB&J on toast. It was an equation that had to be carefully calibrated to achieve the perfect balance.

As Keith and I became more serious, the thoughts of us moving in together where Curtis couldn't "protect me" had my ex beyond rattled. I got a little concerned. Keith had no filters and never slowed down long enough to think about whether Curtis could hurt him in the business world. Was Keith going to disappear like Dillon had?

My lover had a completely chill vibe . . . he loved everyone–whether they loved him back or not. It helped that Keith lived in a different state and had varied business circles from Curtis. While I had the mountains near my home, Keith had the ocean near his home and was six hundred and seventy miles out of Curtis' reach.

I was on cloud nine with Keith because he met my number one core need; he made me feel loved, and oh-so cherished. It was like jumping into a pool of water after being lost in the Sahara Desert for . . . let's see, my entire life! Keith told me he loved me at least five times a day and told me how beautiful I was at least four times a day. He brought me flowers, gave me long hugs, and oh . . . what a lover! I felt like the luckiest girl in the world.

Now, because he had no filters, the first time I saw a Facebook post of Keith out to dinner with another woman in his hometown, it broke my heart. Hoping for a reasonable explanation (*maybe it was his sister*), I called him.

"We have a long-distance relationship, baby. Don't be upset . . . you know you're my most beautiful, favorite girlfriend!" Keith reasoned.

Fuck that! I'm in love with you! I stayed composed and got off the phone. I was so hurt! *How could he still want to date other women? What we have is so beautiful! Why on earth would he mess that up?* I needed to get small . . . climbing into my bed, I wrapped my arms around a pillow and slid down underneath my covers.

However, after an hour or so, my knowledge from Byron Katie took over, and I became peacefully broken-hearted. *This sucks! But you're not a hostage, Ramona, and certainly not a victim.* I called Keith back and peacefully told him our relationship was no longer working for me. No ultimatums, no tantrums.

"Wait, baby, don't do that!" Keith begged.

"Keith, I want you to live your life, and date all the women you want to date, baby. I just won't be one of them."

After a slight pause, I said, "Goodbye, sweetie." Click.

Warrior Wisdom:

The years I spent remodeling Curtis's homes allowed me to ground myself again and get quiet inside. Discovering peace through the teachings of Byron Katie changed the trajectory of my life. Adding to that, discovering the true nature of energy through the teachings of Bob Doyle opened up an empowering world of joyful manifestation–to where I would never be the same.

It would have been so easy to revert back to the "fruitcake" when Keith came into my life; I had waited for him for such a long time–and I was so in love with him.

When you are in love, letting that person go is beyond painful. But if you focus on your own value and self-love, it's a win-win. Because you will either end up with the person you loved stepping up and into the space you are holding yourself in–or someone else stepping into that healthy, empowered space. Either way, you end up with someone who loves you and treats you well. Because you chose to love yourself and did not stay in a situation that wasn't in your best interest.

Energy is very complex, with so many factors at play. Take a look at every single thing in your life right now. If there's something you don't like, ask yourself, "What belief am I holding that supports this being here?"

Our beliefs emit an energy. I learned so clearly that if you do not value yourself, you will attract people who support that belief and don't value you either. If you want people in your life who love and respect you, you first have to love and respect yourself. We attract everything in our lives just like a magnet, based on the energy we emit from the beliefs we hold. If you have chosen to hold onto the role of a victim, you will attract more people to victimize you. Harsh, but true.

Einstein said, "Everything is energy and that's all there is to it. Match the frequency of the reality you want and you cannot help but get that reality. It can be no other way. This is not philosophy, this is physics."

Sometimes, we can be holding onto beliefs we are not even aware of. Here's one thing to remember: With the people and circumstances you have in your life, know that you have the belief (meaning the energy) to support them being there. It would be impossible for things in your life to be there if the energies didn't match. If you want to change your circumstances, change your beliefs that attract those circumstances.

Another thing to remember: The energy of wanting *something and the energy of* having *something are two* very different energies. *If you want a particular thing in your life, be grateful for that thing from a calm state of simply appreciating it, like you've had it for years. Don't come from a desperate state of wanting and wishing for it. Your energy has to match actually having it to actually attract it and receive it.*

CHAPTER 20

Wow . . . This "Self-Love" Bullshit Really Works!

Two days later, I was sitting across from Curtis at a restaurant; we had just placed our dinner order. *This is weird*, I thought; *Curtis is now comforting me.*

"What an asshole," Curtis declared after hearing my story. I looked at him incredulously.

For doing the same thing you did throughout our entire relationship? The irony is killing me! I was no longer the girlfriend who was being crazy and irrational. Now, I had magically become an intelligent woman who had every right to kick Keith to the curb.

Whatever his reasoning, it felt good to have Curtis's support. However, it was my own resolve that allowed me to walk away. I had already *been there, done that*. I wasn't going to spend "another" ten years waiting for someone else to decide to be in an exclusive relationship with me–it was a no-brainer. As much as it broke my heart to leave, I felt an inner strength knowing I had spared myself from being in an unhealthy relationship. It was empowering to know that I deserved better.

A month later, to my surprise, Keith called me. We made small talk for a minute, then I told him I needed to go. Torturing myself by talking to a man I was in love with was not my idea of a good time.

"Wait, baby, I need to tell you something," Keith said urgently. Sensing my demeanor, he spit it out. "I'm ready to be the kind of boyfriend you want me to be."

It had been Keith's choice. No turning into a fruitcake. I thought my heart would burst. I really loved this man!

Over the next two years, I put Keith in "time-out" one more time before he finally realized I was completely serious. And just to clarify, this wasn't a game to me. I was willing to break my own heart and walk away for good. I wasn't going to spend one more fucking second as a hostage in my own life.

The time came when Keith wanted me to move in with him–the ultimate relationship litmus test. It cemented what he had been saying, and his actions had finally showcased. I was his only one.

Curtis did not trust Keith any further than he could throw him. After hearing my news, in one last attempt to get me to stay, Curtis offered to buy the home I was leasing and pay me $10k a month if I would just, "Stop this nonsense." Bless his big, lion heart.

"I'm really in love with him," I said quietly. "Just be happy for me. I'll be fine."

And so was the end of our fourteen-year saga.

As Keith and I finished moving into our new place, we stood out on our deck and watched the sunset on the ocean. Keith wrapped his arms around me, and I had never been more content and happy in my entire life.

This is what heaven feels like.

Keith and I flew home to my neck of the woods the following football season for the weekend. We planned to attend a college game. His all-time favorite team just happened to be located in my state. Keith and I weren't married–so I still had to pretend to like sports. Truth be told, anything I did with my new love was exciting. His spontaneity was a magnet for anything and everything happening unexpectedly. It cracked me up that he and Curtis couldn't have been more opposite. But in the end, it was my adventures with Keith that had me grinning from ear to ear.

While we were in town, Curtis, whom I still spoke with a couple times a week, bit the bullet and invited Keith and I up to his house for dinner. It was like bringing my boyfriend home to meet my father, who owned a shotgun. Curtis threw everything he had at Keith.

"Hey Keith, you should come hang out with me for the day. I could teach you how to be a real man," Curtis joked.

"You bet!" returned Keith, not even phased. "I'd love that, brother! We could go golfing or dirt bike riding . . . they make the best tuna fish sandwiches at the Creekside Country Club. I was just there yesterday . . . " Keith enthusiastically pulled a napkin out of his pocket and revealed some french fries he had saved from his lunch the day before. "Want to try some of their fries? They're absolutely delicious!" His words held all the excitement of a little kid sharing a priceless treasure with his best buddy.

I giggled as I watched Curtis's mouth drop . . . *I thought I was the only one who could make you speechless.* As I took in the scene of these two, my giggle turned into a belly laugh.

"What the fuck, man?" Curtis finally said . . . laughing until he had tears in his eyes.

It took all of three hours for Keith to win Curtis's approval. *Finally! Thank God!* These were the two most important men in my life. It was a relief knowing that one of them no longer wanted to have the other one taken out!

The next day, Curtis called me and just spit it out; "I need you back here. You're the only one who knows how my life works," he admitted matter-of-factly. I was relieved to discover that instead of trying to lure me away, Curtis wanted Keith and me to move into the north wing I had remodeled at his primary residence and return to work. This included everything from choosing his clothes to managing his properties. I had a hunch the PB&J had been a deciding factor as well.

When I told Keith about Curtis's request, he looked at me for a second and said, "Sure baby, sounds like fun!"

Surprised, I loved that Keith was always game for a new adventure. He knew Curtis and I had no romantic energy–only a protective bond that he respected. So, just like that, Keith decided to work remotely, and we moved back to my beautiful home state–next to the mountains he enjoyed so much. In the meantime, there were more adventures afoot...

When Keith and I planned a special getaway four months later in the Sawtooth wilderness, Curtis was the only person we told.

Surrounded by beautiful mountains with Douglas fir and ponderosa pine trees, Keith and I walked barefoot down to the dock. He was wearing surf shorts and a seersucker blazer with no shirt. I wore the beige sundress I had picked up at a thrift store three years before.

Our dear friend Sunny was standing at the end of the dock, even as her husband Jack was taking on the role of videographer. Sunny had acquired her minister's license just for us.

We said our wedding vows, expressing the depth of our love and devotion to each other. Keith kissed me as his new bride–and to everyone's surprise, did a backflip into the water. Then we both paddle-boarded around the lake with my bouquet of flowers on the front of my board. From that day forward, I always had fresh flowers from my most perfect hubby. He either picked them himself or bought them for me. *How did I get so incredibly lucky?*

I called my kids from the cabin to tell them the news the following morning. They were all happy for me, but couldn't resist giving me a hard time–since they already knew about it from Keith's Facebook post! Thanks to Keith, every second of my life was now documented on social media.

My kids had already initiated Keith into the family with their incredibly sick sense of humor and off-color conversations. He not only passed with flying colors, he fit right in and took the lead with being more outrageous than any of them.

The following Sunday, Keith and I visited his mother. She lived just thirty minutes from Curtis's home, in which we now lived. This woman was among the classiest, kindest souls I had ever met.

As we visited, she said to me, "Dearest one, I have a special request for my Christmas present this year."

Being July, I thought it was a little odd. But I smiled and said, "Anything for you, Mom!" I adored this woman, and I meant it wholeheartedly.

She clapped her hands together with delight and continued. "I would like you and Keith to attend church with me every week for one year. After church, I'll fix us a lovely Sunday dinner."

The smile on my face froze into a catatonic state as I suddenly felt queasy. *Shit! You've got to be kidding me!* I had expected her to ask me to refinish a piece of furniture or install a new faucet—she loved how I could fix anything she needed around the house. *Please . . . not that! I'll build you anything you want!*

I looked into her blue eyes, sparkling expectantly. How could I possibly say no to this sweet woman? So, just as Keith had been willing to sacrifice for me, this was my first loving sacrifice as Keith's new bride. Walking through the chapel doors the following week, I let out a big sigh of relief–feeling almost fireproof, when I didn't spontaneously combust!

Settling into our new life and home, Curtis quickly realized the added value of Keith coming into the picture. Keith had the biggest *little black book* of any man on the planet–he never forgot a face, name, place, or story. This made Keith an excellent connector in business and the dating scene.

With such remarkable recall, he was like a human map–happy to talk to anyone about where they were from, he always knew more about their home state or country than they did. Keith never acted arrogant or tried to appear more intelligent; he just loved talking with people. The more he knew about the area a person had grown up in, the more they had to talk about. It didn't take Curtis long to realize how incredibly smart Keith was.

Every morning, as I cooked breakfast in the main house (the central area of Curtis's castle-style home), Keith would come into the kitchen with a towel wrapped around his waist; soaking in Curtis's hot tub had become his morning ritual. I personally never tired of seeing that sexy chest of his! He would tell me how beautiful I looked after giving me a big squeeze and a smooch.

Keith would then pour himself a Diet Coke and sit down to talk to Curtis about the stock market or various business deals he had gotten wind of. More than once, I caught myself shooting Keith an adoring gaze. I knew he was doing this entirely for Curtis's benefit; Keith had his own clients and absolutely no desire to work one minute more than he was already working.

My husband had only worked full-time for about seven years when he first got his MBA degree. And even during those years, he was up at the crack of dawn to get some surfing in before he headed into his corporate financial planning office.

This I knew: Keith was one of the few people who realized what was truly important in life. He needed to be out in nature like he needed air. His love for life was extraordinary, and contagious. I found myself enjoying the beauty of everything around me more than I ever had–more than I'd ever known I could. It was ironic and miraculous; I'd fought for this man and won him. He'd fought for me and won me as well. I would never be the same.

Warrior Wisdom:

Keith was everything I wanted in a man–and then some. He showed up in my life without me even searching for him. He came into my awareness because his energy matched mine; I was what he wanted, and he was what I wanted. *First, I had set the intention for what I desired via journaling. And Keith was drawn into my world as a result of that journaling. There are no coincidences.*

Of course it didn't happen like it does in the fairytales. In my life, I've noticed the times we get derailed do serve a purpose. We don't always have to shut people out forever when they disappoint us. If I took that approach, I would be all alone.

CHAPTER 21

I'm So Happy!
But Wait, I'm Still an Alcoholic

Keith loved my lifestyle because we were always on the move. Within eight months, I turned three of Curtis's five homes into successful Airbnb's. I assembled outstanding cleaning teams at the three locations and created a rigorous one hundred and seventy-two-point checklist for each property. Everything was followed to the letter.

For one of my projects, I was staging an investment home that Curtis was going to sell. The family who occupied this property had moved out over two and a half months prior. To my horror, they had left their dog Apollo behind in the garage. Apparently, they would drop food and water off from time to time. The dysfunction was unbelievable. I couldn't believe this garage had been Apollo's world for two and a half months! My face contorted in fury. *What the hell?*

Apollo was a Rottweiler/Blue Heeler mix. As I stood in the doorway, this adorable caramel and black pup cocked his head. He was so happy to see someone! He padded nervously over to me, his head lowered. It was obvious he was completely traumatized. As I took in the scene, I became even more sickened at what he must have gone through. Glancing around at the conditions this poor pup had been compelled to live in and where he was forced to defecate.

An angry tear stole its way past my defenses, sliding down my cheek and landing on my heart, piercing through to the center–just as Apollo already had. I knelt down and held him in my arms, cuddling him and speaking softly. "Your life is changing right now, sweet boy . . . it's changing right fucking now." I returned from the garage into the house and found my husband in the kitchen.

"Hey, baby! They left a whole box of Lucky Charms in the pantry!" Keith announced, crunching away happily. "Where did you get the mutt?" he asked, playfully rubbing the top of Apollo's head.

I told Keith where I had just found him. One thing I loved about Keith was he never dwelled on tragedy or sadness; instead, he got really excited to have a new member of our family. "Do you want some cereal, buddy?" Keith said as he offered Apollo some of his prized find. "He loves me already!" he declared as Apollo wolfed down the cereal in his hand.

"Of course he does. How could he not?" I said to my most perfect husband as I planted a kiss on his lips. Apollo was now officially our pup; he became my shadow from that day forward, which was fine by me!

Understandably, our new pup had abandonment issues. He followed me from room to room, no matter where I went. It broke my heart when he would lower his head and back away whenever one of us picked up an object–Apollo was afraid of everything. Whoever had made Apollo so frightened is lucky I never saw it first-hand. I wouldn't have thought twice while hiring three or four _____s (fill in your preferred badass gang) to find this person and beat the living shit out of them.

Over the following weeks, due to Apollo's separation anxiety, Keith and I quit flying because he was too big to come, choosing to drive to our destinations instead. This beautiful pup brought Keith and I so much joy! Having Apollo was like the cherry on top for living the best life you could ever imagine.

Our routine became making a big loop to check in at all Curtis's homes. Don't misunderstand, I still worked my ass off, but I loved every minute. This was my happy place. And . . . the busier I stayed, the better I could keep a handle on my drinking.

Keith was always making the most of every minute by riding his motorcy-cle, snowmobiling, golfing, or surfing–depending on which location we were residing at for the month. He was the ultimate example of living a healthy, happy life.

As I completed projects on the properties, I was able to manage the book-ings on my phone. As Keith and I traveled the same loop for the next year, there was no more physical work to be done. This left me restless and trying to figure out what to do with myself.

So, when Jessie and her husband Max made me a grandmother, I put down my power tools and took up crocheting. Being a grandma was the absolute best . . . sheer heaven! The first baby afghan I made ended up sprouting a little tail on one corner–it was like trying to wrangle in mischievous kittens! Laying tile was a cakewalk compared to this. Thank goodness Jessie already knew I did things differently than most in any given situation. Staying true to her kind heart–she loved it.

As happy and perfect as everything was, my alcoholism was progressing. I wasn't drinking to numb my feelings, escape, or cope. I had an amazing life! I was drinking because I had kept my mind sick with drinking for years, and I was even sicker when I didn't drink. I would be shaking and feeling queasy if I went too many hours without alcohol. Having my next drink was always on my mind.

Once I reached a certain point, I didn't have a shutoff valve–I just wanted more. My cherished, beloved Keith had to take the brunt of me getting too drunk and turning into a scary, evil bitch. I'd say terrible things, yelling at the man I loved so much. The next day, as I woke up through the pain of my nausea, my mind would play back my actions, being spared from noth-ing. Reliving the ugly scene from the night before was the ultimate torture. I would hate myself for the way I had acted . . . I was always so very sorry. Keith was my world!

My husband had a gift of never letting anything phase him. He had one mood–happy and optimistic. He would forgive me, and I would try to recover from the utter contempt and disgust I felt toward myself. We continued to go everywhere together, and after a week or so, our lives would return to being perfect again. Until the next time I got too drunk.

After one of my particularly bad episodes, I had finally surfaced two days later and was in the kitchen making breakfast. Keith was out in the hot tub. I was attempting to keep my composure while blocking out the hideous images of the scene I had caused in my head.

Curtis came into the kitchen and sat down. I felt his energy. He had a way of saying things exactly as they were. The man never sugar-coated anything, but I knew he truly cared about Keith and me.

"Ramona, hon, you've got to get a handle on this," Curtis warned. "Keith isn't just going to take this forever."

"I know," I quietly answered with tears in my swollen eyes. "I can't fuck up the best thing that's ever happened to me. Keith is the love of my life." I dried my eyes and tried to buck up and get my head back in the game.

The dangerous thing about alcohol is not just the state it put me in when I was drunk; it was the state it slowly knocked me down to in the aftermath. The self-hatred, guilt, shame, and petty blame pointed toward those closest to me in an effort to justify or make sense of why the hell I chose to keep drinking! It was a deep shithole, a prison . . . with no hope of ever getting out.

The pathetic, despicable state I found myself in was precisely what fueled me for needing to get numb again. It was only a matter of time before it happened again. This time, while drunk, I smacked Keith with the back of my hand, square in the face–while he was driving.

Keith drove home with blood running down his face amid my freaking out and screaming. He packed his bags and left. The next day, I woke up with the familiar horror of images from the night before. Mortified, panicked, shaking, and sick, I called Keith, but this time he never picked up. At the end of the day, he finally called to tell me he was leaving me. He had been at the courthouse to request a divorce.

I couldn't believe what I was hearing. I wanted to rewind the last twenty-four hours–this couldn't be happening. I begged and pleaded with Keith, but he was very different now. Something between us was broken–I had broken it. Crushed it to smithereens. Keith wasn't coming back. I drank so much that I ended up in the hospital. And guess what? He still didn't come back. It was my worst nightmare–really happening. I had driven my knight in shining armor away.

The self-loathing I experienced was almost more than I could bear. I had to sit with the realization that our perfect life was over. It hurt to breathe. I honestly could not see a life without my Keith.

There was no one there to blame or have pity on me. Coincidentally, this happened precisely when most of the world was forced to isolate–so it was easy to be "quarantined." I deserved to be separated from the rest of the world with my self-destructive behaviors. I didn't leave the north wing of Curtis's home for four months. Beyond walking Apollo in the neighborhood, I kept myself completely shut off from everyone . . . even Curtis.

I quit drinking heavily, although I had to drink enough so I wouldn't shake. As I brought my trembling cup to my lips each night, I hated Keith with my entire being. He had pulled the rug right out from under me. How could he do this to us? I thought he loved me.

I began to journal every night to simply cope. I wrote:

I'm still here, I'm still breathing, I will still be here tomorrow, I'm still alive.

Those words gave me a solid point to focus on in a world that had turned completely upside down. Tapering off alcohol became a robotic process. I was in so much pain from losing the man I had waited so long for; the torture my body went through while detoxing was secondary.

Eventually, I began to journal:

I'm still here! I will still be here tomorrow! I'm still alive! I can do this!

Those words gave me a slight semblance of identity that went beyond the self-loathing.

Finally, after watching a Tony Robbins seminar to try and keep my sanity, my journaling became:

This is MY life! I choose! I decide! I create my world! I'm staying right fucking here!

I wrote it over and over, filling pages. Writing those words chased away my split-second thoughts of ending my pain through a finality from which there would be no return. Day by day, in a world where there was just me again, it was time to take back my power. No one else was going to hold my hand or do it for me.

Because taking my life back was in my thought process, I came across the audiobook, *Girl, Wash Your Face* by Rachel Hollis. Rachel has an incredible, inspiring story. She wrote one of my favorite quotes: "If you can't get through the front door, try the side window. If the window is locked, maybe you slide down the chimney." Rachel's book woke something up in me and reminded me that I still had dreams I had not yet achieved.

Curtis and I had acquired one patent together, but I still had more than forty ideas in my design book. Slowly, I got to the point where I was excited to put my focus back into creating something again.

Having the will to not drink was a daily challenge, a constant battle within my head. But when I quit poisoning my brain, it began to heal. And I realized a painful truth; I never, ever would have gotten better if Keith hadn't left.

Warrior Wisdom:

Despite living the best life I could have ever dreamed of, I still fought with the need for alcohol. Alcoholism is a disease; just like all diseases, it worsens over time. Many people can drink, even heavily, and never become alcoholics. Just like being predisposed to getting a particular disease, if you carry specific genes (which they have now identified), you will be predisposed to becoming an alcoholic if you drink. It would be better stated to say that someone "contracted alcoholism" rather than someone "became an alcoholic."

We don't say that someone "became" disease ridden. Nor does someone with a disease have the shameful stigma. A person who drinks and develops alcoholism is no different than a person who eats food and develops a disease. Neither of these scenarios were deliberate, nor could they be controlled from happening. I'm not trying to be insensitive here, I'm simply stating facts that many people aren't aware of.

It all concerns our genetic code and what we are predisposed to. Knowledge is power, my friends. My addiction had created a constant back-and-forth dance in my head . . . Should I drink? Shouldn't I drink? That battle was always present; it never went away. Much more on this topic later.

Despite losing my clients, my marriage, my best friend, my school, and Curtis on and off for years, the hardest thing I had ever experienced was when Keith left.

It would have been so easy to give up the fight when I lost my Keith. Turns out, his leaving created a path to getting my life back. As painful as it was, I stayed in the game. Our brains are incredible things; they want to be strong to operate our bodies. We just have to give them a fighting chance.

Regarding my precious Apollo, I speak up about things close to my heart.

*Dogs are pack animals by nature. Having a dog and not allowing it to be part of your family (pack) is cruel and hurtful.

*If you want a mellow pup, keep it clean by taking it to the groomer every six weeks and allow it into your space.

*Dogs need a job; get healthy rawhide bones or bully sticks to chew on. And it will keep them from chewing on things they shouldn't.

*Raise your bar of excellence and walk your pup daily; it will benefit both of you.

*Dogs are like toddlers; they require constant love and attention. If you haven't bonded with your pet, you haven't taken the time to truly care for it. Harsh but true.

Going back to work on my inventions was the best therapy imaginable at this point in my life. It was something I was good at, and I desperately needed anything I could get my hands on for positive reinforcement. When we are in our darkest hour, anything that can give us the tiniest bit of positive comfort, validation, or reinforcement will serve us. It's a beginning.

When we look back on our lives, we realize that nothing ever stays the same. It's a constant ebb and flow. This fact of life is crucial to remember when we are at our lowest. The horrible things that happen in our lives due to our own actions can be soul-crushing. Every single one of us is here for a reason; we all play such an important role. Forgiving ourselves and doing right by others is the only way out of the pain.

I genuinely believe we have a Creator who loves, understands, and forgives us—whether we are religious or not. Fuck shame and fear, they are the enemy. Know that you are loved!

Knights in shining armor are amazing, yes. But start with the hero inside yourself . . . it's what truly sets you free. Find the things that bring you joy. No matter what shitstorm life hurls in your face. Seek out experiences to spark happiness in your heart. Hold onto that, feel that, feed that. Choose to let go of what's killing you and drink in what gives you life. YOU, my friend. You and your energy are what will create life-saving change.

CHAPTER 22

The Accountable Fairytale

When my world quit working for me, I had to find a new way. After four months, I was finally in a space to be accountable. Keith had tried to stay in touch with me, but I couldn't even speak to him. It was just too painful. Now, I was in a space where I could have that conversation with the love that I had lost.

As I fought back the tears on the phone, I told Keith, "I've got something to tell you . . . but you need to let me say what I have to say without interrupting." Even though I hadn't spoken to Keith in four months, I still knew him well enough to know if I didn't require this, I wouldn't get a word in edgewise.

"Okay, baby," Keith promised. His ready warmth surprised me.

In a shaky voice, I began, "Sweetie . . . I caused this. No one else, just me. I chose to keep my mind sick instead of seeking help. You *had* to leave for me to get better." I covered my mouth to muffle my crying.

"Can I talk now?" Keith asked after a moment.

"No," I choked out in a whisper. I had to come all the way clean. Trying desperately to compose myself, I finally continued. "I wish things were different. I wish you were still in my life." Silently weeping, I found the courage . . . and whispered, "I still love you."

Then, in famous Keith style, he simply stated, "I still love you too, baby. Okay, maybe I'll come back home."

Huh? I sat on the other end of the phone, speechless.

"Okay," I cried in shock. My body felt like a limp noodle. I couldn't believe this was really happening. By the grace of my Creator, my *knight in shining armor* was coming back to me!

"I'll see you in about four hours . . . I had the best ride today! But I'm even more excited about seeing you again . . . my little wifey-wife!" Keith announced happily.

We got off the phone and I fell to my knees. Apollo came over and nudged my face with his nose–obviously concerned about my state. I hugged my sweet pup. "He's coming home!" I blubbered.

Keith and I went down to the courthouse a month later to get remarried. As we walked into the city court building, hand in hand, the court clerk informed us that because of our recent pandemic, they hadn't got around to finalizing our divorce, so we didn't have to bother getting remarried. We both looked at each other, and doing his best Forrest Gump impersonation, Keith said, "That's good. One less thing to worry about."

Oh my heart! I love you so much!

I was so grateful for my extraordinary life. It could have turned out so differently. I felt gratitude to the depth of my bones. Everything I came across appeared so much sweeter. I started watching *Chefsclub* videos on Facebook when Keith and I went on road trips to visit Curtis's properties. The food they prepared looked so beautiful! And through their fabulous videos, I discovered what a creative outlet cooking was. As it turned out, I was a pretty good cook. *Who knew?*

When Keith and I were at Curtis's primary residence, a typical evening at the house looked like this . . . I prepared a gourmet meal for the four of us; Keith, myself, Curtis, and Curtis's date. Keith would be giving the back story on every high-profile player from whatever football or basketball game they were watching. Once in a while (not always), I would shoot Curtis a text and tell him to put his phone away and pay attention to his date. I loved our family. It couldn't have been more perfect. I was in utter bliss again, and I didn't take a single moment for granted.

Warrior Wisdom:

Being accountable and owning my own shit was my saving grace, not just for us as a couple but for me personally. I had already learned with Bruce that becoming right with someone I had wronged, with no excuses whatsoever, is what set me free.

Besides, what has holding on to "being right" ever done for anyone? If you want to experience the most forgiving, compassionate side of someone, acknowledge what you have done and validate how your actions made them feel. And most importantly, as Byron Katie would say: don't expect them to do the same–that's their business, not yours.

Receiving a second chance with my beloved Keith felt amazing, renaissance-like. I experienced a sort of rebirth. It almost felt like I had cheated death. Things I once took for granted–now brought me joy. I also experienced an identity shift; I remembered the importance of pursuing something that got me excited to get out of bed in the morning!

It's funny; if anyone had told me before I met Keith that I would be living in Curtis's house, with my husband, eating dinner together every evening as a family–I would have asked them if they had been smoking crack! I did not see that one coming. However, I had also been journaling about how much I appreciated having a peaceful relationship with Curtis for years. And that's exactly what I ended up with. Curtis became the most thoughtful, caring friend that both Keith and I could have ever asked for.

CHAPTER 23

Of Course I Have an Appointment!

The following January 2021, on a bitterly cold day, tragedy struck my life once more. My sister Rita called . . . I hadn't spoken with her in months. What she said stopped me in my tracks.

"Mom was taken in an ambulance to the hospital last night. When they arrived, she was nonresponsive. She's really sick," Rita cried.

"Is she going to be okay?" I choked out. My stomach felt like it had dropped to the floor.

"I don't know," Rita said devastated. "The nurse told me they have her stabilized, but we can't talk to Mom, and with all of the restrictions, visiting her is out of the question."

We both cried together on the phone, visualizing our mother alone and unable to reach her. *Non-responsive?* I felt my gut clench in anguish.

"Thank you for telling me," I finally said. "I love you, Rita. Keep me posted . . . okay?"

"I will," Rita answered. "I love you, too, Ramona."

As I ended the call, I sat down on my bed. I was wracked with guilt. Out of six adult children, I was the one child who never called or went to visit our mother very often. Keith had only met her one time. I loved Mom dearly, but it emotionally shut me down for days on the rare occasion I would go see her or call. She had become immobile eight years prior because of her weight. My mother hadn't been out of her house in years. It was so painful for me to see her in that state–she was still so young! And I was powerless to do anything about it.

Darren (my younger brother), and his family had moved into Mom's house so they could care for her. My mom, born to be a grandmother, loved having my brother's two girls growing up in her house. It had been the joy of her life. She had the same relationship with my two beautiful nieces that I had with my grandmother, perhaps even closer. It's funny how relationships have to skip a generation sometimes to become really close.

When Rita called me, I hadn't seen Mom for months. *Am I ever going to see my mother alive again?* And after everything I had been through because of alcohol . . . I *still* felt like I needed a glass of wine to cope with this unexpected stress. Although I never became violent with Keith again, the internal argument I had going on regarding staying sober came out in full force after that call with Rita. To drink or not drink? The glass in my hand won out.

Mom was in the hospital for three weeks and then transferred by her doctor to a skilled nursing facility with a secluded section. No one in our family had been able to visit her for over a month. My choice to avoid seeing my mother in the past because it was too painful . . . now made me feel ashamed. And no longer having that option brought forth a desperate yearning to see the mother I loved so dearly.

I began calling the skilled nursing center where my mother was being cared for. It made me crazy that each time I called, the phone would ring for ten minutes with no answer. *What the hell is going on over there?*

When I spoke to Rita, she told me she hadn't gotten through either. One day, I decided to drive over an hour to my mother's care center.

I walked up to the entrance and found it was locked. I pushed the ringer–nothing. This was ridiculous. I began pounding on the glass door and hitting the buzzer repeatedly. Finally, after several minutes, a young man in a white smock and face mask came to the door. He displayed awkwardness in every sense of the word with his seemingly fearful energy towards me. *I'm going to call you "Awkie" for short,* I thought. Awkie cocked his head and looked at me like he was inspecting my mask, then asked if I had a scheduled appointment.

"Yes," I lied. Awkie let me in, and we walked to the front desk. As I entered the facility, I felt a shudder. The energy at this place felt like nothing was right. In a word, it was *frightening.* I couldn't figure out why a place meant to help and heal people felt so wrong.

"Sign your name here," Awkie said flatly. Next, he told me to put my forehead before a light to take my temperature. Finally, I followed him back to where my mother was.

I felt like I was walking through a morgue.

I passed elderly people sitting alone in wheelchairs, but none of them even looked at me as I tried to acknowledge them by making eye contact. Having to wear a mask made emotion almost impossible to read or show. I thought of visiting my great-grandfather in a nursing home when I was young. *It never felt like this!*

As I entered my mother's room, she saw me and began to weep. I rushed to her, hugged her, and cried until I could finally regain my composure. Protocol be damned, I ripped my mask off and kissed her on the cheek.

"They won't let me go," she mumbled, slurring her speech.

I looked at Mom more closely. *What the hell happened? Did you have a stroke?* She began to cry again. Through her sobs, she mumbled, "I can hear the babies screaming all night, and I can't get anyone to help them!"

What the fuck? I hugged her even more tightly.

"What babies, Mom? What happened?" I asked, trying to keep the shock out of my voice. My mother repeated herself again and kept crying. I looked her in the eyes and squeezed her hands. "It's okay, Mom. I'm here now. I'm going to find out what's going on."

I tried to keep my composure as I walked out and found a nurse. Even though I desperately wanted to, I didn't yell . . . I spoke slowly and deliberately, with a face that said I wanted some answers. "Excuse me," I began, "What happened to my mother?"

The nurse spoke cautiously to me. "Your mother's fine. She had a bad reaction to a sleeping med, but she'll be just fine."

"How long has she been like this?" I asked.

"Just today," the nurse answered–a little too quickly.

"She's hearing babies scream in the night," I insisted. The thought of it made me sick to my stomach.

"I'm sorry," she repeated. "It was just a bad reaction to the sleeping pill we gave her. We won't give it to her again."

I couldn't find the words. Instead, I just turned around and returned to Mom's room, where I comforted her. The virus had left her body so weak that she could no longer stand. She was still so large they had to use an electric lift to move her. How would she ever be able to go home again?

"I love you, Mom. You'll feel better tomorrow, I promise." I held her hand until she dozed off.

Choking back sobs, I went into the hall again and found a nurse. "I want to speak with a doctor," I said, covering my mouth to ebb my unstoppable tears. The nurse informed me the doctor only came in once a week–and only the "appointed person" could speak with the doctor. This was my older brother Kyle because he was the one who had checked my mother into the hospital.

Composing myself, I asked the nurse, "When are your visiting hours?"

She thought for a second, "I don't think we have visiting hours," she answered with a shrug. I walked away thinking, *Then why the fuck would I ever need an appointment?*

On my drive home, I called Rita and told her what had happened. Rita listened, then spoke with apparent panic in her voice. "I was able to see Mom for a short visit two days ago, and Ramona, she was slurring her words then! The nurse told me the exact same thing!"

Another alarm went off in my head. *Something is very wrong!*

Rita called our brother Kyle and told him he needed to schedule a meeting with the doctor immediately. Kyle agreed.

The next day, I was back at the care center. I stood there pounding on the glass and ringing the bell for five minutes—all while watching Awkie at the front desk as he refused to acknowledge me. When he couldn't stand my constant barrage, he finally walked over to the door.

"Do you have a scheduled visit?" he asked, with no apologies for ignoring me like a little bitch.

"Yes," I lied again, my voice filled with utter contempt. "Of course I have an appointment!" *Dumb-ass!*

We both walked to the front desk just like the day before; looking at the book, he said, "Hmm, I don't see anyone's name on your mother's visitor chart." *Finally! You're actually going to admit something! Idiot!*

"Well, *maybe* if you guys would answer your phone, we could clear this whole thing up regarding appointments," I answered. Glaring at him, Awkie refused to look at me. "I want to speak with your supervisor . . . *now* please," I said, emphasizing my words. Awkie finally looked up at me, then turned and walked away without speaking. I watched him go, thinking, *I can't wait to speak with someone in charge of this cluster-fuck facility!*

I waited. Then I waited some more. I had been in a high state of panic since seeing my mother the day before. Keith and Curtis had listened with concerned looks as I shared my experience with them when I arrived home the previous evening. But there was no way they could understand the panic

I was feeling. Looking at the clock again, I shook my head. *Twelve minutes–seriously? Fuck it!* I walked past the lobby, through the big doors, and back toward my mother's room.

As I turned down the last hall that led to Mom's room, I passed Awkie and a woman in a nurse's uniform walking beside him. We looked at each other as I passed them–they didn't say a single word! My panicked state deepened. I didn't even turn around to see if they had stopped.

I walked into Mom's room and hugged her. "Are you okay?" I asked, as my eyes filled with tears.

My mother slurred, "Don't cry, Ramona . . . I'm ss . . . so glad you're here."

Why are you still slurring your words? I could barely keep my fury contained. *Those motherfuckers!* I began looking around the room to assess what was happening as I held Mom's hand. I glanced over and noticed the quilt Rita had made for her years before. It had delicate bluebell flowers that matched Mom's bedroom at home. Seeing the quilt gave me a slight comfort of familiarity in the moment. Rita had always taken such good care of Mom–all my siblings had, but not me.

A nurse came in to check my mother's vitals, and I rounded on her immediately.

"My mother is still slurring her words. Yesterday, I was told it was a bad reaction from a sleeping pill–I was told you only gave the medication to her once." I raised my brow and demonstrated to Mom. "Clearly, that's not the case here."

The nurse didn't admit to knowing a thing. She said I would have to wait and have my brother speak with the doctor.

Bullshit! You give her meds every day; you know exactly what they are!

After an hour had passed, a nurse came in. "Visiting hours are over," she said.

I gave her an incredulous look. "What visiting hours? Last I heard, you guys don't even have visiting hours." I stood and faced her squarely. "I'll leave when I'm done visiting my mother." I wanted someone, *anyone* who was in charge, to show their face. But this nurse practically ran away. Now, all the nurses just walked around like meek little meerkats whispering back and forth. As the day progressed, no one would talk to me–it was like they all carried a big secret.

A nurse brought my mother's dinner into the room and set it in front of her at 6:30 p.m. After watching my mother struggle to keep the food on her fork, I gently took her fork and matter-of-factly said, "Let me get that for you, Mom."

She shook her head in a defeated gesture, despite obviously feeling famished.

"It's all good, Mom. No big deal," I said.

I'm actually having to feed my mother–the painful thought caused a lump in my throat so big I could barely swallow. *Buck up, Ramona! Get your shit together!* Quickly blinking away the tears, I bit my cheek and returned to my "don't mess with me mode" while I quietly fed her.

After Mom finished her dinner, I held her hand as we talked. "You're a good mom, and I love you so much!" I said, trying to keep my emotions intact.

"Ahh, I wish I had been more present," she said with a tired sigh. That was ironic, given I was feeling the same way with her.

"You raised six kids by yourself," I told her firmly. "The traits I picked up from being your daughter made me a badass mom." We both chuckled. "I wouldn't change a thing!" I added adamantly.

I noticed my mother's speech had improved since I first arrived that day. We sat and enjoyed our time together, talking about everyone in the family and how life was treating each of them. It reminded me of my grandmother holding me all night when Rita and I had been fighting. There was a comforting peace in knowing that everything could be all right . . . even if just for the moment, because we were there together.

That evening with my mom was such a precious experience. I drank it in and cherished it, somehow knowing I would until the day I died. After she dozed off, I snuggled Rita's blanket around her, kissed her forehead, and left.

It was two weeks before my brother Kyle was allowed to meet with the doctor. The doctor told him the only meds my mother had been given was her high blood pressure medicine. He acknowledged that they had once given Mom a sleeping pill, which hadn't agreed with her. *That's it?* He'd also told Kyle that the virus my mother had when she was hospitalized could bring on dementia, and that it wasn't uncommon to have hallucinations with dementia.

Every alarm throughout my entire body was going off. I Googled dementia and learned that hallucinations come in the middle or end stages of the disease. *Mom had been just fine until she went into this wretched care center!* Although not allowed in person, my siblings and I spoke with her on the phone while she was in the hospital. Dementia was not the culprit. It was not causing my mother to fade in and out of slurring her speech!

Kyle had taken the information as factual from the doctor. Rita and I, however, called major bullshit! Two days later, I showed up again. This time, I had Chance (my oldest son) with me. He had driven ten hours the day before to accompany me. Awkie came to the door, announcing that all appointments must be scheduled via email.

Of course they do . . . how convenient.

I pointed my finger and stuck it right in Awkie's face. "Every time I come here, you guys have a new set of rules! I want to speak with the director!" For once, the director just happened to be in the lobby and quickly walked over.

I want you to know something, dear reader. There's nothing I would love more than to call this little prick by his real name. But for now, let's just call him "Satan."

Satan matched my aggression right away. "You cannot show up here and yell at my staff member while sticking your finger in his face!" he shouted.

I looked him straight in the eyes . . . then I got very slow and quiet. "Every time I come here, you guys have a new set of rules. *Maybe* you should have something called a 'staff meeting' to get everyone on the same page. Last week, one of your nurses told me you didn't have visiting hours. *Maybe* we need *a little bit more training here,*" I said in the most patronizing voice I could muster. The humiliation on Satan's face was seething. Yes, I was calling him out.

I continued without hesitation. "I have traveled over an hour, and my son has traveled ten hours so he could be here. You guys never answer your phone, and I was never told about scheduling visits via email. Do you guys check your email as frequently as you answer your phone?" I didn't give him a chance to answer. "I want to see my mother," I said, in my calmest, *don't fuck with me* voice.

Satan then suggested we could do a window visit since I wasn't officially scheduled. It was a beautiful, warm day–and we could visit with Mom through her bedroom window. A window visit? If that allowed me to see my mother, I would take it.

"Fine, thank you very much," I said. Chance and I walked over to the other side of the building. The nurse opened my mother's blinds and then opened her window. The screen was so filthy I could barely see through it. I waited until the nurse left the room; then, glancing at my son, I took the screen off and Chance hoisted me through the window.

As I popped into the room, it not only surprised my mother, it made her giggle. Being over six feet tall, Chance opted to lean in through the window for our visit.

As Chance stuck his head in, he said, "Hi Grandma!" Mom's eyes lit up with an even bigger surprise.

"Well–hello, Chance!" she said, absolutely thrilled. That was the happiest I had seen my mother in years.

I hugged my mother and held her hand as we talked. When one of the meerkat nurses came in, she had a surprised look on her face but said nothing. A different nurse later returned with a big mug filled with fruit punch. We remained very polite to each other, and she shut the door when she left the room. To our relief, the three of us had a nice, long visit. When it was time to go, I climbed out the same window I had entered, replacing the screen before we left.

This became my routine for the next three weeks. Without Chance there to lift me in, it took a little more effort, but I still managed. With all of my improvised visits, I was never asked to leave–not once. The nurses would come and go, often bringing Mom's lunch in so I could feed her, as they knew she needed assistance.

I would go to the front door and request a window visit, and then a nurse would open my mother's blinds and window. As soon as he or she left the room, I would take off the screen and climb through the window. This was much more pleasant than dealing with Awkie, or Satan, for that matter. *Problem solved!*

Now all I had to figure out was what the hell they were giving my mother. If that evil doctor thought I was going to passively believe his bullshit story, he had another thing coming! The days of putting off visiting Mom–just because it was too painful for my baby-ass feelings, were long gone.

Warrior Wisdom:

Satan might have had authority over the care center, but I had authority over my mother. If I wasn't going to stand up for her, who was? Mustering up a few seconds of bravery is all it takes. The bullies of this world are just people. When we are clear about right and wrong, it becomes easy.

Whenever you have the thought "it's too inconvenient" to visit a loved one, spend time with your kids, spend time with your spouse, sibling, parent, pet–whatever . . . I challenge you to inconvenience the shit out of yourself! Because that's where you'll find the good stuff. *The stuff you think you "don't have the time for" can shape you into a person who's passionate about life and the people (and pets) you share it with. We all have great things to contribute to each others' lives.*

I have found that having a "convenient life" is like eating milk toast . . . who was ever passionate about that?

CHAPTER 24

The Truth Will Always Surface

On one of my visits to see Mom, I met her new roommate. Her name was Kathryn. As I hopped through my mother's window, Kathryn grinned at me and clapped her hands together.

"You must be Ramona. I'm so delighted to meet you!" she said with excitement. Kathryn seemed totally healthy to me; in fact, she and I were the same age. I had no idea why she was there, but I loved her immediately. She was kind, outgoing, and had embraced my mother like her best friend. I was beyond grateful to have her there.

The next time I came for a visit, I brought little gift bags for Mom and Kathryn. I had lip gloss, fingernail polish, sugar-free chocolate, and perfume for both of them. I also brought a stepladder, which made entering and exiting through the window easier with the gift bags.

I found a little corner in the shade for Apollo and set out a water bowl for him. I tied my sweet boy to the stepladder and told him to stay–which he gladly did, knowing I was just inside. *You're such a good pup!*

Settled inside their room, I was painting Mom's fingernails and chatting it up with her and Kathryn. My mother was slurring her words less, although she still acted very differently from what I knew was normal. Suddenly, I looked up to see two police officers standing in my mother's doorway. One of the police officers said to me: "Ma'am, we need you to step out into the hall with us."

Annoyed, I answered back. "We're talking right here. Don't try and intimidate me." I didn't want them scaring my mother.

"Ma'am, you are criminally trespassing."

What the hell?

"I checked in at the front door. You can ask the blonde woman at the front desk. Check your facts, officer," I said. Now I was even more annoyed, knowing someone had actually called the police!

Instead of checking out my story, the two police officers proceeded to grab me; I was tackled, shoved down on my mother's bed, and handcuffed. Apollo went absolutely nuts outside Mom's window–barking and growling like crazy.

"You are under arrest for criminal trespassing and resisting arrest," one of the police officers huffed during our little scuffle. *Go fuck yourself! You stupid dick!* I thought as I tried to break free. Kathryn began to cry, and I could see my mother was visibly shaking. The sight of this broke my heart.

"I'm okay, Mom, don't worry. I'll be back, I promise!" I said as the two officers hauled me out of her room.

Satan had seen the stepladder outside my mother's window, which had been a little more than his pride could take. He told one of his meerkat nurses to call the police; she told them I had been sneaking in and out of my mother's room for weeks, and I had refused to leave–*a blatant lie.*

They knew every time I was there. If the nurses hadn't pulled up the blinds and opened the window for me, there would have been no way I could have climbed into my mother's window.

I knew the police had cameras on their uniforms. As I was being escorted out of the center in handcuffs, I asked the woman at the front desk if I had checked in that day. The woman promptly answered, "Yes." Satan was nowhere in sight. When we got outside, one of the police officers took off the handcuffs. I immediately took my phone and started recording the officer.

"Why was I arrested?" I asked him.

"You have been sneaking in and out of your mother's room, and you have refused to leave," he answered.

"I have never been asked to leave! Not one time!" I shouted. "Tell me what you just heard the front desk woman say to me!"

The officer refused to answer me. Instead, he said, "Right now, I need your information."

I repeated what the woman at the desk had said, stating that I had checked in for a window visit. I was desperately trying to make the officer understand.

"I thought we had an understanding. The nurses bring my mother's meals in while I'm here so I can feed her! How can *that* be criminal trespassing?" I reasoned.

The other officer noticed that I was recording. He abruptly took my phone away and put me back in handcuffs, then gruffly placed me in the back of the police car and set my phone on my lap.

"I have a dog over there!" I pleaded with the officer, now getting panicked. I didn't care what they did with me, but Apollo?

"That's your property, not mine," he answered flatly. *Asshole! I can't wait to tell my brother on you!*

I was left sitting in the back of the police car for thirty minutes while they took down my information–not even a statement, just my personal information. Finally, I was released. As the police officer took my handcuffs off, he said, "I think your dog took off."

Racing over to the window where Apollo had been, I was in such a state of fury and panic it felt like I was going to have a heart attack. All I found was the ladder a few yards away and his collar–still attached to the leash.

Apollo had freaked out when the police officers arrested me. When he ran to jump at the window, he had the step ladder after him! With Apollo's history of abuse, he freaked out. He fought and managed to back out of his collar and took off running.

I ran over to a group of people sitting in a patio area. One of the gentlemen said, "We saw your dog take off. We watched it run across Center Avenue! We were so scared it would be hit by a car." My fury immediately turned into terror. Center Avenue had eight lanes of traffic in front of a busy mall! *Apollo is heading north . . . that's where home is, to the north.*

I raced across Center Avenue and into the mall parking lot. Running up to people, I asked them if they had seen a dog. They would say, "Yes, he ran by about ten minutes ago." Apollo didn't even have any identification on him anymore. My mind was racing. *What if someone finds Apollo and ties him up again?* I felt like I was going to be sick. I kept running, screaming Apollo's name. My lungs were on fire.

A truck pulled up next to me. It was the people I had approached and spoken to in the mall's parking lot. They asked me if I wanted some help.

"Yes, thank you!" I answered through my tears. "He doesn't have any identification on him." The kind people drove up and down the streets while we all looked for Apollo. After thirty minutes, I finally had them take me back to my truck at the care center.

I called Curtis first. *He's the power that can make things happen.* I began to sob as I told him about Apollo. Curtis told me to calm down and said he would immediately put a $1K reward on Facebook. Then he told me to call the animal shelters.

After I called the animal shelters, I called Keith to tell him what had happened. "They arrested you?" Keith answered, baffled. That part of the story didn't even bother me. *Fuck getting arrested, my baby is missing!* I ignored his question. My mind was racing . . . *what's my next move?*

Keith was the love of my life, but he didn't understand my attachment to Apollo—not like Curtis did. I wasn't in the frame of mind to be barking orders at my husband. I got off the phone, so I could think. *Someone in this area has to have seen Apollo.*

I pulled into a Walmart. Running as fast as I could, I bought five dry-erase black markers.

Then I wrote all over Keith's white truck:

MY DOG APOLLO IS LOST WITH NO IDENTIFICATION HE IS A ROTTWEILER/HEELER MIX, and my phone number.

I scribbled it out on both sides and the tailgate in big, bold letters. I should have added Curtis's reward–but it never crossed my mind in my panicked state. Sobbing, I slowly drove up the main street and back and forth on the side streets. My heart sank deeper with every minute that passed.

An hour later, I pulled into a park and got out of the truck. I needed to ensure I had written my message bold enough to read from a distance. A kind man in his early twenties approached me amidst my frantic scribbling. He told me how sorry he was and said that he and his friends would keep a lookout for Apollo.

I put my hand over my mouth to try and control my sobbing and nodded at him. Then he asked me, "Do you need a hug?"

"Yes," I choked through my sobs. I was crying so hard my whole body was convulsing. The young man kept saying, "It'll be okay, it'll be okay," through his own tears. I thanked him and got back in the truck. *There's no time to waste!*

I looked for Apollo for the next four hours. I also put my jacket under my mother's window at the care center. A friend once told me she lost her dog while on a cattle drive; she called out for him for hours and finally had to get to her destination with the cattle. She put her jacket on a nearby bridge before leaving the area. After a sleepless night of crying, she returned to the bridge the following morning to find her dog sitting on her jacket.

Maybe this would work with Apollo—perhaps he would return to where he last saw me and stay by my jacket. I became increasingly devastated as every hour passed in my unfolding nightmare.

A blocked number had called me shortly after I began looking for Apollo. I didn't pick up, but when I listened to the message, it was one of the asshole officers telling me I had not signed my arrest warrant and needed to come into the police station to sign it. "Fuck that!" and "Fuck you guys!" I screamed after I had listened to their message.

A blocked number had called me several times now. When I answered their call this time, the police officer repeated his request. I screamed, "I'm a little busy right now! I'm still looking for my dog!"

The policeman answered matter-of-factly, "They found your dog. It's at the Lakeside Animal Shelter."

I was beyond livid. *What the fuck?* "Why didn't you guys tell me?" I asked in disbelief.

The police officer piped up, "We saw you running up and down State Street, but we were busy." It was the officer's way of adding a little *fuck you!* I hung up on him.

That asshole really said that to me—I'm not even kidding.

I cried out to my Creator, "Thank you, thank you, thank you, thank you," the entire way to the shelter. It was twenty miles from my mother's care center. I hadn't even thought to call the Lakeside Shelter because it was so far away. I had no idea how far Apollo ran before he couldn't run anymore and allowed someone to pick him up.

Once I arrived and identified Apollo, they kept him in the kennel and made me return to the lobby and fill out paperwork. My sweet pup hadn't had a rabies shot within the last year, so they required me to pay for it and let them give him a rabies shot before they would release him.

I could have strangled every person in the shelter by the time they finally brought my baby out to me. When Apollo came out, he was quiet–he didn't jump all over me like I thought he would. I was desperately trying to read him. *Does he think I abandoned him? Does he think he's in trouble?* I just hugged Apollo and cried, "I'm so sorry!" over and over.

When Apollo and I got home, I fed him his dinner and prepared his nightly bedtime ritual of one percent warm milk with a bit of monk fruit. After he drank his milk, I laid on my bed with him–yes, Apollo snuggled with me on my bed whenever he wanted to. It didn't matter that he also had a big dog bed . . . lined with another memory foam dog pad inside of that one. And a Minky Couture blanket to snuggle with. I kept his bed right next to my side of the bed; this way, I could reach down and pet him whenever he was having a bad dream.

Now, snuggling together on our bed, Keith was home, and we loved on Apollo and scratched his neck, telling him how much we loved him. Finally, he made the little baby snort sounds he makes when I give him a rub down every night. I couldn't even imagine what I would have turned into if a car had hit Apollo that day. He literally didn't move the next day. He had pushed his body to the limit, running toward home.

Satan banned me from ever coming to see my mother again. One thing this incident did was force me to look outside the box. After researching, I discovered several skilled nursing care centers in the area that would be suitable to care for Mom.

Another thing the incident did was instigate a phone call from Kathryn–my mother's roommate. She told me they had been giving Mom a benzodiazepine twice a day. Kathryn knew precisely what the drug was because they gave her the same thing.

I also learned that Kathryn had seizures; she was in the nursing center due to having no family. I had never wanted to ask because I didn't want to seem nosy or impolite. She told me it was an entire month after she arrived at the nursing center and had already been through two horrific seizures–where my mother would scream for help, and nobody would come–before a nurse came in and threw down a thin foam pad on the floor. "We heard you're a seizure risk," she said.

Kathryn also told me my mom would scream with horrific, violent hallucinations during the night, and no one ever came. She said no one ever came when my mother needed to be changed. I couldn't take what I was hearing. *My mother is in a real, live house of horrors!*

I found a new skilled nursing center right away, but it was two weeks before they had processed my mother's paperwork, and Satan's *evil doctor* signed my mother's release forms so we could finally have her transferred.

Satan informed my brother Kyle that Medicare would not pay for the transfer. We would have to cover that ourselves. *Who gives a shit? Just get our mother the hell out of there!* Satan also lied to Kyle, telling him I had stuck my finger in his face the day I was arrested and refused to leave. I hadn't seen that little chicken-shit since my visit with Chance. But hey, if you're already illegally drugging an entire care center, what's one more lie?

After my haunting call with Kathryn, Curtis got in touch with the federal and then the state agency for reporting elder abuse. I filed a report and told them my story. This action brought forth a full investigation of Satan's house of horrors.

The woman I gave my report to thanked me for coming forward, stating that usually, people choose to be silent when things like this happen. That was beyond my comprehension. She also told me their agency would not be able to tell me the outcome of their investigation.

"Why not?" I asked. *I want this to be on the news! I want the world to know what Satan has done!* How many elderly people had they been over-drugging? Creating a living hell for the helpless, vulnerable people in their care?

"We're not permitted to share the findings of an internal investigation," she answered.

When I finally saw my mother again at the new nursing facility, she told me she had been "shaking like a leaf" before they moved her. After seeing her transfer sheet, I knew why. They had been detoxing the medication out of her system *before* they transferred her.

The reason my mother had quit slurring her words so much was not because they had stopped over-medicating her; it was because she was building up a tolerance! Those bastards didn't even wean her off that sick drug; they just stopped giving all but one milligram to her.

The nurse at the new facility showed me my mother's med sheet that had been sent over with her. Satan's lying-ass doctor had prescribed Mom two milligrams of the benzodiazepine twice daily. The week we informed the doctor of Mom's transfer, he had switched it to one milligram once a day before bedtime. He had also written, "She does very well on this."

As I stared at the report in disbelief, I finally demanded, "Cross that out!" while trying to maintain my composure. "My mother has never been on benzodiazepine drugs . . . that shit has caused horrific nightmares and violent hallucinations! Cross that out!" The infuriating reality of what the previous center had done to Mom (even on her way out) felt like I had been punched in the gut.

The nurse searched my face with a disturbed look. Then she took her pen and scribbled through the notation, writing Discontinue Immediately underneath. I could have hugged her.

I was so hopeful my mother was going to have a full recovery. The staff was kind and took the time to speak with me and answer any questions whenever I came in. I knew she was in good hands.

But my heart was broken the next time I visited. As I sat beside Mom on her bed, she asked if my father was still alive. I softly told her no and wiped her tears as she heard the news. Realization hit me. *I will never have my mother back again.* Rita and I fully believed that our mother's dementia was brought on by the heavy doses of the benzodiazepine that Satan's facility had given her.

Ten weeks later, I spoke with my mother for the last time. We were having a pleasant visit–nothing was out of the ordinary. Then she said, "I don't think Ramona thinks I was a very good mother." Although my mother's violent hallucinations had gone away when they quit overdosing her with drugs, the dementia she now had often caused sad or negative thoughts.

Oh, Momma, you don't know who I am today. She would recognize me on some visits we had–and on other visits, she wouldn't.

I smiled as I took hold of her hand, "Of course you were a good mother," I said. I meant every word.

Mom shook her head in protest of my comment. Clearly, this painful thought had her in a distressed state. I kissed her hand and sat on the edge of the bed.

I looked into my mother's eyes. "Mom, I just spoke with Ramona this morning. She told me you were a wonderful mother! She said she loves you so much!" I cried, smiling at my wonderful news.

Her eyes widened. "She said that?" she asked, surprised.

"Yes," I confirmed. "Those were her *exact words*."

The happy, peaceful look on Mom's face was such a gift. I reveled in the moment where things could be okay–if only for now. I had no idea that would be our last conversation together.

Two days later, my mother developed a staph infection that took her life four days after that. I never saw my mother conscious again.

Rita was with her when she passed. Mom was finally free. I had the privilege to speak at her funeral and tell all her loved ones what a blessing she had been in my life.

A few weeks after Mom passed, I was sitting in church and received a text from the nice man in the park who had given me a hug the day I lost Apollo.

The text said: This is the man you talked to in the park. I gave you a hug :) Did you ever find your dog?

I answered: Yes! Thank you so much! You are such a good person! If you ever find yourself in a bind, please keep my number. I'll be there for you. God bless you!

Now, I know what you're thinking . . . for my dear readers whose jaws dropped when I said, "I was sitting in church." *Yes, I still go to church.* Close your mouth, and I promise we'll talk more about that later.

Warrior Wisdom:

I'm so very grateful for the imperfect mother I was blessed with. She was perfect for me–giving the best she had to give every day. I am who I am because of the mother who raised me. I know I will see her again.

I once attended a training called The Hoffman Process. I was asked to write a hate letter to my mother. This letter was for my eyes only. My gut reaction was, "Why on earth would I ever want to do that?" And this letter had to be at least thirteen pages long! After ninety minutes, I had only been able to write a page and a half.

The facilitator told me to keep at it. As I pondered over what the hell I could write, I began adding to my letter. Then, something completely unexpected happened; a rage inside me was literally unleashed. I began to sob as I wrote furiously. Fifteen pages later, I was finally finished. I had pulled up all the little beliefs I had stored away–and viciously spit them out on paper with no mercy. These were beliefs I wasn't even aware I was holding, hidden deep in the cells of my unconscious.

As I tore up and buried the letter in a ceremony that evening, I felt closer to my mother than I ever had–with a peaceful understanding of what life must have been like for her. After writing the first letter, I was also asked to write a love letter to my mother that I could keep.

My love for my mother allowed me to reconcile all the things that had come up in my other letter and reflect on what life must have been like for her. As I sat by myself under a tree and wrote, it was like pieces of a puzzle all coming together. My mother had my forgiveness, empathy, compassion, and a more profound love than I had ever felt toward her. This exercise was so powerful! I learned that understanding is the door to freedom from painful thoughts.

The situation surrounding the care center affirmed a critical truth: Never be afraid to question authority. Satan, his evil doctor, and the nurses who blindly followed orders seriously harmed the vulnerable people they were supposed to protect. If something feels wrong or off to you, take that as an invitation to discover why you are experiencing that particular feeling. You are feeling that way for a reason! Yes, it could be a hundred different things, but love yourself and those around you enough to find out.

I learned (through my mother's roommate Kathryn) that Satan, the evil doctor, and several head nurses were fired. I would imagine they're all in a bit of a pickle. Case #126473 via Elderly Protective Services.

The criminal trespassing charges against me were dropped. However, the "upstanding police officers" still charged me with resisting arrest. I was ordered to pay a fine and take an online Critical Thinking Class. As I took the class that day, I appreciated the valuable information that was shared. I found peace in knowing that I wouldn't take back a single second I had with my sweet mom. I smiled as gratitude filled my soul for the mother who had allowed me to become the fearless little hoodlum that I am.

That being said, there's an important lesson I can share from my experience of getting arrested: I realized (after the fact, of course) that if I could have shown more respect to the police officers when they first arrived, perhaps they might have shown me more respect in return. The people who succeed in this life don't magically experience only good things. They have simply mastered the ability to adapt to, and ultimately gain, the upper hand in any given situation.

Every person on this planet has the ability to be an asshole . . . or an angel. I can tell you through personal experience, life is so much easier when I succeed in bringing out the angel.

CHAPTER 25

Say That Again?

"**W**hat the hell?"

Sitting across the table from Rita at the Olive Garden restaurant, I listened in shock as my fifty-eight-year-old sister told me that her kidneys were failing.

"I'm going to begin dialysis immediately, and they have put me on the list for a kidney transplant," she said. Her voice was so matter-of-fact it took a couple seconds to sink in.

I couldn't believe what I was hearing . . . *You're only five years older than me! Dialysis?* I knew she had contracted a severe virus in 2020 and had been hospitalized for a few days, but she had completely recovered . . . or so we thought.

Rita sighed and took a drink from her stemmed water glass. "I've been out of the hospital for eight months but suddenly discovered I have seventeen kidney stones!" She shook her head, her green eyes looking at me with an expression I did not recognize in my sister. It was fear–that she was trying to mask with a brave determination.

My beautiful sister brushed a strand of dark hair away from her face and continued. "After what we've been through with Mom, I did my research! I learned kidney problems can happen with one particular antiviral drug the hospitals have been using. So I called and asked the hospital if they had given it to me during my stay. They denied it. But after doing a little more research, I found out this was the standard protocol for *all* hospitals."

I just stared at her, still stunned. Driving home that day, I had a sick feeling in the pit of my stomach. When I got home, I Googled "dialysis." In everything I read, I learned how incredibly hard dialysis is on the body; it basically has to purify your blood every day because your kidneys no longer perform that function.

The only other remedy is having a kidney transplant. The average wait time for people who need a kidney if they don't have a family member who's a match and willing to give one of theirs is five to seven years. My heart wept for my dear sister. Her life was going to be so hard.

I wiped away my tears and Googled "kidney donors" next. Then I discovered something astounding–donating a kidney didn't shorten a person's life by even five minutes! I also learned a person would not be considered for donation unless they were in a healthy state.

Sitting on my bed with Apollo next to me, I unconsciously stroked his back as I absorbed the information I now had. I knew I needed to do everything I could to help Rita. She would have been the first one there for me if the roles were reversed. *I* was the one who had abused my body with drugs and alcohol–not Rita. She had worked her entire adult life to try and be healthy and fit–it didn't seem fair.

Thinking about what I was about to do, my body felt like I was on a roller coaster going straight down at one hundred miles an hour. I picked up my phone and called my sister.

"Hello?"

"We need to see if I'm a match, Rita," I insisted as soon as she answered her phone.

Rita began to cry. "Are you sure you want to do that?" she asked.

"Of course, I'm sure. There's nothing to think about . . . you're my sister–I love you!" My emotions took over as my eyes filled with tears. Breathing through my tears *and* my fear, I added, "It's going to be okay, Rita. We've got this!"

I thought, *If I'm a match, this is meant to be.*

A week later, Rita called me while I was walking with Apollo in the fresh morning air. She told me she had learned about a donor program where they could match you up with another family to do a trade if you're not a match with your loved one. I could still give a kidney on her behalf, and she would receive a kidney from someone else doing the same thing, creating a win-win. As I digested what my sister had just said, the roller coaster was back. This time, it was even more intense, to the point that I actually felt nauseous. *This is real now!*

Determined, I dug my heels in and replied, "That's awesome! Let's fuckin' do this!" And I meant it with my whole heart and soul.

Something happened to me at that moment. Pushing through my intense fear and choosing "all in" to save my sister released a massive shift inside my body. The nausea and the fear were all gone now. It was replaced with overwhelming empowerment, unlike anything I had ever felt. To say it felt euphoric would be an understatement.

But the real miracle came the next day when I realized something pro-found; the internal argument regarding alcohol, which was always present in my head, was gone. Gone! In wonder, I went through my usual routine with Keith, reveling in the gratitude and wondering when I'd come back down and feel that consistent desire to drink. But the relief didn't stop. It continued. In fact, it was as if I had never drunk in the first place. I couldn't remember the last time I had felt so free!

I never had the urge to take another drink again. It wasn't even a conscious thought, or any kind of tug on my body. The addiction I had struggled with for twenty years was no longer an issue, and I continued to marvel. It was as if I'd turned back time, and the compulsion never existed.

Day after day, I woke up the same way. It was like going from a life of black and white to living, glorious color. I realized I was now navigating through life in a completely different version of myself. Keith noticed my huge, unexpected change within a few days. I was on fire; nothing could dampen my mood or bring me down. My sweetheart kept grinning at me, enthusiastically praising me for the transition he was seeing. Even Curtis noticed. He asked me how I was feeling to prompt an explanation for the crazy joy and lightness that both he and Keith were witnessing.

"It's the weirdest thing, you guys," I said as the three of us sat in the kitchen. "I don't even think about alcohol anymore. It's a non-issue. How crazy is that?" They both looked at me in silence. As the weight of what I had just said settled, I was touched when Curtis's eyes teared up. Keith, being allergic to any form of tears (even tears of joy), piped up, "That's awesome, baby!" He came over and gave me a big bear hug while plastering kisses all over my neck.

I started walking three miles and then five miles on my treadmill daily. Walking . . . not running. I'm not a runner–I couldn't run if something was chasing me! But oh, to feel strong in my body was marvelous. I also began to pay attention to everything I put into my mouth, choosing only nutrient-rich food. I felt like a mighty warrior with wings!

My everyday life was more and more a miracle.

When I decided to sacrifice for my sister, I realized an energy showed up for me, unlike anything I had ever experienced. I had been through so many shitshows with alcohol, with that ever-present internal argument in my mind. I'd always needed it to cope when stress came into my life. Or, just the flat-out thirst for alcohol when my life was wonderful.

Within a week, I began journaling every day again; this time my mind was very clear, and strong! Because of my journaling and what I was journaling, I came across an audiobook that expanded what I knew yet again. It was called *Identity Shift*, by Anthony Trucks. Anthony's explanation of identity shift and identity loss was spot-on genius. And for myself? I was definitely having an identity shift!

I am no longer The Alcoholic. I am Ramona, the Winged Warrior.

Next to my husband Keith, Curtis was the closest friendship I had ever known. He had been my mentor since the day I met him. Through my identity shift, I came to know another truth; I did not need Curtis's approval or his validation. For the first time in well over a decade, I felt the power of standing on my own two feet.

The state of being I found myself in was extraordinary. I suddenly understood Keith's frame of mind perfectly–like anything was within my reach.

I found out that I *was* a close enough match with Rita. Before I could get too excited, the doctor told me, "Your kidneys are nothing to write home about, but you're still in the game." That line may have offended some people, but I didn't care. I was over the moon at the news. As I told Rita, she again expressed her gratitude.

"I'm the one who is so incredibly grateful, Rita. You brought about a true miracle." I went on to tell her how my addiction had vanished, and we both cried with gratitude.

The last step was going in for an interview with several of the doctors to be assessed for "mental stability." They needed to know whether I was sane or not. The whole concept made me chuckle. *Clearly, I'm not sane–but what has that got to do with it?*

I walked into a large boardroom, where four professionals were my jury. I shared my experience of having my addiction lifted in front of this board of directors.

As I saw their concerned looks, I instantly regretted sharing that little piece of information. I was still marveling over what had happened to me. A doctor came forward and shared his concern about relapsing after I donated.

This procedure would be very difficult to go through physically and mentally. They all agreed unanimously.

Then, another doctor made a suggestion. She seemed the most relatable of the four doctors in the room. She had kind, understanding eyes. "Why don't we give it nine more months? This would put a year of sobriety behind you. It will give you time to increase your stability before donating a kidney." Her request seemed reasonable.

"I completely understand your point. But have you *ever* had a patient tell you they have experienced what I have?" Reiterating my miracle felt vital to me. I wanted just as much information from them as they wanted from me.

The doctor—who was by far the oldest in the group, replied with raised eyebrows, "To be quite honest, alcoholics don't usually want to donate a kidney."

I chuckled. "Mea culpa," I said, shrugging my shoulders. "But I *do* want to give a kidney, and this *was* my experience."

The doctor—whom I labeled a "newbie" within the board, suggested I join an AA group to stay strong. *Argh! You definitely aren't getting it. How could you? You've never been an alcoholic—or alleviated from it miraculously.*

"Here's the problem I have with that," I began to explain. "My addiction is gone. I don't want to go into a program that will reinforce my identity of being an alcoholic. I plan on continuing to live my life, getting stronger every single day. If I focus on alcohol (either drinking it or not drinking it), that will be my experience for coping. By the grace of God, I no longer have that internal argument going on in my head. Alcohol in my world doesn't exist anymore. I'll even go as far as saying that I've discovered an *addiction hack* if you will."

He gave me a long, thoughtful look. "At least agree to come in for blood tests whenever we request," he said.

"I think that's a great idea!" I answered, allowing my enthusiasm to spill out all over them. I went home and called Rita to tell her the plan. My dear, sweet sister was so understanding.

"We'll do it together. We can get healthier and stronger every day–together," she said.

"Fuckin A!" I agreed.

Rita hadn't let dialysis slow her down one bit. She had just returned from Vegas, where she had performed with her bagpipe band. She had opted to drive so she could cart her dialysis machine with her to use every night. She needed to keep her strength up because they would be performing in Normandy for the eightieth anniversary of D-day.

As I braved ahead, my little miracle couldn't have come at a better time. Keith's heart disease was progressing, though you never would have guessed it. He was either golfing, riding his dirt bike, or gardening daily. He was addicted to life. The old Ramona would have freaked out and done everything she could to numb out to the situation.

But my new superpower had left me in a state of mind where I could handle everything that came my way. I woke up each morning feeling such extreme gratitude–and it humbled me to my knees. I kept working out. I kept eating healthy. I kept enjoying every moment I had with Keith. I was present. I was joyful. I had purpose.

Thanks to the miracles and my grateful acknowledgment of them, I was now navigating through life in a different, fully elevated version of myself. Every morning, I woke up to an extraordinary life. Keith had seventeen stents in his heart, with only one of his stents that wasn't completely occluded. His heart had become inoperable, and my husband was placed on a heart transplant list. Even this news wasn't too much for me to handle. Everything, every moment, became so much sweeter with my lover and best friend.

When the doctors gave us an update on Keith's condition, Keith told everyone, "Good news! I don't have to have any more stents!" We weren't going to waste one day of this treasure we called life. I'd never experienced a person with more excitement and gratitude for daily life than my incredible husband. And now, after experiencing my own miracle, he and I were operating on the same wavelength of joy.

Keith's doctor spoke to us at one of his monthly appointments regarding his daily activities and learned that Keith had just returned from snowmobiling.

The doctor shook his head. "Keith, I don't even want you driving . . . let alone snowmobiling!"

Keith calmly answered, "I'd rather be dead, brother." His greatest fear was having to spend his last days or even minutes sitting down–let alone being stuck in a bed. If anything, Keith ramped up his need for unbridled joy on a daily basis. I had never felt a deeper love for my beloved husband, and I reveled in his exuberance of life.

Warrior Wisdom:

By the grace of God, when I made the decision and commitment to sacrifice a part of me for the life of another, my addiction was lifted. It's as simple as that. There was definitely a Higher Power in play. Miracles can happen, because one happened to me. I know how real the disease of alcoholism is. I struggled with it for over twenty years. I would never, ever say something that made light of any addiction or disorder.

As one of my mandatory tests, I was required to have a colonoscopy. They removed two pre-cancerous polyps. I would have never gone in for a colonoscopy in a million years; it just wasn't on my radar. The doctor told me ninety-eight percent of colon cancer can be prevented with regularly scheduled colonoscopies every ten years. Easy peasy. Put this on your radar, my dear readers.

They say "hindsight is 20/20." That cliche couldn't be any truer. My life at that time was unfolding in Divine Order. I was going to have to be stronger than I ever imagined.

Life can be so much kinder when we recognize the value of our trials. We can feel gratitude for the strength we have acquired rather than being a victim of our circumstances. Then, we can find the empowered state within ourselves to love and empower others.

When we look back on our life, I think we can all identify moments in time when we've had to face a challenge that made us stronger. Where we were forced to flex everything we had to survive. And more importantly, where (in retrospect) that newfound strength showed up to benefit us in our time of need.

As Rachel Hollis once said, "Life isn't happening to us, it's happening for us."

CHAPTER 26

Oh Sweetheart . . .

In 2022, on Mother's Day, I gave Keith a kiss goodbye as my beautiful, active man left on his motorcycle to take a ride for a few hours on one of the nearby mountains. We were spending the day at one of Curtis's homes in a beautiful canyon. All of my children and some of their in-laws were there for the holiday.

Keith drove his motorcycle up to about 8,000 feet and then stopped to call me. He called my cell phone, despite knowing I didn't have cell service at the house, so he could leave me a voicemail–something he loved to do. Then he called the landline so we could talk. He told me what an incredible ride he was having (in my honor since it was Mother's Day) and how beautiful everything was. It made my heart smile to talk with him and hear that he was having such a good time.

Never being one to stay on the trail, Keith got his motorcycle stuck in a deep snowdrift about an hour later. He called me on the landline a few more times while he was trying to dig his bike out. About 6:30 p.m., I started to panic and told him to forget the bike and start walking out. Keith let me know it had started snowing, but he was fine. My thoughts went to what I had seen him wearing when he left–a long-sleeved riding shirt and breastplate with riding gloves. *Oh, babe . . . you've got to be freezing!*

Everyone but Conner had already gone home. I called 9-1-1 and gave them Keith's coordinates. Search and Rescue were immediately dispatched. An hour later, my twenty-six-year-old Conner grabbed his jacket and a big trash bag.

"I'm going to go look for him, Mom," he announced with certainty. He wasn't interested in my response if I planned on arguing with him. He cut holes in the top and sides of the trash bag so he could slip it on to keep him dry. Then he grabbed a blanket off one of the beds, a lighter, stuffed a couple of newspapers in his shirt, and headed out toward Keith's location.

I received a call from Conner twenty minutes later, telling me he had just spoken with Keith over the phone. Keith had mentioned to Conner that he was "actually pretty warm now." Hearing this news, Conner floored his truck–knowing that hypothermia must be setting in.

I spoke with my husband once more after that, and then his phone died.

About an hour later, the Search and Rescue coordinator called me. He told me a complete white-out had settled in on the mountain, making it almost zero visibility. He had sent out twenty-five trained men to look for Keith. I couldn't believe it; there wasn't even a hint of snow at the house we were in, just one mountain over. *This is May, for hell's sake!*

As the news sunk in, my heart dropped to the floor. "My son is out there looking for him," I choked.

The coordinator yelled, "You need to get on the phone with your son right now and tell him to get off the mountain! We don't want this getting any more serious than it already is!"

"I will, I will!" I whimpered. My state of panic went to a level I didn't know existed. I couldn't even take a deep breath.

When Conner answered his phone, I thanked God to the depths of my soul to hear his voice. "Conner! You need to get off that mountain right now! Twenty-five men are up there looking for Keith; you are not dressed warm enough to be up there. Please! Come back right now!"

Conner was shivering so hard I could barely understand the slew of curse words he was shouting in frustration. Two hours later, when Conner came through the door, the broken-hearted look on his face was indescribable. I grabbed him and hugged him as we both sobbed.

As the evening inched by, I wanted to be alone. I felt like there was a ticking time bomb inside my chest. Conner wouldn't leave me but went down the hall into the master bedroom.

I sat alone in the kitchen at the house, paralyzed with fear as I waited for another phone call. *It's almost midnight . . . why can't they find him?* Sitting with my hands locked together and pressed against my lips, I wouldn't allow myself to think or reason about the probability of the outcome.

Then, out of nowhere, the most comforting and peaceful feeling washed over me and through me . . . lingering. To my surprise, I found my panic and terror were gone. I could breathe again. I sat with this new feeling for several seconds as a loving "knowing" came into my thoughts . . .

Oh, sweetheart. And I knew that my Keith had gone home. It was the most tender, surreal moment of my life.

A second team on horseback and two helicopters started the search again at first light. They found Keith's body at noon that day, sitting up against a tree. The autopsy said the primary cause of death was exposure, and the secondary was cardiac arrest. Meaning, when Keith's body began to shut down due to hypothermia, his heart condition put him into cardiac arrest.

His official death was listed as May 9 because that's when they found him. But I knew it was on May 8. By the grace of God, I had been comforted since 11:30 the night before when I felt Keith leave this earth. My beloved husband was really gone.

Keith's death left everyone in such a state of shock; he had truly touched the lives of everyone he knew. I decided to speak at his funeral. That morning, I prayed that I would have the same comfort and peace I had felt the night of his death so I could honor my sweetheart by sharing how very important he had been in my life.

In the days, weeks, and months that followed, I had to learn an entirely new level of self-care. At first, I tried to be brave by facing each new day via mechanically going through the motions of my usual activities. As every hour passed, however, I would become increasingly nauseous. Finally, I would be sick, violently retching in the bathroom. Retreating from everyone, I would break down and wail until no more tears were left. And then it would begin all over again.

As time passed, I began to feel more and more frail. I finally decided that whenever the wave of extreme sadness came out of nowhere, I would let my tears flow freely without trying to hold them back–no matter where I was. This was so much kinder to my body and psyche–and right away, my nausea stopped.

I came to terms with the fact that I couldn't handle crowds or even noise– so I didn't. I spent a lot of time alone with Apollo because that gave me the most comfort. My sweet pup had sensed my pain from the very beginning, and slept next to me ever since.

A couple months after Keith's death, I confided in Curtis about how incredibly hard it was becoming to carry my grief. It was like a heavy, painful weight . . . one I couldn't put down. Never having even one minute of relief, I was beginning to question how much longer I could handle what I was experiencing. We were both struggling; when Keith died, Curtis posted to the world that he had lost his best friend.

After confiding in Curtis, within three days, he had gathered knowledge from people he knew worldwide and offered me some help. I began IV ketamine therapy. This literally saved me. From my very first treatment, I woke up the next day feeling peaceful. Slowly but surely, the debilitating weight decreased until it was gone. And I continued to not need alcohol or even want it.

Whenever I started feeling really sorry for myself, I could hear Keith's playful voice laughing, "Oh, brother!" It's something he would say whenever he thought I was being ridiculous. And then I got to remind myself that Keith taught us all how to live–I couldn't let this beautiful gift he gave us be in vain. The best way I could honor my beloved husband was to live a life that would make him proud.

I put my daily mantra on Curtis's fridge in the main house.

It reads:

What would Keith do? What will make today extraordinary?

Today is all we have . . . make it count!

Keith left such a legacy . . . I know he will never be forgotten.

Warrior Wisdom:

I'm so incredibly sad when I think about having to finish this life without my Keith. But I'm so grateful I met him when I did! I'll be reunited with my sweetheart again someday–and then we'll have forever.

Today, when I think of my beloved husband, I picture him riding the most perfect wave, climbing the most beautiful mountain, skiing the most glorious slopes, and smiling down on me.

I've experienced some painful times in my life. But everyone *has experienced painful times–that's just life. We are all capable of being our own guru. We are all capable of navigating through the challenges that come up for us.*

My only advice to anyone mourning the loss of a loved one is do what works for you. We are all different. No one has the right to tell you what you should or shouldn't be doing if you haven't sought out their advice. You know what you need during this time more than anyone else. You know what loving self-care is . . . and what it isn't.

Losing Keith changed me in a profound way. I found myself having compassion and tolerance for everyone, no matter what the circumstance. You never know what's going on in the life of another. Driving home the day they discovered Keith's body, a truck sped around me, and the driver flipped me off. I'm sure I was going slower than I would normally drive.

I was too numb to care at the time, but I have never forgotten that lesson. Thinking back on that day, and the numerous times I have been rude or impatient with other drivers, it humbled me in an instant. I no longer feel the need to judge when someone isn't driving the way "I think" they should be driving. They could very well be navigating through some rough roads in their own lives.

Regarding ketamine therapy, there are many things to know and understand. Go to <u>https://insightfamilypractice.com</u> and learn how it works by *interrupting communication between neurons in the brain and the spinal cord, allowing the central nervous system to reset.*

I share my ketamine experience with you, my dear reader, because it changed my life. The self-love and peace I have acquired is mind-boggling. I still go in once a month to this day. In case you haven't noticed this about me . . . I have no secrets. If something works for me, you can bet your ass I'm going to blab it to the entire planet!

My number one priority has become joy and happiness. I've found this through self-care and showing the utmost kindness to every person I come across. My husband gave me a wonderful example of doing just that. Keith's joy was being out in nature. My joy is my grandchildren, children, work, and Apollo. My inner circle is very small. When you follow your bliss, whatever it is, it's so much easier to be strong.

CHAPTER 27

Gratitude and Grace

L ife went on, and I was focusing on my health. I needed to be as strong and healthy as possible; I was going to be there for my sister. Rita was going to get my kidney and get her life back.

When she called me one night, I picked up, assuming it was one of our normal, sisterly check-ins. I loved the relationship I now had with my sister. But that evening was anything but normal. Rita was on her way to the hospital.

I listened intently as she told me a young man had been killed in an accident that day. This man was listed as a doner, and he matched Rita on a cellular level–an even better match than mine! She had been given forty-five minutes to arrive at the hospital and receive his kidney.

As her husband drove her, we both wept for the young man who had lost his life, and in turn, given Rita hope for her life to continue.

That evening, I was filled with dichotomous emotion: being so grateful my dear sister would receive a kidney with such a high probability of being successful, and at the same time, feeling seriously let down. Committing to give a kidney had taken more courage than I ever knew I had. And the miracles that followed had changed my life. Even with Keith's death, the urge to drink had never returned. So why had it ended *this* way? It didn't make any sense. The doctor had told me it was good that we were a match because no hospital would have taken my kidney on a trade.

As I thought about everything, I felt a panic settle in. *Will I get to keep my miracle? Oh God . . . please, please don't take this freedom away!* I felt so incredibly humbled in that moment. That's when I knew. I would not, could not, keep these miracles all to myself. This had all taken place for a reason, and I wasn't going to let any of it be in vain.

I was beyond relieved when I learned that Rita's surgery was successful. After she was strong enough, I spoke with her on the phone, and we marveled at the course of events that had come to pass.

"Isn't it funny, Rita?" I mused. "You still saved me."

"I'll never forget that you were willing to do this for me, Ramona," Rita replied with emotion in her voice.

"I feel like this was a test, Rita. I was given an opportunity to make a sacrifice for you. And when I accepted that sacrifice, I was given the most wonderful miracle I could have ever imagined!" I cried. "I think I'm going to write a book. I'll just tell everyone, 'if you have an addiction, donate a kidney!'" I laughed through my tears, totally joking, of course.

"Fuckin' A!" Rita laughed. It was probably the pain meds talking, but that was the first time I had ever heard a single swear word come out of my sister's mouth.

Speaking of who curses and who doesn't in my life . . . let's address the elephant in the room that I promised to discuss. "Why on earth," you may have been asking yourself, "does a potty-mouthed woman like this still go to church?" That's a very fair question.

I started going to church because I love Keith's mother dearly, and it gave her comfort. And supporting my sweet mother-in-law brought me joy. I have continued going to church because it now gives me comfort as well. I discovered there are good, kind people in the congregation, and it feels nice to connect with other people in my area. No one has an agenda; they just offer their support and love. And to be clear, my miracle with my addiction was between me and God. Religion had nothing to do with it.

Curtis asked me once, "So, are you going to keep going to church?" I smiled at his curious comment.

"Yeah, I am. It gives me peace. I'm actually not even breaking the rules anymore . . . now that I quit drinking and popping pills–except for my potty mouth. That's pretty fuckin' cool when you think about it," I said with a wink.

"God help them!" he replied with a laugh. "Just try not to lead anyone astray."

"Maybe you should come with me. I could bring a fire extinguisher the first time you walk through the chapel doors–just in case," I joked.

Curtis raised his eyebrows. "Are you sure you're not still on drugs?" he answered, his voice dripping with sarcasm.

"Never mind, we wouldn't want to cause an uproar. You would just be hitting on all the women," I quipped. The things I could say (and get away with) as Curtis's friend were one of my true pleasures in life. There was no end to the sarcasm we dished out to one another.

Attending church was completely different now. I was living a life of integrity for my best self. And not one bit of it had to do with the wonderful X-Factor faith. Is this faith true? Absolutely. It's absolutely true for millions of people, just as millions of others choose different religions that are true for them. We all get to choose the experiences that resonate with who we are as individuals. And we all get to be right without telling anyone else that their "right" is "wrong."

Do I think *anyone* will be judged for "not" choosing a particular religion in their life? No, I do not. If you are joyous with the life experience you have chosen to live, that's wonderful! Keep doing that! I believe our higher power wants us to be happy. If you choose to suffer in oppression with rules or practices that do not resonate with who you are, at the end of your life, you will have suffered in oppression.

I'm happy sharing my beliefs because they're mine–and mine alone. You get to have your own beliefs, and I respect that one hundred percent. I personally believe that when I die, I will be received with nothing but love and honor. And I believe the same is true for the people who have lived under every rule they deemed necessary to follow.

If we come to a point in our lives where we discover the beliefs we have held no longer serve us, we can peacefully let them go and feel gratitude for the experience. We don't have to feel resentment or judgment . . . *unless we choose to.*

I found freedom in recognizing the value of my *own* path. I made amends with the people I injured. I asked for their forgiveness, and they forgave me. Making peace and also forgiving myself was every bit as important. In doing so, my heart and conscience felt right again.

In writing this book, many close family members and friends had no idea about any of the details in these chapters; this is so true for many people with an addiction. We can create two versions of ourselves in our suffering. The choice to own all of these parts of my journey in black and white was a huge breakthrough.

If I have learned anything through my life of fairytales and street fights, it's grace. Grace will put us on the road to understanding and compassion; it's what allows us to be okay when our life doesn't take the path we thought it should.

Life is always changing and evolving, and we are the directors of this incredible experience. What an amazing gift we have been given as human beings on this earth.

Keith's beautiful voicemail that he left me within five hours of his death will always be with me, giving me the priceless reminder that he sought out joy until the last day of his life:

"Hey baby! Happy Mother's Day! I'm having the *best ride* . . . in your honor. It's beautiful up here! You should see how green everything is. I can see the whole valley . . . so peaceful. Okay, sweetie, I'll try you on the land-line. Love you, bye."

I know he's up there having the best ride, in the most beautiful place.

I pray that each of you find your own wild ride, your own beautiful truth, and live your best life–every single day. I will be cheering for you!

Warrior Wisdom:

Aside from telling everyone who struggles with alcoholism, "Just donate a kidney," I want EVERYONE who has carried the burden of addiction to know there is a version of their life that is so wonderful, so free, and so empowering! I want this version of life for everyone who wants it too.

As with all the other things I have shared that have come into my life in my time of need, once again, something came directly into my path not that long ago. I had the opportunity to hear about a new method of treatment for alcoholism. The company is northstarcare.com, and they are changing the world. Through Northstar, I learned that because they have identified the genes that predispose someone to alcoholism in our DNA, they are now able to correct this through certain supplements and medications. To the point a person can actually be "cured" from alcoholism.

I can't tell you how excited and relieved I was to hear about this treatment. Having something to share with you, my dear readers, was an answer to my prayers! A lecture given in 2023 by Dr. Amanda Wilson showed it has been eighty-five percent effective to date! Here is the link. https://northstarcare.com

Please . . . do not resign yourself to living anything but the life you were meant to have. We were put on this earth to experience joy and bliss. Yes, life is hard . . . and so painful at times. But if you have suffered with alcoholism, it no longer has to dictate your world. Fuck alcohol! It is possible to regain control of your thought process and your life. We all have a superhero inside us, just waiting to be unleashed! Know this, too: the best superheroes work together with others when they need help, to lift them, and inspire them exponentially. You are never alone.

Regarding religion . . . any religion. I was able to embrace mine again when I lost any critical judgment toward myself or others–judging them by assuming they were judging me. I no longer had the fear (of not measuring up) and guilt that I used to associate with going to church.

I believe this is something our youth can experience whether they are following all the rules or not. It's about making peace with oneself. It's a result of loving and accepting ourselves and what we want in life, absolutely and completely. Having a congregation to meet with and support (while also feeling supported) is just a bonus. I feel accepted and loved, because I love and accept myself. *I like where I am and the peace I have found.*

Let's choose to make every day extraordinary. Let's choose to see the good and beauty in everything. Let's choose to become powerful warriors by empowering, supporting, and protecting those around us. Let's choose unbridled joy!

This is just an invitation, of course . . . ultimately, **the choice is yours.**

The End

As you go on in your own life and make your sacred choices, whatever they are, I want to hear from you, my dear readers. Your triumphs will give more meaning to my life and this book. If you are struggling, remember–you are never alone. We empower each other via finding solutions. Know that I am always your biggest fan in this crazy adventure we call life. We are all connected. The powerful, energetic bond of love between human beings is so strong. Feel it! Revel in the knowledge that it will always be there.

Please join my community on my website and Facebook, full of others who are finding and loving their own superpowers. I invite you to join us in having a safe place to declare the most perfect "you" that has emerged within yourself. And celebrate all the fairytales and street fights of this life. My mailing list is also an excellent option to keep up-to-date with new snippets of Warrior Wisdom that I feel honored to share with each of you. We are all in this together!

Ramona's Top 10 Principles to Live By

1. **Become somebody's #1, "You're fucking awesome!" fan (especially your own!)**

   I challenge you to take on this role for every child, spouse, friend, or beloved pet in your life. Make it a point to shout aloud to the world what you love about them. If you are your own #1 fan first and foremost, it will become much easier to show up for others.

2. **Summon your courage!**

   Yeah, this is hard, but you know what's worse? Sitting in the aftermath of a trial and realizing you acted out of fear. To this day, I take opportunities to speak with my adult children, to acknowledge and validate the pain I caused them when I checked out of my life. Even as adults, it's vital for them to know that they were always worthy of my love. It's important to create a space where you can communicate with those you love by owning your inactions and bravely asking for forgiveness.

3. **Rise above it!**

   This one is all about our exes. Getting along with them is a choice . . . a big one. When I decided to actively put my love for my children in front of my pride, I discovered that a peaceful life isn't only possible but is realistically wonderful. That's why I invite you to learn how to praise your ex-spouse at any given opportunity. This kindness might feel out of your comfort zone, but set the intention over and over, keep it constant, and don't give up. Your kids are part of your ex-spouse, and they will feel your energy personally . . . negative or positive. So keep it positive!

4. **Embrace new forms of treatment to facilitate healing!**

If you have endured childhood trauma, PTSD, anxiety, depression, grief, or self-confidence issues, I encourage you to explore the possibilities of ketamine therapy. It has been transformative for me. The self-love and sense of wholeness I have cultivated are ten times more potent than any love I have experienced from another person. I feel complete and solid in my own being. I urge you to engage with a professional to explore whether this could be a powerful tool for your own journey.

5. **Bring it on!**

Seriously, my friends, there's nothing better than a true badass who refuses to be afraid of life's challenges. Every shitstorm that comes your way is an opportunity for growth. Do your best to see it that way. Numbing out to difficult situations doesn't get you through them, it simply keeps you stuck exactly where you are. Face the terror and fear head on. You "will" get through it, and become a stronger, more capable person to take on the next obstacle.

6. **Every day, write it down!**

Make it a daily practice to journal about the things you want in your life. Write from a point of simply appreciating each item on your list, like you've had them for years. You will be amazed at the things you can manifest. Remember Einstein's quote: "Everything is energy, and that is all there is to it. Match the frequency of the reality you want, and you cannot help but get that reality. It can be no other way. This is not philosophy. This is physics."

7. **Get back up!**

In the street fight of life, just remember–the last one standing wins! Failure is a part of life. Don't let it define you. Most successful people have failed more times than they have succeeded. Failure is simply a way of learning how "not" to do something. It's a necessary part of success. But the most vital action you must take is to simply "get back up!"

8. **Erase the stigma!**

Shaming yourself or a loved one for being an alcoholic is no different than shaming yourself or anyone else for having any other disease. Healing from this disease is hard and takes time. At Northstar care, you will learn long hidden facts; such as, the alcohol epidemic is literally ten times bigger than the opioid epidemic. It has to be taken head-on, and I know it will be the fight of your (or their) life. Here is the link again to connect with invaluable resources: *https://northstarcare.com*

9. **Carve out your own path!**

We were put on this earth to have our own experience, not the experience our parents told us to have. Lose any beliefs that keep you stuck in an unsatisfactory life. Focus on seeking out joy every day instead. When you take on this new perspective, you will find what resonates with you. You might even circle around and have a stronger conviction to be right where you started, because it will be something you gave yourself the freedom to choose. Whatever it is will feel wonderful because "you" chose it.

10. **All you need is love!**

Give your children unconditional love. This means allowing them to fail and learn from their mistakes, teaching them through example, and respecting their individual paths. When we meet our maker, if we have lived a life of unconditional love toward our family and fellow human beings, I personally don't think we have anything to worry about.

About the Author

Ramona Baxter is an author and speaker known for her entrepreneurship and inventive spirit. Born with an innate curiosity and a drive to make a difference, Ramona has built three dynamic businesses–always drawn to the world of invention and radical solutions. Throughout her career, she has even patented an idea that revolutionized industries. Wherever she has seen a need, like on-site childcare for single mothers in school, she finds a solution.

Ramona's life is a testament to the power of passion and the resilience of the human spirit. After experiencing a true recovery miracle firsthand, she has become a powerful resource for anyone seeking inspiration, guidance, and a path toward freedom from addiction. As a mother of four, grandmother, and fairy dogmother, Ramona continues to inspire others to embrace their magic, give their inner warrior wings, and unleash their inner superhero.

Facebook page link here: **Winged Warriors**
Website link here: **fairytalesandstreetfights.com**
Email list sign up here: **ramona@fairytalesandstreetfights.com**
Her Instagram handle is **fairytalesandstreetfights**

Reviews

"What truly sets this memoir apart is its authenticity. The author doesn't sugar-coat her experiences or present herself as flawless. Instead, she embraces her imperfections, using them as stepping stones toward growth and self-discovery. In doing so, she not only empowers herself but also empowers readers to embrace their own humanity.

In conclusion, Fairytales and Street Fights is a profoundly moving testament to the indomitable human spirit. Through her compelling narrative, the author proves that even in the darkest of times, there is light to be found. This book is not just a story—it's a powerful reminder that we all have the strength within us to overcome life's greatest challenges."

–Ramona DeHoyos Stark

"Ramona's vulnerability and honesty throughout her book are what make it so powerful. She bares her soul, sharing both her triumphs, as well as her darkest moments. It takes immense courage to reveal oneself in such a raw and authentic way, and she has done so with grace.

Despite the challenges she faced, she persevered and found a way to rise above. The lessons she drew from her experiences are truly invaluable, and they serve as a reminder to all of us that we have the power to overcome any obstacle life throws our way."

–Dennis A. Conforto, Podcast Host & Producer of *Just Saying The Obvious*

"It takes courage to write about your own life and to make sense of it so that others can be impacted by what you have learned. The book, Fairy Tales and Street Fights, contains the life experiences of Ramona Baxter, author. The narrative made me smile, laugh, and cry. It describes a full and rich life. A life full of good times and bad times. A life of good and not-so-good choices. A life that depicts great successes and disappointing failures. A life that spans the spectrum of emotions from tremendous joy to deep sadness. I would encourage anyone to read this book about life's ups and downs, building resilience of the human spirit, and empowerment through self-love and kindness."

–Janet Schmidt, International Best Selling Author of *Journey to Self-Awareness and Hope*

"Ramona has recreated her world from a very early age and shared it with all of us like a beautiful secret. Her words and her story are so powerful that I can't count the times I laughed and cried during this amazing journey.

This is an honest and human story about family, upbringing, and most of all choice and empowerment. Her "Warrior Wisdoms" are not to be missed, as they are the perfect summation of each chapter.

Ramona Baxter, I thank you from the bottom of my heart for sharing your journey from "Wamona" to Ramona, to Ramona the amazing storyteller."

–Misti Mazurik, Director of Operations, RHG Media Productions

"This is a story of surviving on one's terms with all the pitfalls and attempts at life changes but still finding courage to survive it all, intact. This author shares her personal struggles, sharing an after-the-fact account in her Warrior Wisdom of growth from what she lived through, holding herself accountable with a new perspective. I found that to be especially enlightening because I, as the reader, could understand her growth and what she learned.

She isn't shy about sharing her struggles, coming face-to-face with herself and all she has gone through. Adjusting and adapting to how she wanted to live her life was welcomed openly. We struggle in life because that's what our journeys through life are. I found this book to be well written, describing how a person can make their dreams come true with focused determination.

It is an honest account of a life being lived and finding peace with it, especially with the ones she loves."

–Steve Zeiger, International Best Selling Author of *My Lights*